THE SUICIDE BATTALION

armchair general series

Canadian Cataloging in Publication Data

McWilliams, James L.
  The suicide battalion

First paperback ed.
Includes bibliographical references.
ISBN 0-920277-53-5

1. Canada. Canadian Army. Battalion, 46th.
2. World War, 1914–1918 — Regimental histories — Canada. I. Steel, R. J. II. Title.

D547.C2M29 1990   940.4'1271   C90-093651-7

Design/Cover   Mark Waters
Cover Photo   National Archives of Canada
Map   Loris Gasparotto, Brock University

Vanwell Publishing Limited
P.O. Box 2131, Stn B
St. Catharines, Ontario
L2M 6P5

Distributed in Great Britain and Europe by:

Spa Books Ltd.
P.O. Box 47
Stevenage
Herts SG2 8UH, UK

THE SUICIDE BATTALION

James L. McWilliams
R. James Steel

Vanwell Publishing Limited
St. Catharines, Ontario

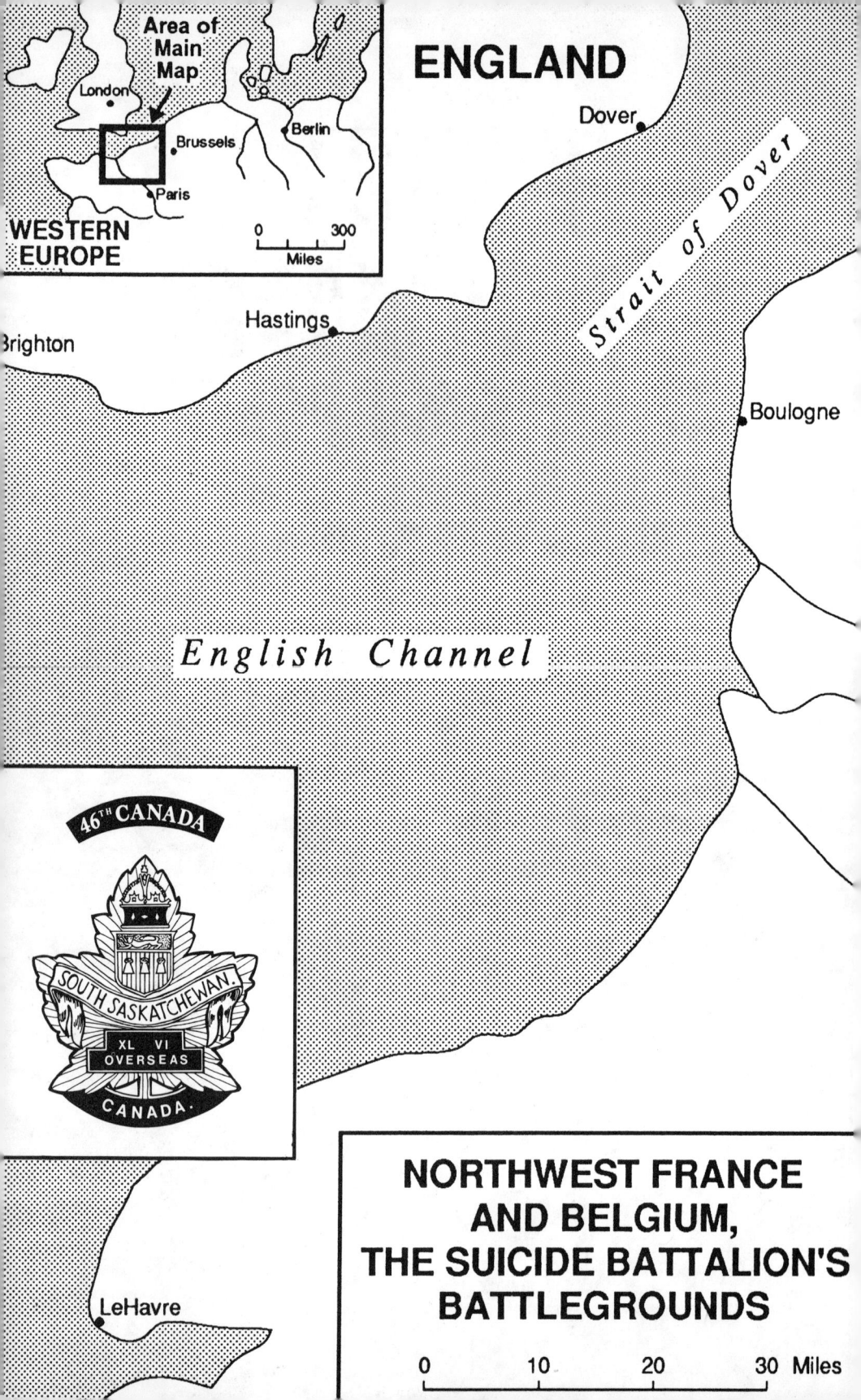

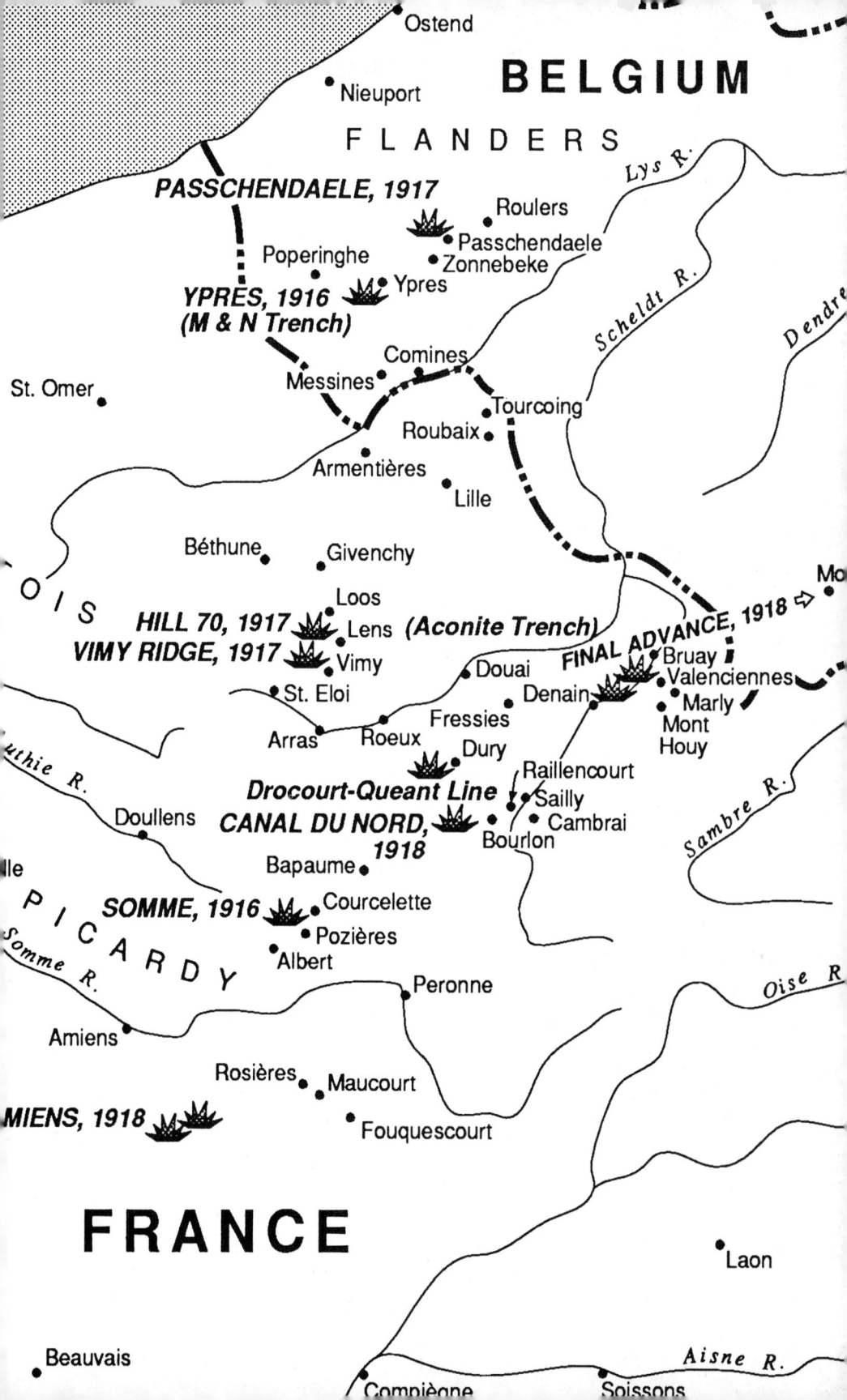

Contents

Acknowledgements/*8*
Preface/*10*
Prologue/*11*
1 Call to Arms/*13*
2 Sewell and Bramshott Camps/*19*
3 To the Front/*29*
4 Over the Top/*35*
5 The Somme/*43*
6 Regina and Desire/*55*
7 Winter Below the Ridge/*69*
8 The Battle of Vimy Ridge/*79*
9 The Summer of '17/*89*
10 Aconite Trench/*99*
11 Passchendaele/*107*
12 The Second Winter/*127*
13 The Spring of '18/*135*
14 Something in the Air/*141*
15 Amiens/*149*
16 The Drocourt-Queant Line/*161*
17 The Canal du Nord/*171*
18 Pursuit/*183*
19 Valenciennes/*195*
20 Peace/*203*
The Bond That Binds/*209*
Appendix/*211*
Notes/*220*
Bibliography/*222*
Index/*224*

Acknowledgements

We are extremely grateful to the following, who have so kindly assisted in the research for this book by providing interviews, photographs, and private papers: Professor J. V. Bateman (Victoria), Mrs. Betty Bell (Medicine Hat), Canadian Forces Records Centre (Ottawa), Mrs. D. Couser (Winnipeg), Mrs. Thomas Dann (Lyn, Ontario), Mrs. Arthur Dawes (Naicam), Len Donkersley (Powell River), Mrs. Victor Ellis (Pilot Butte), Mrs. R. G. Ennis (Vancouver), William O. Harris (Calgary), Mrs. M. E. Hodson (Saskatoon), Dorothy M. Ingram (Brandon), Arthur McClellan (Vancouver), Mrs. Sarah Ann Prescott (Bienfait), J. A. Pringle (Vice-President, University of Saskatchewan, Saskatoon), Mrs. W. A. Shepherd (Mission City, B.C.), Mrs. Gladys Sheridan (Nipawin), Major A. Stow (Moose Jaw), George Tomlinson (Saskatoon); and the Moose Jaw *Times Herald* for the use of its archives.

Special thanks are due to: Douglas MacGowan of St. Catharines, who was a constant source of information on the C.E.F. and who allowed us use of his private library; Miss B. Wilson, military specialist with the Public Archives in Ottawa, who always went out of her way to assist us; Don Graham and the Saskatchewan Department of Culture and Youth, who made it possible for us to interview so many veterans by providing a grant to cover some of our expenses; E. D. ("Mac") McDonald of Keighley, Yorkshire, who came out of the blue with trench maps, books, and documents, to say nothing of hours of taped memoirs; R. E. Steel of St. Catharines, who so willingly produced maps and drawings as we needed them; Carlotta Lemieux of Regina for her editing and her guidance in many matters; and the ladies of the Moose Jaw Public Library for their unflagging interest and assistance.

We also owe a debt of gratitude to our long-suffering wives, who prevented us from starving to death during the endless hours of research and writing.

Of course, especially to be thanked are the following veterans of the 46th Battalion who assisted with letters, interviews, questionnaires, photos, and encouragement: George Anderson, Colin Bond, Jim Broomhead, Gordon Brown, L. W. ("Pat") Burns, Jim Butterworth, Douglas Carmichael, Stan Colbeck, John Copp, W. H. S. Dixon, Sam Downey, A. J. Elliott, Harold Emery, Jack Featherstone, George Fountain, J. H. Frank, Fred Gillespie, Pat Gleason, Ernie Harris, Hartley Hea, Percy Hellings, Thomas Hewitt, Stanley Hickley, R. H. Howes, Jack Huckerby, Ernie Jenner, George Johnson, W. S. Jones, Bobby Kears, Fred Kemp, George Kentner, Charles Lock, E. D. ("Mac") McDonald, N. B. MacDonald, Donald MacKay, Don McKerchar, John P. G. McLeod, Neil J. McLeod, Doug MacPherson, Bill Manners, Bill Musgrove, Ted Oakley, Tommy Rea, Tom Scott, Charlie Skeates, A. A. ("Spike") Smith, Thomas Smith, Curry Spidell, D. R. ("Bob") Stevenson, Bill Sully, Sidney Tallis, Frank Taylor, Morley Timberlake, B. A. ("Bob") Tingley, George Tomlinson, John Walker, J. S. Woodward, Percy Young.

We also wish to express our thanks to the Public Archives of Canada for permission to reproduce material from the *War Diary* of the 46th Battalion and to the Saskatchewan Archives in Regina for permission to quote from a collection of tape-recorded interviews with ex-members of the 46th. Every effort has been made to credit accurately the sources of all material used in this book, but we shall welcome any information that will allow us to correct any errors or omissions.

To everyone who assisted in any way we would like to express our sincere thanks. We must also say that while no effort has been spared to ensure that the facts in these pages are accurate, the responsibility for error is ours alone.

J. L. McW. and R. J. S.

Preface

This is the story of an infantry battalion in the First World War. It is in no way an official history; generals, grand strategy, and political events are seldom mentioned. This history belongs to the infantrymen—a few lieutenants, several sergeants, and numerous privates. The narrative includes many personal accounts, some written sixty or so years ago and others recalled more than half a century after the event by retired farmers, railroaders, executives, and labourers. For a brief time they all shared one common experience—they were all members of the 46th Canadian Infantry Battalion (South Saskatchewan).

The 46th is the subject of this account, but it could as readily have been the 8th Argyll and Sutherland Highlanders of the British Army; or the 42nd Queensland Battalion, Australian Expeditionary Force; or the 180th Windau Regiment in the Tsar's army; or France's 165th Regiment of the Line; or possibly even the 99th Reserve Infantry Regiment of the Kaiser's legions. This is not written in praise of any individual or unit or nation. It is merely the typical story of a battalion of men caught up in the ghastly reality of war.

Like many units in the armies, the 46th on occasion referred to itself as "The Suicide Battalion." There were many units which could justifiably bear that name in The War to End All Wars. It is to all the Suicide Battalions of that war that we dedicate this account.

Prologue

On 28 June 1914 Archduke Franz Ferdinand of Austria-Hungary was assassinated at Sarajevo, Bosnia. The assassin was a young Serbian. Austria, long anxious to blot out the little kingdom of Serbia, seized upon the murder as a means to that end. Egged on by the bombastic and unstable emperor of Germany, the Austrian government demanded a most humiliating list of guarantees from Serbia. The Slavic kingdom's almost complete compliance was brushed aside and Austria declared war against her. Thus the conflict known as The Great War, or The War to End All Wars, sputtered into history.

Austria and Serbia were hardly significant in themselves; they were merely the first two casualties. As they fell into the conflagration they dragged others in with them one by one, each causing the flames of war to shoot higher. All Europe would soon be ablaze.

Tsarist Russia creaked into action in support of Serbia. Germany in turn slipped her well-oiled war machine into gear to back the Austrians. This gave France her chance to avenge the shame of 1870 by engaging Germany in support of her new-found ally, Russia. Germany, anxious to destroy France, attacked her flank by the simple expedient of advancing through Belgium. This action was to bring Britain into the war.

Far from the scene of the coming Armageddon, one of the Britannic lion's cubs was enjoying a glorious summer. On the prairies of Saskatchewan the big news event in every town and city was the local fair. The murder at Sarajevo did make a few lines on the front page, but it was not as spectacular as the Kraftchenko case in Plum Coulee, Manitoba. Besides, who knew where Sarajevo was? Those Ruthenians, as the newspapers described them, were always doing some fool thing anyway. But during the last days of peace, "that row in Europe" gradually came into prominence. The front pages of the prairie newspapers carried threats of war and the rattling of sabres from continental Europe. Speculation as to Britain's role began.

Nevertheless, western Canadians still looked on as spectators. The Moose Jaw *Evening Times* of 30 July announced: "Expected That Two Thousand Ruthenians Will Leave This City for the Seat of War." There followed a generally sympathetic story of the excitement and patriotism stirring within the Austrian community in Moose Jaw and district. The next day the Regina *Leader* published a list of Austrian reservists who were leaving Regina to join their regiments. They were to sail on the *Victorian* on 4 August.

A day later there seemed to have dawned a realization of Canada's imminent involvement and the *Leader* was spilling with excitement and stories of local men volunteering for possible war service.

On Sunday, 2 August, crowds of nattily dressed gentlemen in boaters and suits were photographed outside the Regina *Leader's* office waiting for news of the war. "Four Great Powers Now at War," trumpeted the *Leader* on Monday. But still Britain stayed out. Excitement was at fever pitch.

The fourth of August was a let down. The *Leader* announced with a disappointed air, "Armed Neutrality Only." However, enthusiasm picked up in numerous small articles which told of volunteers from every social strata. That night thousands gathered outside the *Leader's* office to hear the latest war news. They were not disappointed. The official announcement was received that evening: Britain had joined the Allies—and when Britain went to war, the Empire went with her.

CHAPTER ONE

Call to Arms

Oh, we don't want to lose you,
But we think you ought to go
For your King and your Country
Both need you so.
We shall want you and miss you,
But with all our might and main
We will thank you, cheer you, kiss you,
When you come back again.
"Your King and Country Needs You,"
a popular recruiting song

It was 17 December 1914. Lieutenant-Colonel Herbert Snell looked over the order he had just received from Ottawa. The instructions were clear—begin recruiting 220 men for the third Canadian overseas contingent.

Herbert Snell was an energetic and dedicated man. Born in Stockbridge, Yorkshire, in 1880, he had come to Port Hope, Ontario, with his parents when he was eleven years old. As a young man he had headed west to seek his fortune and eventually established a ladies' wear store in Moose Jaw, where he soon won election as an alderman. Then, in 1913, with characteristic vigour the 33-year-old merchant had taken command of the newly raised 60th Rifles of Canada.

The weeks before the declaration of war had been frustrating. Long beforehand, Snell had forecast the coming conflict. During that last summer of peace, his store and the large comfortable house on North Hill had seen him less and less. His small, spare figure could daily be found signing recruits or inspecting the new armoury, which was nearing completion. When war was declared on 4 August, Herbert Snell and his beloved regiment were ready for it. Like so many other militia regiments, the 60th confidently awaited its mobilization call. Nothing happened.

It was becoming painfully obvious that something had gone awry with Canada's carefully prepared mobilization plans. Sam Hughes, Falstaffian minister of defence, had scrapped the detailed plans and had instead sent out 226 night telegrams instructing local commanders to begin recruiting. Thus the established military administration had been circumvented and control lay in Hughes's powerful hands. Existing units were ignored and numerous "overseas battalions" were being raised by gentlemen whom Hughes considered to be both prominent and politically safe.

Within two weeks Moose Jaw had seen three groups of men leave for the war. The Princess Patricia's Canadian Light Infantry had gobbled up 106 men on the eleventh. Shortly afterwards 250 men were dispatched by Snell to Valcartier to form part of the first contingent. On 18 August a party of 18 British reservists left for the Old Country. Meanwhile the 60th Rifles sat encamped on the Exhibition Grounds in Moose Jaw waiting to be called.

As autumn dragged on, excitement turned to frustration. In November, Snell dutifully raised a large draft of men for the second contingent. When the men left for Britain, he was ordered to remain behind. The chances of going over appeared so dismal that he stood for re-election as alderman. On 14 December the voters gave him a large majority, but the next day the Moose Jaw *Evening Times* carried a headline—the ultimate insult to the city's would-be warriors: "Moose Jaw Nurses Are Now in France on Active Service." Nurses Fraser and McCurdy had arrived overseas with No. 2 Stationary Hospital. The ladies of Moose Jaw were in France before the men.

The twenty-first of December found brothers Fred, Will, and

Earl Gillespie walking up North Hill to the Armoury. They had recently come from Ontario, but jobs in the West were scarce and prospects looked bleak. The war offered them at least some excitement.

There were few recruits that day, but despite this, they had over an hour's wait for their medicals. By late afternoon Fred and Will were members of the third contingent and officially on leave until after Christmas. Earl had been turned down on medical grounds but his twin brother Ruben would join Fred and Will on 31 December. The drab winter had taken on an air of excitement for the Gillespies.

After Christmas the recruits began training, but first they were issued their kit. Each man received one pair of long woollies, a shaving kit, and later a decrepit Ross rifle. They "fell in" on the Armoury floor and were introduced to the intricacies of squad drill. Their performance was not quite what their sergeant had hoped for and as a result they were run three times around the race track at the Exhibition Grounds next door. "They just about killed us that first day," recalled Fred Gillespie. "Luckily for us, Doc Bayly stepped in and put a stop to it."

The first three weeks were not what the keen young recruits had envisioned. They had no uniforms, and some of them were poorly dressed for winter. They also had to provide their own lodgings and meals. Early every morning the rookies appeared at the Armoury to take their daily dose of drill, P.T., and route-marching. At noon they broke off soldiering and headed for Yip Foo's Café, where they would have their dinner in relays.

Lieutenant-Colonel Snell had been hard at work and soon conditions began to look up. The men were given straw-filled paillasses with which to bed down on the Armoury floor. A caterer by the name of Stover was engaged. He hauled a granary up to the north end of the Armoury and began dispensing enormous meals to the growing crowd of recruits.

The men were working into excellent shape. Each morning, before breakfast, they doubled seven city blocks down the hill to the post office where they would "about turn" and double back up to the Armoury. Route-marches to Belbeck and back, patrols and skirmishing in the ravines of Wellesley and River parks were giving them confidence and spirit. Although they had no band, there was plenty of music en route. This was provided by lusty voices and a button-accordion played by a most singular redhead. The members of his platoon had shaved one another's heads, but they had done his flaming red hair Mohican-style—in a wide band from back to front.

Despite their nondescript appearance, they mounted sentries at the Armoury twenty-four hours a day. The long winter woollies that had been issued to them came in handy during those cold winter nights, patrolling back and forth under the northern lights. Fortunately the winter of 1914-15 was relatively mild. There was little snow and they got by in their civilian clothes.

The Moose Jaw contingent was not the only body of men in the area. Estevan and Weyburn had their small quota, and Regina was collecting a company in Alexandra School. One of the Queen City's earliest recruits was Vic Syrett. He came from a military family and had already seen two older brothers enlist. Vic felt he had to answer the call to arms, but being only sixteen posed a problem. Although the army did accept buglers at that age, this seemed no use to Vic as he could not play a note. But "where there is a will"—so young Syrett joined the 95th Saskatchewan Rifles to learn the art of bugling. By Christmas he felt proficient enough to request a transfer to the third overseas contingent. He was accepted.

During these early months each contingent was a separate entity, a mere collection of men to be fed into the war machine, but on 1 February all that changed. It was on that date that the 46th Canadian Infantry Battalion (South Saskatchewan) was authorized by Ottawa. The Moose Jaw *Evening Times* trumpeted the news: "Headquarters of Forty-Sixth Battalion Here—Six Hundred Troops to Mobilize—Lt. Col. Herbert Snell Gets Command."

The new commanding officer immediately requested Ottawa to renumber his battalion the 60th. He was turned down by the minister of militia because it was "not desired that the battalions of the C.E.F. should hold any class or clan distinctions." Nevertheless, the new 46th carried on in the manner of a rifle battalion. Both the Moose Jaw and Regina contingents were officered by men from rifle regiments and the men were being trained in the quick-tempo manner peculiar to such regiments.

The 46th was to consist of four companies, each to be of double strength and under the command of a major. A regiment must have a band, so a vigorous recruiting campaign was instituted, and by March a fine brass and reed band had been assembled under the direction of George McClellan, the bandmaster of the 60th Rifles, who had previously been a French-horn player with the Highland Light Infantry. With him came his son, Fraser, a first-class bass player and band sergeant, plus a majority of the members of the 60th's band.

The Armoury began to take on a more martial air when the uniforms started to trickle in during March. Within a month most of the men were completely outfitted, and in late April the battalion was ordered to provide a draft of 5 officers and 250 other ranks to leave for England immediately. Moose Jaw, Regina, Weyburn, and Estevan were all to contribute. The Moose Jaw quota was to be 82 men, and they left the city, cheered on by the crowds, on 7 May. Meanwhile the main body of men remained behind, continuing with their training, guarding local ironworks and government grain elevators, and impatiently waiting for the day when they would move to Camp Sewell in Manitoba—the first step on their way to France.

On 26 May word was at last received—the 46th would entrain for Sewell on Friday morning, only two days away. The train was to pull out of Moose Jaw at 6:40 A.M., so the Moose Jaw quota was up early that Friday morning. As the troops formed up, it became evident that thousands were coming to see them off. At six, led by their band, the men of Headquarters and C Company marched out of the Armoury and down Main Street to the tune of "The Maple Leaf for Ever." It was a rousing scene, described with enthusiasm by the *Evening Times:*

> There was another immense crowd at the C.P.R. depot this morning to join in the hearty send-off given the Moose Jaw quota of the 46th Battalion. . . . The men made a pleasing picture as they crowded round the carriage windows. Their sunburnt faces and fine physique told, in many cases, of wonders per-

formed physically by their training at the Armoury, and the expression was freely heard that "the third contingent possesses the finest set of fellows yet." The old song, "Tipperary," was changed to "It's a long way to Manitoba where the wheat and barley grow," and on one of the carriages was scrawled the words "Berlin or bust." There was a noticeable lack of flippant boasting which have characterized the send-offs to other contingents, and even the Kaiser's name was not taken in vain.... When the bell sounded for the train's departure the crowd burst into one long cheer, which was sustained until the echoes died away on the rumbling of the wheels.[1]

And so the volunteers of Moose Jaw set off to join the rest of the unit, which had been collected at Regina. Within an hour the 46th Canadian Infantry Battalion (South Saskatchewan) would be brought together for the first time.

CHAPTER TWO

Sewell and Bramshott Camps

Hell hath no fury like a non-combatant.
C. E. Montague

When the train pulled into the small siding at Sewell, the men were more subdued. Camp Sewell was hardly impressive. "Crowding off the trains, the men look out over a tumble of sandhills clothed with sparse brown grass and ground cedar. Bluffs of discouraged poplars dot the rolling plains; while here and there scrub oaks and evergreens struggle up to the crest of sand ridges. To the south of the railway track lie the long, white-tented lines of the camp."[2]

Although Sam Hughes had recently renamed the area Camp Hughes, to the men of 1915 it was always "Sewell." The name became synonymous with the word *sand*. The perpetual prairie winds made Sewell sand a part of every activity, from shaving to route-marching. The men of the 46th were to get to know these sands well, for they remained at Camp Sewell for nearly six months. They found themselves brigaded with the 44th, 45th, and 53rd battalions. Soon other troops poured into Sewell and the rows of tents stretched farther and farther out onto the prairies.

For each unit the routine became similar. From the sounding of "Reveille" at 5:30 A.M. until "Lights Out" was played at 10:15 P.M., the time was filled with inspections, physical training, musketry, route-marches, lectures, and drill. "Beds were paillasses filled with straw," recalled George Tomlinson of the

Medical Section. "These had to be rolled up every morning before breakfast and were placed in neat piles in front of each tent. The sanitary arrangements consisted of rows of pails, with a hen roost to sit on and let your tail piece hang over. Ablutions were performed in the open air at a series of long wooden troughs with a cold water tap at one end." But it was not all drill and discomfort. In off-hours there were recreations—football, baseball, and boxing—and occasionally there were visitors' days. And it was during this period that the men of the battalion were able to size one another up and to coalesce as a unit.

The 46th had its share of colourful characters: Private Bashmakoff, whose father was a general in the tsar's army; Private Youkitanie of the Imperial Japanese Army; and ex-guardsmen such as Sergeants Stamper and Broadstock. One of the most popular men was "Old George" Tomlinson of the Medical Section. Tall and unpolished, with a most impressive handlebar moustache, he was completely unflappable, and despite his youthfulness he had several years of military experience—hence his nickname. The regimental sergeant-major was Harry Monger, his snow-white moustache and military bearing reflecting his twenty-nine years of service around the Empire. Then there was the adjutant, Captain George Dann, who was largely responsible for molding the superb battalion the 46th was destined to become; and the least soldierly-looking officer of all, Captain James Sabiston Rankin, a Weyburn lawyer, rather roly-poly and "country gentleman" in appearance, who had served in the Highland Light Infantry in his native Scotland and was known as Jock—but for all his military background, he was unable to keep in step with the brass band (though he did somewhat better with the pipes).

The 46th Battalion had three bands. In addition to the original brass and reed band under Bandmaster McClellan, a pipe band was also taking shape under Sergeant George Allen, a former Scots Guards piper. And since the 46th had declared itself a rifle regiment, it had to have a bugle band. Unlike the brass and pipe bands, which were part of Headquarters Company, the buglers were attached to the various companies and only played together on parades. Captain Dann taught them a special call, which he himself had composed, and when it rang out it could be distinguished from all the other bugle calls at Sewell as the 46th's own regimental call. Captain Dann also chose the regimental march, suggesting "Punjab" in memory of his days in India. Of course a second march was required for the pipe band, and Jock Rankin, the pipers' number one promoter, suggested "Scotland the Brave." And so were chosen the regimental marches of the 46th.

During the summer the battalion also acquired a badge. It was a maple leaf bearing the Saskatchewan coat of arms, the designation "South Saskatchewan," and the Roman numerals XLVI. A long correspondence followed with Ottawa, seeking approval for the badge. Colonel Herbert Snell was not a man to wait for ever, so the badges (one cap and two collar) were made up for each man and issued in mid-September. Five days later Ottawa approved the pattern.

This all added up to a pleasant enough life, but the men were anxious to be off to France. The disastrous battle of Loos was being described by the papers as a great victory and the turning point in the war. While the struggle for Loos raged on, the 46th completed a twenty-mile march in the pouring rain thousands of miles away. It seemed that the war would be over before the battalion ever left Sewell. In fact, a popular marching tune of the 46th ended with the lines: "When the war is all over we'll be out in Sewell Camp,/When the war is all over we'll be there."

To be sure, a draft of 250 men and 5 officers was sent overseas in September and new recruits were enlisted to make up the numbers, but the main body of men remained in Manitoba. What was going to happen to the 46th? Would it spend another winter at home? Would the authorities continue to break it up into small drafts until the unit ceased to exist? Or was it possible, could it ever happen that the 46th would be sent to Britain and then to France? Every man from Colonel Snell down waited and hoped.

Then word came. The 46th and 44th would entrain for Halifax on 18 October. A wave of excitement swept these units while the rest of Sewell sank into despondency. There was a quickening of pulses as each soldier contemplated the future and prepared for departure. Private E. D. ("Mac") McDonald, a bank clerk from

Moose Jaw, sold his civilian suit to another private for ten dollars, knowing he would not need it for some time.

It was early morning when the two battalions boarded the four trains that were to take them to Halifax. The soldiers already aboard cheered wildly as their train pulled out. Thousands of others outside returned the sound, and the contingent headed east—all except the private who had bought Mac's suit. He had deserted during the night. The troop trains made few stops and six days later they arrived in Halifax, but the long journey in the immigrant cars with little to do except gossip had made every man aware of the dangers that lay ahead. The thought of crossing the stormy Atlantic, filled with lurking submarines and possibly the famous German raider, *Emden*, had made everyone edgy.

The 46th was to sail on the S. S. *Lapland*. This four-funnelled White Star liner was considered to be fast. It had already survived one narrow escape when explosives were discovered hidden aboard in New York harbour. Memories of the *Lapland* vary according to the accommodation enjoyed. Those who were fortunate enough to be located in the passenger cabins remember her as a marvellous ship. Others, like the English recruit Bobby Kears, recalled: "It was a high narrow thing and it rocked back and forth all the time. What a boat! We had hammocks way down near the bottom. . . . We sat on the floor and laid our equipment on the floor under them. But soon I was sick. Oh my, was I sick."

Before dawn on 23 October, the S. S. *Lapland* put to sea—alone. This increased apprehensions. She looped far south of the normal shipping routes, maintaining radio silence, but six and a half days out of Halifax, dusk found two silent streamlined shadows approaching from the east. The destroyer escorts, as sleek as greyhounds, had arrived. The Royal Navy received a hearty cheer. Next day the English coast came into view. To the expatriate, the sight of those Devonshire cliffs brought a lump in the throat. The Canadian-born stared in anticipation. The fog eventually blotted out the sight and the S.S. *Lapland* slipped into Plymouth harbour.

The following morning a warm sun dispersed the fog to reveal the legendary city of Drake and of the *Mayflower*. The troops were quickly disembarked and loaded into trains, which the railroaders in the battalion jokingly dubbed "vest-pocket editions of the CPR." Packed eight to a compartment, the plainsmen then occupied themselves staring at the countryside as the trains rolled across southern England.

The 46th detrained in the dark at a village named Liphook, where the men formed fours and began the three-mile march to their new home, Bramshott Camp. "I never saw a road in my life that was waving so much," recalled Percy Young, who was noted for having the smallest feet in the battalion. Fred Gillespie also remembered those three miles: "That was a hard march. We all seemed to have sea legs, and, oh my, it was a dreadful march up there. It took everything out of you to make it those three miles."

It was past midnight when the weary column entered Bramshott Camp. It was then discovered that billets had not been arranged and that there was little or no food available. No preparations had been made because the 46th had not been expected. Major-General Sir Sam Hughes (he had been knighted that year) had decided to dispatch twelve thousand reinforcements to Britain without notifying either the Imperial War Office or his own representative in Britain, Brigadier-General J. W. Carson.[3]

Bramshott Camp, which was not far from Aldershot, was an ancient, ramshackle affair of slate-lined huts. It had recently been vacated by a division of Imperials (as the British were called) and had stood forlorn and neglected until the previous day. Rations were in short supply and there were not enough to feed the men properly.

Percy Young later recalled those first days in England: "We were in there three days before our regular rations started. The fellows had to go out of camp to get something to eat and some of them just kept going. Sergeant Broadstock, myself, and one other young fellow were sent to London to pick up three of our men under guard. We brought back thirty-nine. The military police had picked them up and we brought them back all happy as could be. The boys had gone all over the place. Some even went to their old homes."

Meanwhile, Colonel Herbert Snell was having his own problems. His wife and baby had followed him over as planned, but upon reaching England they seemed to have vanished. The authorities in London never did notify him of his family's whereabouts, nor could they tell Mrs. Snell where the 46th was stationed. Finally, three weeks later, the Bank of Montreal contacted the frantic husband and the family was reunited.

Days soon became more settled, and in later years the men would describe this as the happiest period in the 46th's history. New comfortable huts were built, and the high-collared Canadian uniforms were replaced by more comfortable and more serviceable British Army issue. The new huts were the best the 46th ever encountered. "Our furnishings comprised of three barrack-style tables with two benches to each table," wrote "Old George" Tomlinson of the Medical Section. "There were twenty-five men to a hut, and for heat a large coal stove stood in the centre. Three planks about six and a half feet long and a foot wide, a couple of low wooden trestles eight inches high—these items completed our bedsteads. For a mattress we were supplied with a cotton paillasse to be filled with straw (scores of bales had been dumped on our parade ground). For a pillow, a round cotton bolster was issued. This was also filled with straw. For our further comfort each man was given two blankets. Now our boudoir was complete. In these surroundings we wrote letters, played poker, and swapped yarns."

Reveille was at six followed by "physical jerks" and general clean-up of huts and gear. Breakfast followed, and at nine "fall in" was sounded and the daily inspection of boots, buttons, rifles, and individuals began. Training was usually prefaced by the instruction to "forget everything you learned in Canada." Primitive hand grenades were made by filling jam tins with dirt, powder, bits of iron, and a long fuse. Bayonet training was spurred on by a cockney NCO, who would roar in mock rage as the men plunged at the dummies dangling before them, "Fink it's your muvver-in-law!" Rifle practice was another part of the training—one of the most popular, for the Ross was an excellent target rifle. Route-marches were the least popular, especially the twice-monthly, twenty-two-mile ones.

Meanwhile, Christmas came (the first away from home for most of the men) and New Year's, and both were celebrated in style, but as 1916 rolled on one problem sorely bothered the men of the 46th: Why were they not in France with the 3rd Division? The battalion had been raised as part of the third contingent and was superbly trained and in readiness. Yet when the 3rd Division had been formed in December 1915, the 46th found itself left out. Battalions junior to the 46th were included, and this fact rankled. Although policy was never explained to the men, the reason was that only one Saskatchewan battalion was to be included in each division. When it was decided to convert the ten regiments of Canadian Mounted Rifles to infantry battalions, the 1st CMR from Saskatchewan became part of an entire brigade of mounted rifles in the 3rd Division. This left no place for the more junior 46th.

In December the British government had asked for twelve Canadian battalions for Egypt. The Canadian government had offered as a counter proposal a fourth Canadian division to be sent to France with the first three. Consequently, on 26 April 1916, the 46th found itself in the 10th Infantry Brigade, 4th Canadian Division. The 10th Brigade consisted of: the 46th; Winnipeg's 44th Battalion; the 47th from the Victoria, Vancouver, and New Westminster area; and the 50th from Calgary. The men liked to consider themselves as part of a "crack" western brigade. The two other brigades in the 4th Division were the 11th (54th, 75th, 87th, and 102nd battalions) and the 12th (38th, 72nd, 73rd, and 78th battalions).

Finally it seemed certain that the 46th was destined to see action, for the 4th Division was to go to France sometime during the summer. Training proceeded at an intensified pace, and the 46th rehearsed for a possible immediate move.

Meanwhile, the 1st Division in France had suffered appalling casualties in the Battle of Mount Sorrel. Trained reinforcements were needed desperately. On the night of 15 June long lists of names appeared in the huts of the 46th, notifying the men who were to leave for France next day. The following morning the battalion went on parade. Colonel Snell's voice broke as he read the orders. His beloved battalion was being broken up: the 46th was to send nearly eight hundred men in drafts to France. Most of A Company would go to the 58th Ontario Battalion, B Company men were to go to the 13th Royal Highlanders, and C Company to the 16th Canadian Scottish. D Company men were to be distributed amongst the drafts. Colonel Snell wept when the parade was dismissed.

On 16 June, the day that the 46th was broken up, the brigade received its first commanding officer: Brigadier-General W. St. Pierre Hughes, the younger brother of Sir Sam Hughes and former commander of the 21st Battalion. His appointment was looked upon as political by almost everyone. On that same day, as the originals marched away from Bramshott, the first replacements were disembarked—192 men from Edmonton's 51st Battalion. The trickle soon swelled to a flood as the authorities attempted to rebuild the shattered battalion with partially trained men from every corner of the Dominion. Men arrived from the 53rd Prince Albert Battalion and the 71st from Woodstock, Ontario, but the largest draft was provided by the 65th Battalion from Saskatoon, which contributed 507 men, some of whom claimed never to have fired a rifle.

If there was one thing remarkable about the draft from the 65th it was the large number of brothers. There were the Cairns, Hugh and Abbie, both keen footballers from Saskatoon. Their bunkmates were Jim and Dick Butterworth, farm boys who had left their sod shanty near Coleville to join up. The nominal roll of the 46th now also included six members of the Tallis family: the brothers Edgar, Victor, and William, well-known musicians in the Borden district (and descendants of the sixteenth century composer, Sir Thomas Tallis), William's son Arnold, and two nephews, Sid and Harold.

There was magnificent material in the new drafts, but most were woefully lacking in training, so an intensive regimen was embarked on with the men at both the rifle and bombing ranges from dawn to dusk. The 46th would have to be fully trained within two months or it would lose its place with the 4th Division.

Before these two months were up, tragedy had struck the battalion. It happened on 5 July. The new Mills bomb, a hand grenade designed to replace the homemade jam-tin bombs, had arrived. Colonel Snell took a keen interest in the weapon and he personally supervised much of the training. The Mills was a frightful tool of war for the rookie. The thought of holding all that explosive in the hand, activating it by pulling out the pin, and then stepping back to throw it as the seconds ticked off was an unnerving experience the first time around. One of the new men, in panic to get rid of his bomb, bounced it off the parapet of the trench. It lay there ominously silent as the man stared, horror stricken. Colonel Snell and the bombing sergeant, standing a few feet away, saw what had happened. Both rushed to grab the bomb to throw it out of harm's way. They never made it. The grenade exploded, badly wounding Colonel Snell and two others. The terrified private was killed.

Herbert Snell was not expected to live. He was badly cut about the face and chest, one eye was gone, and several pieces of shrapnel were lodged near his heart. Nevertheless, he began a remarkable recovery. Fifteen days after the accident General Watson, the divisional commander, visited the colonel in hospital and was able to promise him that he would wait until September for Snell to rejoin the 46th.

Throughout that busy summer the 46th trained hard. The rigorous training whipped the new men into fine shape. "I cannot think I was ever so happy as I was at Bramshott from the time the battalion arrived till June 1916," Private Mac McDonald reflected many years later. "That spring and summer in Bramshott was absolutely marvellous. We marched; we played; we sang; we drank. We marched over every inch of those roads around Bramshott, and if there is anything more thrilling than marching as a private, in a platoon, in a battalion, in step, I've never experienced it."

During July further small drafts joined the battalion from the 80th and 74th, two Ontario units. The glorious summer rolled on. August arrived and many a prairie soldier's thoughts drifted westwards as harvest time approached. But suddenly the reveries were shattered—the 46th was to leave for the front. On the night of 10 August the battalion entrained for Southampton. There the men boarded the old side-wheeler, *Princess Clementine*, and began the short crossing to Le Havre, or "Le Harv" as the Canadians pronounced it. And at last, early on the morning of 11 August 1916—nearly two years after many of the men had enlisted—the 46th Canadian Infantry Battalion (South Saskatchewan) arrived in France.

CHAPTER THREE

To the Front

> *The future means little to us; we are here, and no matter how eager we may be to get away from it, deep down in our hearts is a feeling of pride that when the call came we answered it.*
>
> T. S. Hope, *Rage of Battle*

Lieutenant-Colonel Herbert Snell, who had led and trained these men, lay in hospital in England as the 46th Canadians marched through the docks of the ancient port of Le Havre, treading in the footsteps of centuries of soldiers, including more than one thousand of their own original battalion. By breakfast they had been quartered in warehouses piled high with bales of cotton. It was a pleasant day, lolling about on the soft bales. Although none realized it, these bales would be the last soft beds for many months.

Before dusk the men received two days' rations and boarded several tiny railway cars, each bearing the loading instruction: "40 hommes, 8 chevaux." This legend was to become familiar during the ensuing months and years. "To make tea we used to dash up to the locomotive and hold our mess tins under a pipe while the engineer filled them with hot water," wrote the young bugler, Vic Syrett. "I could run faster than the train and used the opportunity to climb through the hedges, pick a few apples, then run to catch my car."

The battalion detrained at Steenvoorde in Belgium, and it

received a disappointing message at this time—Lieutenant-Colonel Snell would not be rejoining the battalion. The new commanding officer was Lieutenant-Colonel Herbert John Dawson. A professor at the Royal Military College in Kingston during prewar years, he had raised the 59th (Brockville) Battalion for overseas service. Now he was taking over a western battalion. The new colonel was a strict disciplinarian and a stickler for spit and polish. Few men in the 46th ever recalled seeing Dawson smile, and he soon had a collection of nicknames, of which "Old Stone Face" was the most descriptive. However, his students had long before dubbed him "Dismal Dawson." That name arrived in France with him, and it stuck. Many of the officers were disappointed that a complete stranger, who, it was rumoured, was a close friend of St. Pierre Hughes, had been given the battalion. The men grumbled but accepted resignedly. But it was only a matter of days before opinion began to change. "Corps H. Q. couldn't have picked a better man. Dawson was a natural commander," was the verdict of the New Brunswicker, Private Bill Musgrove. "He was very strict but with a regard and respect for his men. Before we went over on a raid or attack, Dawson wanted to know all the enemy positions, their machine gun posts, the weakest point in their line, etc. The men had the greatest confidence with Dawson planning their moves."

The men of the 46th were now experiencing billets for the first time. Harold Emery, a former butcher from Pilot Butte, would write: "We usually stayed in a barnyard. We slept in sheds or a barn while the officers slept in the farmhouse. The barns were mostly paved with stone for drainage and were pretty uncomfortable. But tired we were, and we slept rather well."

Sergeants were normally able to find slightly better accommodation, as was testified by Sergeant A. C. Scott. Tickler, as he was known (because of his ability to procure the jam of that name), wrote home: "Six of the other sergeants and myself were put into a deserted hen-house for a few days, and we called it home for the time being. We got nicely asleep the first night when the rats started in. They chewed up our clothes and everything in general. We did not mind that so much, but when they started walking over our faces we immediately raised an objection. We got busy and rustled a few candles, and the lights succeeded in keeping the rats quiet. We got nicely asleep again, and were enjoying wonderful dreams of beating up Heine, when we were awakened by the old reliable rooster. He couldn't be driven from his old home. To wind up the experience, the next day we started by casting sidelong glances at each other. The end of it was that we all beat it back to our hen-house to read our shirts."[4]

This became a common practice. On one of the first days after crossing the Channel, George Tomlinson, the medical corporal, was quietly accosted by a fastidious bank clerk from Regina. The man was agitated and tears began to roll down his cheeks. He looked cautiously from side to side and then whispered desperately, "I—I just found a louse in my shirt." Soon everyone had the telltale itch, and all ranks began "reading their shirts." Even officers were not immune. The tubby Scottish "country gentleman," Captain Jock Rankin, was often spotted, hands in pockets, scratching away at the pesky creatures. Once, on parade, Jock, who always maintained his sense of values, was obliged to scratch a most delicate spot. Snickers broke out in the ranks behind him. Unabashed by such boorish behaviour, he turned—still at attention, of course—and asked, "What are you laughing about? You itch just as much as I do."

The day after the battalion arrived in Belgium, the men were out on a route-march when a dispatch was received ordering them up to the front immediately. "Our battalion 'fell in' at 1 P.M. in heavy marching order," wrote Lieutenant John Copp of Saskatoon. "We marched steadily (except for a ten-minute break each hour) until 9 P.M. when we arrived on the hill above Poperinghe. I figured that we marched thirty-three miles that day with heavy packs, and we had nothing to eat from noon until nearly ten that night."

Orders announced that A Company of the 46th was to go into the line. These would be the first troops of the 4th Division to do so. They would be met by scouts from the 18th Battalion of the 2nd Division, and that night the company was to be taken into the 18th's reserve trenches two hundred yards behind the firing line. The initiation would take place at a spot known as the M and N Trench on the southern flank of the infamous Ypres Salient. This portion of the front was relatively quiet and had been chosen for the 4th Division's baptism of fire. Each night another company would move up until all four had been in the reserve, support, and firing lines.

The men of A Company bumped along the pitted road in lorries that night while the sounds of gunfire grew steadily louder. When the convoy halted, the troops dismounted in a muffled clatter and moved down the remnants of a road to Hell Fire Corner, where they turned east toward the front. Strange shattered figures, which had once been trees, loomed on each side of the road. The night sky ahead and to each side was almost continually alight from the glare of the flares that the enemy sent up. Sounds became individualized—the crack of a rifle, the sudden clatter of a machine gun, the crash of a lone shell, or the thundering of an isolated barrage—all were heard interspersed by silence along this "quiet sector." Men marvelled that it was possible to approach such a place without being torn to pieces, but the silent trek through the communication trench known as Chicory Lane was completed without casualties.

Every man carried his own vivid images from his first time under fire. Jim Broomhead, a pint-sized sniper, wrote: "It was pitch dark except for the starshells. The fellows who were to instruct me in my style of work were standing on the firestep and seemed unconcerned that the enemy was only about one hundred and fifty feet away. As far as I was concerned, I was scared to death."

To Private Emery, the former butcher, the protecting breastworks were impressive. "The duckboards on the bottom were in excellent shape. In fact, they were the best trenches any of us were to see from then on."

"Every night each of the four Lewis guns had to fire a thousand rounds," recalled Mac McDonald of Moose Jaw. "That ammunition of course had to be carried into the front line, and I can tell you it was extremely heavy. We used to move around from bay to bay firing off our Lewis guns, much to the annoyance (which was volubly expressed) of the people in those bays. I often wonder if we hit anything. We hadn't the faintest idea of where we were firing except that it was in the general direction of the German trenches."

For some, their baptism of fire was more brutal. "On our first trip into the line, my platoon, No. 8, along with the rest of B Company, was marching along the road when we came to Hell Fire Corner," wrote Lieutenant Copp. "The Germans apparently had a range on this spot. Shrapnel shells started bursting overhead, and one burst directly over my platoon. I had five of my men wounded including my platoon sergeant. One of my men had a broken leg, and as we had no first-aid man along, I had my first experience at trying to set a leg." Later that night Lieutenant Copp and his men took their places with the 18th Battalion in the firing line. "I was standing right near a sentry looking over the parapet of the front line. He was peering over, watching what was going on, as he was supposed to do. Bullets were coming over all the time and one caught this chap in the middle of the forehead and he fell dead at my feet."

On the night of 17/18 August, D Company took over in the firing line. It was the last company of the 46th to go into the line for this tour. The next night the battalion would be relieved by the 44th. The approach through the communication trench had been completely smooth. The forward trench was occupied and a small patrol went out into no man's land. Jock Rankin's batman, Ted Oakley, recalled that night: "We had our first fatal casualty a few minutes after taking over. A chap named Harrison was a member of a party sent out into no man's land. He just caught a stray bullet in the head. It made us realize it was no picnic we were on."

On 20 August the battalion moved out of the line and back into billets. The men had had their first mild taste of warfare. They had behaved well and their schooling was now complete. The next time into M and N the 46th would be on its own. The men would be solely responsible for their sector and would at last be taking on the "wily Hun" after two years of frustration.

Despite this elation, it was a subdued battalion which gathered at Ridgewood Cemetery that day to pay its final tribute to the first to fall. As "The Last Post" sounded and No. 437026, Private William Harrison, was lowered into his final resting place, few failed to wonder who was destined to follow. It is doubtful that any of the men gathered there realized how terrible the 46th's sacrifice was to be.

CHAPTER FOUR

Over the Top

Death is not an adventure to those who stand face to face with it.
                Erich M. Remarque,
                All Quiet on the Western Front

A feeble moon illuminated the tense faces. The night was filled with the commonplace sounds of their new existence—the random pop of rifles somewhere down the line and every so often a short burst of machine gun fire. The moon was suddenly obscured by clouds, and a nervous enemy shot up a flare to flood no man's land with its ghostly light. It was midnight, 16 September 1916. Fifty grim-faced men, relative strangers to this world of stealth, huddled behind the breastworks of M and N Trench. They were the first raiding party of the 46th. In ten minutes they would test the German defences.

The 46th had completed several stretches up the line since its initiation over a month before, and the men were beginning to feel like veterans, although they had yet to go over the top. Their surroundings had become familiar as had the bays of M and N Trench. The "trench" was in reality a long wall of sandbags and bully-beef tins stretching southwest from St. Eloi. Each bay was designated M or N 1, 2, 3, etc.—hence the name. The Canadian line wound along a valley and was completely dominated by the Germans on Messines Ridge. Due to this fact, the walls of M and N were inordinately high, except where streams meandered through the line. Duckboard walks raised above ground level kept feet relatively dry. Fortunately the weather had remained pleasant.

In front of M and N lay a no man's land of shell holes and patches of scrub grass. Three hundred yards away was the German wire, tumbled by shells and waving tattered shreds of clothing in the wind. At the top of the gentle slope lay the shattered remains of Wytschaete. Once a pleasant town of over three thousand citizens, it now lay ruined, roofs sagging amid grey rubble.

Trench life had already become routine—nights of strenuous work parties and patrols in no man's land followed by days of comparative rest disturbed each afternoon by "rum jars," a gift from the enemy. "Rum jar" was the name given to a type of German trench-mortar shell, which was shaped somewhat like the jars in which the rum ration was brought and which travelled so slowly that its flight could be predicted quite accurately. Sharp-eyed sentries were posted in each bay to shout out directions such as "Rum jar on the left!" This information would send men scampering to the right while the bomb tumbled through the air to land with a terrific explosion near the spot predicted.

The 46th soon learned to respect the lumbering rum jar. "It was about noon, and a lovely day, but Fritz was sending over rum jars," wrote Harold Emery, the former butcher. "The first one just burst about ten feet from our bay, and a minute or so later one burst really close but to the left of the bay. It seemed so close that Major MacKenzie went to take a look and took me with him. There were others in our bay, but they were ordered to keep a lookout through the periscope. When we saw what the rum jar had done we were both shaken. No one was alive, but the sides of the trench were spattered with bits of bodies."

Daybreak was "stand to" time as every man mounted the firestep to repel a possible enemy attack. Rifle inspection followed while cooks in shelters of corrugated iron and sandbags prepared the inevitable breakfast of bacon and bread, washed down by tea. The rest of the morning was usually quiet. After the noon meal an afternoon of hide-and-seek with the rum jars was the norm. The new Stokes mortars were occasionally employed to retaliate. This weapon could put as many as nine shells into the air at one time and played havoc with the German line. Unfortunately the Hun had developed an unsporting habit of shelling the line severely in reprisal for a Stokes bombardment.

Daily life varied according to the soldier's duties, but the men soon discovered that night was the deadliest time. Jim Butterworth, one of the homesteading brothers from Coleville, recalled: "You could become so tired and exhausted that you would lean against a wall or stump and be asleep in seconds, and still, at the slightest sound, be wide awake. You didn't move a muscle but your eyes took in the darkness around you. If the noise was continued, you simply slid slowly to a prone position and very cautiously and silently prepared your hardware for prompt action. If the noise was not repeated, after a steady silence of about five minutes you simply fell asleep again."

Gas was the latest German terror weapon and the troops had been issued with a primitive gas mask known as the P.H. helmet, "made out of a shirt material which made you resemble Donald Duck. Your ears and everything were covered and your collar was fastened tightly around it." The 46th endured its first gas attack while back in support near La Clytte. Private N. MacDonald was there: "The gas warning sounded and we lost no time taking refuge in our P.H. helmets. When the 'all clear' sounded a little later, we felt elated that we had successfully withstood our first gas attack until one of the men discovered that one of the eyepieces was missing from his helmet and he should have been a casualty."

As soldiers, the men realized that casualties were inevitable, yet they were new to the game and each death struck home. When a popular sergeant was killed, some of his men knelt and kissed his cheek. Death had already torn apart one of the brother combinations. Private Edgar Tallis, one of the three musical brothers, had been severely wounded on 6 September. Five days later he had died. But the deaths had all seemed so impersonal, like an act of nature. A stray shell while moving up, a random rifle shot, or a blast from the trench mortar—it almost seemed that there was no human element involved.

On the night of 8 September all this changed. That morning Captain Bertie Philbrick of B Company had asked the adjutant, Captain Dann, to persuade the CO to let him lead a small patrol over to the enemy line to capture a prisoner. George Dann had laughed and pointed out that the supply of Military Crosses had just run out and that Bertie should wait until more came in. However, Philbrick was not leg-pulling, so the colonel eventually gave him permission to go if he wished, and only if conditions were "satisfactory."

The nights had been exceptionally quiet and 8 September was no different. At eleven Philbrick and four volunteers from Battalion Bombers and Scouts went over the top and vanished into the silence. Everyone waited tensely, but no sounds came back. Evidently Fritz was neither overly alert nor aggressive.

An officer at Battalion Headquarters later described that night: "Then came the shock, for about forty-five minutes later the usual 'Adjutant on the phone please' came from Signals, and the message came through that a man of the raid party was just back and reported that Captain Philbrick was badly wounded, and that the three other men were bringing him in. We at once got in touch with Tomlinson. . . . The next word received was 'we can hear them!'—'we can see them'—'both fronts very quiet,'—'they are just coming in over the parapet,'—'he is in a very bad state, has a severe wound; appears to be suffering and rather delirious. I am going to use a hypo and apply dressing. Afraid he cannot last much longer, but will get him to the Brasserie Dressing Station by going over the top.' "[5] It was all to no avail. Captain Bertie Philbrick died on the duckboard floor of M and N Trench.

It was shortly after this that Divisional Headquarters ordered the first official raids to be carried out by the 4th Division. In mid-September seven battalions were to raid the enemy all along the Ypres sector. The tragic truth was that raids were costly. The more haphazard the venture, the more costly it could become. So the 46th's first official raid was going to be planned to the smallest detail. Zero hour was set for 12:15 on the night of 16/17 September, and the raiders from the prairies were to penetrate the Hollandscheschuur Farm Defences.

The raiders consisted of two bombing squads of eleven men

each, led by an officer. These men were loaded down with Mills bombs, which were to be hurled into dugouts as the attackers swept through the German trenches. Engineers would accompany the raiders to destroy with explosives any machine gun emplacements located. Four scouts and two special observers from Brigade Headquarters completed the first wave. In addition, there was to be a covering party consisting of six snipers and two four-men Lewis gun sections, who would establish themselves at the point of entry into the enemy trench and provide covering fire both to right and left while the bombing party advanced each way along the trench.

The raiders were all dressed for this type of work. Balaclava hats and sweaters provided lightweight comfort and replaced the conspicuous silhouette of the tin hat. Badges were removed, and all ranks were forbidden to carry maps or even letters with them. Such information found on the body of a fallen raider could assist the enemy in his intelligence gathering.

While the raid was in progress, the trenches held by the 46th were to be manned by a skeleton crew. The forward company would be withdrawn two hundred yards to a support trench, and only a handful of sentries, two in every third bay, would man the front line. One platoon in the support trench was also equipped to join in the raid if the attackers required assistance.

An essential element of the attack was the accompanying artillery and mortar barrage. The German position was to receive an intense bombardment commencing at zero hour. Five minutes later this fire would switch to a box barrage designed to cut the objective off from all possible enemy reinforcements. This stage was to last twenty-five minutes. The rate of fire would then drop off and die out. Finally—a diabolical touch—the barrage would open up once more for three minutes at zero plus sixty minutes. This was to catch the relaxing enemy as he brought up his reserves and surveyed the damage.

Thus it was that fifty men from the 46th stood fidgeting nervously in their trench that night. Jim Broomhead, the pint-sized sniper, described their initiation: "Some officer gives us the signal, and over the top we go in single file. The first one out is a huge French-Canadian Indian by the name of Vandale. He was one of the bravest men I ever knew. It ended up he was the first one of our fellows into the German trench. Jimmy Jackson and myself being snipers are the last out of the trench. We hardly got through the wire when all hell breaks loose. Our own artillery had opened a barrage on us! The officer had sent us out too early! Shells are crashing everywhere and the Germans are throwing up flares so it's bright as day. The din was tremendous. I wasn't even clear of our barbed wire when I see that huge Vandale running back to our trench. That was enough for me! I turns and gives a great running jump and comes crashing down on top of the officer who had sent us out early."

The raid was disintegrating into a fiasco as the men piled back into their trench out of the covering barrage. The enemy, now alerted, had begun to retaliate. To make matters worse, the "Officer Commanding Raid" was in a daze, possibly from being jumped upon by Private Broomhead, though Jim had another explanation: "I noted that he was rather tipsy and didn't seem to know what was going on." It was at this moment that Lieutenant Cattell stepped into the breach. Broomhead later recalled: "Then I could see another officer standing on the parapet, with blood streaming down over his face and waving his revolver over his head yelling, 'Come on boys! They know we're coming! Come on lads, lets go!' So out we go again."

This time the raiders reached the enemy trenches as the bombardment shifted. Miraculously, there were no casualties. The bombing parties split left and right to begin their deadly work. The sappers found a crater, which they labelled a machine gun emplacement, and blew it up. Meanwhile the covering parties had arrived and had "opened up a rapid fire in the general direction of Berlin." The right-hand party moved to the point arranged and then bombed the enemy line. The left party, led by Sergeant A. R. Walker, proceeded sixty yards up the German trench and accounted for six enemy killed plus an unknown number in a dugout. Fortunately for the raiders, the line was lightly held and the enemy seemed demoralized. A total of ninety Mills bombs were thrown.

Broomhead was a sniper in the party facing left. "I'm laying there with my rifle stretched out in front of me, popping off shots at anything, when I hear this shouting: 'Don't shoot Jim, don't shoot!' There, within six inches of the end of my bayonet, appears the fat face of a middle-aged German with short-cropped reddish hair. He was paralysed with fright and was being boosted out of the trench by members of the raiding party. That was our prisoner—the first one taken by the 46th."

By zero plus nine minutes the raiders had accomplished their task. Still without casualties, they withdrew.

They began congratulating themselves as roll call was taken, but then it was discovered that one man was missing. Volunteers immediately went back into no man's land, a spot now exceptionally unhealthy. The missing man was found, lost and creeping about, and the party returned unharmed.

The next morning the official report went in, and as official reports tend to do, this one spoke of the raid in glowing terms. There would probably have been a few snorts of derision from the raiders had they read the opening lines: "The minor operation as pre-arranged was successfully carried out on the night of the 16/17th September, 1916. At 12:10 A.M., on the 17th, the party left our parapet and laid down in front of our wire for five minutes, while our Artillery and Trench Mortars bombarded the enemy's lines. The barrage of fire lifted at the right moment, and the party rushed into the enemy's trenches."[6]

Despite the early confusion, everyone was happy. Brigade Headquarters had its prisoner, the colonel had a glowing report to submit, and General Watson was overjoyed. The happiest of all, however, were the men of the 46th, for they had just proven themselves.

CHAPTER FIVE

The Somme

If a giant plow could have been made to plow back and forth, twenty-four hours a day, and then have Lake Ontario emptied on top of it, and if a million shell holes as big as a swimming pool were added, then you'd have the Somme, the way I saw it.
Letter from Pte. Jim Broomhead, 46th Battalion

During the 46th's tour of duty on the Ypres front the first three Canadian divisions had moved south to the Somme area. This left the new 4th Division as one part of a polyglot formation made up of British, Belgian, Australian, and Canadian troops. This collection was named Franks Force after its commanding general.

The day after the 46th's first raid, Franks Force was disbanded and the 4th Division became part of the British 9th Corps. The ordinary soldier knew nothing about these administrative changes, nor did he much care. What he did notice was the new emphasis on training. On 24 September the 46th had been drawn west to St. Omer. While in reserve there the men learned to handle the British Lee-Enfield rifle, a vast improvement on the cumbersome and delicate Ross rifle. Sir Sam Hughes had insisted the Canadians be armed with the Ross, designed and manufactured in Canada, but the weapon had proven to be completely unsuited to the muddy conditions of trench warfare and it jammed after several rounds of rapid fire. It was a sign of the waning of Sir Sam Hughes's star that the dependable British rifle was at last being issued to the Canadians.

The training emphasized co-operation with artillery and aircraft. An attack seemed imminent, for many practice assaults were made behind an imaginary "creeping barrage" which advanced one hundred yards every three minutes. Each man had his helmet marked with chalk to assist friendly aircraft in spotting the advancing troops.

Two changes in appearance also occurred at this time. The men received new respirators, or gas masks, and the old cloth P.H. helmet was discarded. The new respirators were tested with tear gas and proved to be very effective. The other change was of a heraldic nature. Each Canadian division was issued with a rectangular "patch" to be worn on the upper arm as a distinguishing mark. To make identification easier, the patches were colour-coded and another design was placed above the rectangle. The 46th wore a semicircle above the patch and the entire insignia was coloured green. Unlike the majority of battalions which wore metal shoulder titles, the 46th had, as a remnant of its rifle regiment origins, a red and green cloth shoulder flash with "46th Canada." This was always referred to as the "jam label."

While at St. Omer the battalion proved to be popular with the local inhabitants. The young French girls were particularly taken with the kilted pipe band. On one march through the city a bevy of the bolder mademoiselles skipped from the crowd and, giggling and laughing, lifted the bandsmen's bright red kilts for all to see. The pipers' faces were soon as red as their kilts, but manfully they continued to play, undeterred by such behaviour.

On 3 October, the 46th left St. Omer in the familiar "40 hommes, 8 chevaux" box cars. They were going to "where the action was"—the Somme. The Somme front received its name from the minor river which flows through the gently undulating hills of Picardy. Marshy bottomlands surround the river, but the Somme uplands are dry and chalky. In 1914 the major cities had been Amiens, Albert, and Bapaume, which ran in a straight line from west to east-northeast. The Germans held a line which lay astride the Albert-Bapaume Road in the vicinity of the village of Courcelette.

As the troops approached the summit of the road from Warloy to Albert they were startled by an apparent apparition that rose into the sky beyond the ridge. A golden figure of a woman loomed before them. In her outstretched arms she bore a naked child. The figure was hanging parallel with the horizon, face down, holding the babe earthward. It was the famous Golden Virgin of Albert Cathedral, maintaining her precarious station above the city despite the damage caused by German shells. Legend had it that the Allies would lose the war should the figure topple. To the men of the 46th it seemed a rather fragile hope of victory.

From the summit, the Somme battlefields could be seen as rows of slight ridges beyond Albert. Old trenches, craters, and shell holes stood out as chalky white scars. The area between was a hive of activity: horse lines, supply dumps, airdromes, tent lines, gun parks and marching troops. All appeared to be jostling one another for room.

The weather had turned wet and cold, and good billets were not in abundance. Most men slept in water-logged shell holes and in the dugouts of a brickyard, the roofs of corrugated tin or tarpaulin being supported by "old rusty Hun rifles." The 46th scouts and snipers had it better—they were billeted in a house. "It had been knocked about a good deal, but the front of the house was fairly well intact. About thirty of us were in one room. The windows and doors were plugged with cardboard, old blankets, and groundsheets. There was a hallway with a very smoky old stove."

After a short time the battalion was ordered to form up on the Albert-Bapaume Road. A Canadian battalion was returning from the front, and the 46th was to give it a hearty welcome. Jim Broomhead described the scene which was indelibly scribed on his memory that day. "Both bands proceeded up the road while we lined up along each side. Pretty soon the bands reappeared playing full blast. Behind them was a very small group of weary, mud-caked kilties. There were more in our two bands than walked behind them. There had been an attack the night before and this pitifully small band of men was what was left of one battalion."

On 10 October, the 4th Division relieved the 3rd Division on the Somme front, and within a week the first three divisions had moved north to the Arras and Lens area. The 4th Division was on its own again, this time as part of the 2nd Corps.

The conditions were unbelievable, and even the British official history abandons its normal restraint when describing the Somme sector of October and November 1916: "Here in a wilderness of mud, holding water-logged trenches or shell-hole posts, accessible only by night, the infantry abode in conditions which might be likened to those of earth-worms, rather than human kind. Our vocabulary is not adapted to describe such an existence, because it is outside experience for which words are normally required. Mud, for the men in the line, was no mere inorganic nuisance and obstacle.—It took an aggressive wolf-like guise, and like a wolf could pull down and swallow the lonely wanderer in the darkness."[7]

The men of the 46th formed their own impressions as they went up on various work parties. Past the derelict tanks and dead horses they squelched, loaded down with trench mats, Stokes shells, tins of water, barbed wire, small arms ammunition and the like. The Albert-Bapaume Road was lined with abandoned and shattered equipment, and mingled with that were the remains of what were once living men.

When, all too soon, the 46th was ordered into the line, the men saw even worse. Sniper Jim Broomhead, twenty years old, recorded the scene. "I got my first glimpse of death and its stench at Poziers. The dead had not been removed, and they were piled three deep. What an awful sight! At about Poziers we marched in single file about five yards apart. Now we came to the trench. God forbid anybody from seeing what I saw. Our barbed wire was fairly well intact, but it hung full of dead Canadians and Germans, like birds on telephone wires. The parapet had been kept built up, but you couldn't avoid the arms and legs that were sticking out of it."

The continuous rain which had fallen since the 4th Division's arrival served to make a terrible situation even worse. The Canadians had taken Thiepval Ridge during the last days of September. Now they had been ordered to continue the advance. This meant giving up positions on the ridge for ones full of water in the valley. The mud was indescribable. Bugler Vic Syrett of

B Company wrote: "Our transport lines had weigh scales, and it was found that a man's clothing became so coated with half-frozen mud that together with his boots and puttees they weighed in the neighbourhood of 120 lb., and in one case, 145 lb."

The Germans looked down into this quagmire from the Ancre Heights where they had an unlimited field of fire. The enemy had dropped back into Regina Trench, which lay just behind the crest of the heights. This made a very difficult target for the Lahore Battery, which was serving temporarily as the 4th Division's artillery. Nevertheless, these crack Indian Army gunners kept up a continuous bombardment on the enemy in his well-protected position.

To the men in the line, the appalling conditions were only a part of the horror. For the first time, the 46th was to learn that heavy casualties were involved in simply holding a position. Death was everywhere. It came suddenly and picked a man here and another there. This is what they had learned at M and N Trench. On the Somme it was different. Death snatched whole handfuls of young lives at every turn.

John Copp, the officer commanding No. 8 Platoon, sent four men back for water one night. By one o'clock they had not returned. Finally a lone man appeared, dripping and exhausted, to report that the party had been shelled and he had returned to bring assistance for the others. "So I sent four men back with a stretcher," related Copp. "By seven or eight o'clock I wondered what had happened because they hadn't returned. Finally I was informed that a shell had made a direct hit on the lad on the stretcher and wiped out the entire party as they were carrying him back."

Private Harold Emery had a similar type of experience. "Two of us had chosen to sleep near the entrance of a dugout about twelve feet down where the steps had taken a left turn. A shell burst and sealed the entrance and I can only guess that it was three or four hours before the diggers reached us. Both of us were unconscious. I later watched them digging for the rest of the men, but the mud and water were pouring into the hole as fast as they could dig. It was about noon the next day that they had to give up."

The young bugler, Vic Syrett, who was now employed as a

runner, also had an unpleasant brush with death. "One night I was nearing our company trenches when a German battery opened up. It was throwing dirt all over me, and of course steel was flying everywhere. I jumped into a shell hole for protection and put my hand squarely into a dead German's face. He had been there for some time of course, and I didn't enjoy his company, but better there than in the open, even if the hole was half full of water. It made an impression on an eighteen-year-old."

Several methods were tried to make the ordeal more bearable. The battalion went into the line in halves. Colonel Dawson and the adjutant, Captain Dann, took one half in one night. Twenty-four hours later they would be relieved by the other half under the new second-in-command, Major Milt Francis, and the assistant adjutant, Lieutenant J. S. ("Woody") Woodward, formerly Canada's youngest alderman.

In the trenches themselves various methods were adopted in the hopes of bettering the lot of the men. "At a supply dump we were issued thigh-waders like fishermen use," recalled Jim Broomhead. "You never got a matched pair; maybe one size six and one fourteen, but they did help. They kept your feet fairly dry and that was a big item."

"Because of ghastly weather and the heavy shelling, the nightly rations from our transport lines on the brickfield at Albert couldn't get through," wrote Vic Syrett. "So many men were getting sick that in desperation someone got the bright idea of sending up packages of Symington's Pea Soup powder, and every man was also issued two small cans of 'Sterno' to enable him to make his own *hot* soup. I'm sure that this soup and the small ration of British Navy rum at 'stand down' every morning were the two things that enabled us to survive."

Eventually it would come time to pull out of the line and go back into billets, and in the darkness the men would file, shambling and splashing, along the ditches shown on the maps as CTs (communication trenches), back over Thiepval Ridge—now moving overland—through the grim depression known as Death Valley, along the shattered streets of the once-lovely village of Courcelette, where Battalion Headquarters was situated in a captured German dugout, and onto the Albert-Bapaume Road.

The Albert-Bapaume Road was in constant use, crowded with men and supplies moving up by night. During the day, labour battalions slaved over its pulverized surface in an attempt to keep the life line open. At all times this road came under continuous fire from the German batteries back of Ancre Heights.

On arrival at their billets, the weary footsloggers would thankfully collapse in their rat-infested "bivvies," where they would immediately fall into a restless sleep, tortured by recent sights and memories. "We managed to get a piece of corrugated iron," recalled Mac McDonald, "and decided to build into the side of a bank. Sure enough, we unearthed a dead body. We had just come out of the line, we were dead tired, and the only part of the body which showed was a leg, so I slept that night with a dead man's foot six inches above my head."

Morning would come all too soon, and with it came "spit and polish." Every man had to get his filthy gear back into barracks-room condition. Buttons and the 46th cap badges would soon (reluctantly) be gleaming, and coats, caps, and trousers brushed more or less clean. Then roll call would be taken and inspection carried out. During one of these vastly unpopular rituals a German long-range shell landed on one of the billets, utterly destroying it. For a time, there was almost no grumbling about inspections.

While out of the line, a number of men would be detailed to collect the rations for their particular unit. Jim Broomhead described a typical ration party: "Along the road would be a line of horse-drawn wagons full of gunny-sacks of 'gourmet' food. There were scores of men from scores of units there for their eats. The guy on top of the wagon would lift a sack and call out, '46th Scouts.' Somebody out of the darkness reaches up and grabs the sack.... Then the man might say, '44th Bombers.' Somebody grabs that sack—maybe a 46th man. Everybody grabbed everything they could, and it always backfired. So we'd head back to the 'Albert-Hilton' and dump our half-a-dozen sacks. Maybe only one sack actually belonged to us so maybe we landed up with three bags of sopping wet bread, or maybe one whole sack of canned butter, and of course sacks of bully beef or beans. Now you could have a hot meal.... You'd take a Player's cigarette tin and stuff it with your shirt tail, or better still, a roll of bandage. Then you soaked the whole works with candle grease. It would last a lifetime. Now you take your bully beef and the pork and beans, hang it over the burner, and in no time you had a hot meal in your mess tin. Sometimes you could even dry out the bread."

When they were out of the line, the men tried to relax by playing "penny ante," writing letters, "reading their shirts," or yarning about the girls and home. There were often makeshift concerts put on by talent from the division. For most, relief came with a few glasses of the red or white French wine.

Mac McDonald wouldn't settle for the cheap wines from the *estaminets*. "On one occasion while we were billeted in Albert, we discovered that with a little bit of jiggery-pokery we could get bottles of whisky out of the Expeditionary Force canteen which had been established in Albert. The method was simplicity itself. Only officers were allowed whisky, but our officer's batman got hold of the small army books on which notes and messages were written. I wrote, 'Please supply the bearer, John Jones, who is my batman, with a bottle of whisky,' and signed on it our Lewis gun officer's name. Off went the batman with three francs and back he came with a bottle of whisky. As long as we could find the three francs we were in clover."

Private Syrett remembered one highlight. "We had our first official bath in Albert in late October in the big wooden vats of a winery. About a dozen were in the same water at once, and Lord knows how many before us. The water was filthy, but we were worse."

The officers also looked for ways to escape momentarily from the spectre of muddy death. Woody Woodward, the assistant adjutant, later reminisced: "We were lying around this cheese factory in Albert where our billets were. I got the idea that we should have a cocktail party, so I got a lot of liquor and mixed up a cocktail that had liqueurs, whisky, and everything else in it. Everyone got tight as a nit, and in the midst of this, Dizzy Dawson wanted an officers' conference. There was one officer who never took a drink, Lieutenant Young I believe it was. He was the only sober one in the bunch, so we dispatched Mr. Young over to the OC's conference to represent C Company. Dizzy didn't like that one bit. I was not one of his favourite officers after that."

Soon it was back into the firing line again. Then word came that the 44th Battalion would attack Regina Trench. (The plan of attack sent out by Brigade Headquarters was printed appropriately enough on the back of spare copies of last will and testament forms.) The operation was scheduled for 7:00 A.M. on 24 October. The 46th would supply one company to provide covering fire, repel counterattacks, and send forward a digging party to connect Regina Trench with the Canadian line.

A composite company from the 46th was detached under Captain Jock Rankin, and in pouring rain they dug saps out toward the German lines. Then the attack was suddenly postponed twenty-four hours, and the troops huddled in the muddy ditches until 7:00 A.M. on the following day.

"We were standing in the trench," related Lieutenant Copp, "waiting for seven o'clock, when a shell hit direct at one end of the trench where five of my men were standing with me and blew up the whole trench. One of the boys was buried up to his neck—he was killed—another was buried up to his waist, and the chap at the end of the trench was too. I was buried up to my knees in mud and I could pull myself out, but the other fellows, we had to help them get out. This was about six-thirty in the morning so it was pretty upsetting to start an attack after that, but it was part of our job."

Zero hour came and the 44th went over the top. Then came the 46th's turn, as Lieutenant Copp described. "Just after 7:00 A.M. Lieutenant Woodcock led off with his No. 5 and 6 platoons to go over several hundred yards to our left to reach the trenches where the 44th had just jumped off from. I followed with my 7 and 8 platoons. About halfway across to the 44th's lines word comes back to me that Woodcock had been killed. So I proceed to the front of the company to lead them to our objective. The machine-gunning and shelling were very heavy, and just as we were approaching the 44th's line I saw Lieutenant Horan standing at the junction where we were supposed to turn right. He called out to me, 'Copp, don't bring your men to this corner. It's suicide!' We were about forty yards from there at this time, so I jumped out of the shallow trench we were in and led my company overland to our objective. It was a wise move as the Germans had their machine guns trained on that corner and were mowing down anybody who came that way. Lieutenant Horan was killed at that spot about a minute after calling to me."

Meanwhile the 44th's frontal attack had become a slaughter. "In a ghastly few minutes well-nigh half the attacking force have been cut down," wrote the 44th's historian. "Hardly have the men of the leading platoons stepped up on top when they are met by an appalling concentration of machine gun fire from front and flank—mowing down the waves as they come into the zone of fire. With terrific suddenness the enemy barrage bursts along the front. The entire area churns and spouts with bursting shell—as guns of all calibres pound the front endlessly. The supporting barrage is almost non-existent—a few guns only come into action."[8]

A battle patrol was hastily organized by Lieutenant J. S. Woodward to establish contact with the 44th. Woody, who was rather rotund and a jocular sort, found the going rough. "I had a sergeant and ten men—bombers and so forth—and we started to crawl around in the front line. And of course we were pretty well exposed because the Germans could see what was going on and they were firing those damned whiz-bangs at us. It was about a mile we had to go around this front. The damned whiz-bangs kept firing at us and we kept ducking our heads down. However, we found that the line had been established and there had been no counterattack. It took us a couple of hours of course to get down to Brigade Headquarters, which was reasonably far behind the lines. I got there tired as hell, and these whiz-bangs coming at us the whole time had scared the pants off me. I collapsed in a chair and muttered, 'These goddamn whiz-bangs, these goddamn whiz-bangs!' The brigade major got pretty worried; he thought I was shellshocked."

During this time, John Copp's platoons 7 and 8 had begun their assignment of digging a communications trench from the 44th's line to Regina Trench. "We got into position all right. There was a little bit of trench there so we started digging and getting as deep as we could to get cover. But we were only about two feet down and some of my men were killed right there while they were digging. About eight-thirty, I sent a young fellow named Cooper—he was a stretcher bearer and also acted as my runner—back with a message to Battalion Headquarters telling them where we were and what we were doing."

Meanwhile, in the 46th trenches, Jock Rankin attempted to keep abreast of the situation. Private Ted Oakley, Rankin's batman, remembered that morning vividly. "It was horrible. All that day Jerry knocked hell out of us. A whiz-bang landed at the back of the trench six or seven feet from my head. It took me months to get over that. If I was anywhere near the front I could hear shells coming at me from every direction. That shell killed one of the most popular chaps in the battalion, a fellow named Red Horning. All I got was a piece of casing through my coattails. Major Rankin was in charge that day and he surely proved his worth. He never left the front trench all day."

Jock Rankin continued to try and direct affairs, although there were periods when no communication could be maintained with the detached platoon. By eight o'clock the situation was critical. The 44th's attacking force had been crushed—the living were pinned down in no man's land. The front line was now held in the 44th's sector by four machine guns and the remnants of the 46th's composite company. At 8:52 Headquarters ordered Lieutenant Copp to withdraw his party to the 46th's lines. The message was carried by Private Cooper who had already made the trip once each way. Rankin sent out two runners, Walter Nurse and Dan McFadden, to try to establish contact with the platoons under Lieutenant Steel who had taken over command after Horan had been killed. The two runners were also to carry messages to the 44th's survivors.

As the parties gradually returned, Captain Rankin organized the defence and prepared for the expected counterattack. By eleven o'clock the situation seemed to be clearing up. On the left, the 44th was being reinforced after its disastrous assault, and the 46th's own lines were now held in sufficient strength to withstand an attack. A few minutes later, large numbers of the enemy were spotted coming over the ridge in front. The snipers and machine gunners opened fire and accounted for fifty or so Germans. The attackers withdrew and by 1:00 P.M. Rankin reported, "Situation normal."

That night the 46th was relieved around nine o'clock by a British battalion. John Copp led the 125 survivors of B Company out. "We came to the Albert-Bapaume Road and were told we would have to go to X-eleven-A, better known as the Chalk Pits. So we took a path to the left of the road towards the Chalk Pits. It was raining and cold and muddy, and it was maybe ten or twelve miles. My men were awfully tired. There was no question about that. They had been in since Monday night—this was Friday night. They'd had no rest, no sleep, not even a place to lie down in during that time. We marched along for an hour or so and I decided we'd better stop and have a rest. They'd just lie down in the mud and have a few minutes rest and I'd say, 'All right boys, let's get going again.' They'd get up, and I'd lead off again. Each time I did this I found that a few never could get up and they'd just lie there in the mud. Our company was getting smaller. We got out to X-eleven-A about four in the morning, but I only had six men with me."

The attack had been a complete failure. Recriminations surged back and forth, with the divisional commander and the brigadier each suggesting that the other was the bungler—for bungled the affair had certainly been.[9] The obvious loser would be St. Pierre Hughes, for his brother, Sir Sam, was about to be sacked as minister of militia. This would make the younger Hughes's removal a simple process. The less obvious losers were the men of the 10th Brigade. Many had paid for the incompetent planning with their lives.

CHAPTER SIX

Regina and Desire

"He's got fifty medals. . . ."
"Yeah, but he'll never die in a lousy trench. . . ."
"God, no. Generals die in bed."
"Well, that's a pretty good place to die!"
                    C. Y. Harrison, *Generals Die in Bed*

The tenth of November found the 46th in bivouacs. The troops had arrived back at the Chalk Pit that morning and were looking forward to a day or two of rest. Reserve specialists had been brought up to replace those who had just come out and there was the inevitable clean-up.

Morale had begun to suffer. Victory seemed further away than ever. Casualties mounted daily, and everyone had but one overriding desire—to get out of the Somme. "By the time we had been at the Somme for a while no man cared how serious his wound was, just as long as he got a Blighty," wrote the sniper, Jim Broomhead. "Someone might be missing from the section and the question would be asked, 'Where's Joe So-and-so?' The answer might be, 'Oh, he got a DANDY Blighty—lost his leg you know.'"

Meanwhile the division's objective had not been taken. Regina Trench still lay behind the summit of Ancre Heights, and most of its length was in German hands. On 21 October the 11th Brigade had seized a portion of the trench west of the 46th's sector, but then had come the ghastly blunder of 25 October. The 10th Brigade had gone back into the line on 3 November and had seen heavy action since. Now, during the ninth and tenth, the weather had been unusually fine and as a result the Germans were being treated to two days of howitzer fire.

For the men of the 46th the day of rest on 10 November was short lived. At 5:15 P.M. Operations Orders arrived from Brigade Headquarters. The 46th was ordered back into the line at once to make another attempt on Regina Trench. The attack was to be launched within seven hours. This left little time for planning.

The assault was to be made by two companies of the 46th and two of the 47th from New Westminster. The 46th would be on the right, and B and C were allotted the task. The plan was to slip out into no man's land and form up in waves under cover of darkness. There they would await zero hour. An eight-minute bombardment would give them time to move up to Regina Trench. When the barrage lifted the attack would go in. All was very straightforward.

Captain Dann and the colonel worked speedily to produce a set of orders before the battalion left for the front line less than two hours later. By eleven everyone was in the line. Patrols were sent out, and at 11:40 P.M. B and C Company moved out into the fetid mire of no man's land. D Company prepared for its task: to dig a trench to connect the captured section of Regina with Kling Trench. As for A Company, it was to provide carrying parties for the rest of the battalion. Zero hour was set for midnight.

Jim Butterworth, a battalion bomber, recalled those final moments: "Joe Broughton was a real comic in the outfit, and he was always my buddy. Just before zero hour Joe says to me 'Jesus Christ, Jim. I got a sickening feeling something is going to happen to me. If you get hit I'll sure as hell throw you a bandage, but if I get hit, for Christ's sake throw one to me.'" Joe had reason to be nervous; he had already received a minor wound during the 25 October affair.

"My Lewis gun crew was on the very right of the battalion," Mac McDonald recalled. "We were taken out in front of our front line a few yards, surrounded by dead men of previous attacks and the attack went in at twelve midnight."

The hurricane bombardment shattered the night silence at precisely twelve. It churned up the earth on the crest of the heights to an incredible degree, although the destruction was not visible to the Canadians below. But the "special effects" were. "To put the show on the road," wrote Jim Butterworth, "we had the Lahore Battery acting as a conductor of the orchestra—one long, a pause, four short, a pause, two short—the familiar 'Shave and a hair cut, two bits.' Then all hell breaks loose. We had all seen and heard terrific thunderstorms on the prairies. Well, multiply the thunder by three and the lightning by two, keep it going steady, and you have an idea of the bombardment. Our barrage starts in the middle of no man's land and gradually creeps forward. Now we follow the drill as planned. The barrage gives Fritz's front line special treatment and when it lifts we are there with bayonet and bomb. Any Fritz still holding a rifle dies. Others with their hands held high are shouting 'Camerade' or 'I go please.' "

"We were on our way rejoicing," reported Mac McDonald on the right flank. "We were soon on top of a rise so it wasn't so desperately muddy. The only thing was that there were a lot of dead men lying about. We came to Regina Trench, which had been absolutely shattered by quite a terrific barrage and was nothing more than a shallow ditch. We went on. I had got instructions and we went on in front of Regina Trench, set up my Lewis gun in a shell hole, and waited for the counterattack. Well a real counterattack didn't develop although there was a considerable amount—a very great deal—of shelling from the German side. We saw and heard some Germans during the night and opened fire on them with a couple of pans of Lewis-gun ammunition and they disappeared."

Colonel Dawson's official report described the battle for Regina Trench more formally: "Parties of the enemy put up a strong resistance but were mopped up, and many others who retired hurriedly towards Pys when the barrage moved forward were killed by rifle fire and by the barrage. Steps were at once taken to consolidate the new line. Machine gun posts were pushed out in front, and the digging party was formed up between Regina Trench, where it crosses Farmer Road, and Kling Trench. Work proceeded vigorously, and by 4 A.M., reports were received that consolidation was well in hand and that the new connecting trench was well dug."

The 46th, according to Brigade Orders, was to be relieved at this point, but "at 3:30 A.M. it was reported that the 47th Battalion on the left had suffered severe casualties, and information was received that they needed help. Assistance had been given by extending the 46th Battalion to the left, but a counter-attack was looked for. The orders for the relief of the 46th Battalion were at once cancelled, and immediate steps were taken to supply additional supplies of Small Arms Ammunition, bombs, and water to the front line. The Company detailed for working party was moved up to position in the North Practice Trenches to act as support should the enemy launch a heavy attack." Posts were established well ahead of the new line, but these had to be abandoned when they were shelled by their own supporting artillery.

As day dawned, the men were able to take stock of the area they had just captured. Regina Trench, which had so long frustrated the Allies, proved to be a disappointment. It was in such a state of disrepair from the bombardments of the past months that in places it was not recognizable as a trench. Evidently, the enemy had not been occupying it in strength recently but instead had established a system of posts. Despite the fact that many of the dugouts were actually falling in, they had been used as shelter by the Prussian Guards and Saxons who had held the position. Large stocks of food and supplies were stored in each.

Looking back to the ground over which they had advanced, the men of the 46th could see many huddled figures in muddy khaki: rifle fire and machine gun fire from the left had caused many casualties. By moving into no man's land before the attack, the 46th had avoided most of the enemy's retaliatory barrage which fell on the Canadian front line, but casualties totalled over seventy, and the day had merely begun.

There was little time for the men to look over their shoulders. Regina Trench had to be made defensible immediately. The attackers slaved feverishly to reconstruct the battered trench. By digging down to the hard chalk, a dry trench four feet deep was built. Meanwhile the enemy had begun to react, as the colonel's report showed: "Numerous casualties were suffered from artillery fire. The enemy's artillery opened a heavy barrage on the area between Regina Trench and 200 yards in rear of our former front line. It did not seem to be able to locate the exact position of Regina Trench as it fell some ten yards in the rear. This fire continued with varying intensity throughout the day, and was intense at about 4 A.M. and 5 P.M."

"I looked around to see how many were missing," recalled Lieutenant John Copp. "One of my pals, Lieutenant Young of C Company, seemed to be. I couldn't find him anywhere. He must have been wounded on the way over, I thought. So I took a sergeant and a runner and put a white flag on a stick and got out of the trench to start to look for him. The Germans were in their support trench only a hundred yards or so in front of us, but I thought perhaps they wouldn't shoot us if we put this white flag up. I found Young about halfway over. A shell had caught him on the hip and had blown his right hip off. Of course he was dead. I knew he was from Ontario and was an only son. I would have to write his mother. We put him in a shell hole and covered him with some earth, but I noticed he had a signet ring which his mother would probably like to have. I tried to take it off his finger but it wouldn't come. My sergeant said, 'I'll do it for you.' So he took out his clasp-knife and cut the little finger off my pal and gave me the ring. I later wrote to his mother and enclosed the ring. I only hope she received it."

Mac McDonald was also hit that day: "We were waiting for our relief and I was dozing in this shell hole—muddy at the bottom of course. When the next thing I knew I was lying on my back with a terrible pain in my back, and somebody was slapping my face trying to bring me around. There was mud all over my face and hair—I had lost my steel helmet. Apparently what had happened was that I had been hit by a piece of shrapnel and either the force of the blow or the explosion of the shell had put me down in the bottom of the shell hole in the water and mud, face down, and if they hadn't turned me over I would have drowned."

McDonald realized that with any luck at all he was on his way to Blighty. He made his way back to an aid post. On the way he was reinforced by several good fiery gulps of rum from "a good Samaritan." The effects of raw rum on a nineteen-year-old stomach, which was by that time quite empty, may be imagined. The mud-caked young soldier tottered to the aid post near Poziers, where he sat down in front of a stove in the marquee. Suddenly he toppled onto the stove. It tipped over with a tremendous crash of stovepipes and cursing soldiers. McDonald's hands were badly burned. "There was quite a disturbance. By this time I was lying on the floor, quite unable to get up, and the doctor looked at me and said, 'Why, this man's drunk!' And I remember to this day saying, 'Please sir, I'm wounded in the back.' He turned me over, dressed my wounds, and had me put on a stretcher. And lying on that stretcher I heard the guns open for the Battle of Ancre Heights on the thirteenth of November."

That night the 46th was relieved by the 12th Brigade's 73rd Battalion. On the way out two more casualties occurred, but it was for a different reason that Jim Butterworth remembered that night. "As I was about to go into our headquarters I asked where my brother Dick was. 'Hell, Jim, I heard he was missing—last seen wounded.' So, unknown to anyone else, I went back and I spent the whole night looking for Dick. I went around shell holes and saw bodies here and there. I touched their faces and each time thought, no, that's not Dick. I was thankful I didn't find him."

After a time it began to grow light and Jim Butterworth no longer knew exactly where he was. "I saw a German not too far away looking through a telescope. There was only one way he could be looking—at our line. That gave me direction and I fumbled my way back on the crawl till I came close to our line. As I approached, I kept saying, a little over a whisper, 'Hold your fire. Hold your fire.' "

The lone bomber was discovered and taken to see the local commander. After relating his story, Jim was helped onto a limber and sent back to a spot near Albert where the 46th was resting. A long walk took him the rest of the way to the battalion's "bivvies," where he received a hearty rum ration from Jock Rankin. The weary Butterworth collapsed. When he woke, someone was slapping his face saying, "Jim, wake up, damn it! Sober up!"

"Dick had my head on his lap and was slapping my face. 'Where the hell have you been?'

" 'I was out looking for you.'

" 'Why you dizzy—you should have known I'd be all right,' and he chewed me out."

The 46th had taken its portion of Regina Trench. This fortification with the name that reminded Saskatchewan men of home, had been the nemesis of all four Canadian divisions in turn. Now it was captured. At long last this foolish battle could die down. The generals could surely see that nothing more of value could be achieved in this bloody quagmire. So reasoned the victors.

But no, there was another ditch just five hundred yards beyond Regina Trench. It was declared imperative that this new trench be captured before "bad" weather set in. This trench bore the somewhat beguiling name, Desire.

It was 5:45 on the morning of 18 November that Lieutenant Richard Walter Gyles made his final rounds of A Company. For three-quarters of an hour the men had been waiting in Regina Trench, crowded in with its normal complement of men from the 44th. Fifteen minutes earlier the 46th men had received their rum ration. Their bayonets were fixed, for in another twenty-five minutes they would be going over the top. Between them and Desire Trench lay several hundred yards of hell.

The attack was to be made in two waves over a frontage of 150 yards to the right of the 50th Battalion, A Company under Major MacLean and Lieutenant Gyles forming the first wave, and B Company under Lieutenant Guest forming the second wave. Because the tension was overpowering, men reacted in various ways. Some were unnaturally loud and could hardly contain their excitement; others were strangely quiet. All knew what awaited them.

"I was scared and shaking," recalled Private Emery, the onetime butcher from Pilot Butte. "Sergeant Lees came up behind me and helped to push me up the side of the trench and over the top. My knees had turned to water. I like Sergeant Lees for that and I grieved when he was killed later that day."

The attack started according to schedule. "At the appointed time (6:10 A.M.) the barrage opened," reported Lieutenant Gyles, "and every one, as far as I know, got over the top and proceeded to get under the barrage. The line was fairly strict but seemed impossible to keep absolutely straight owing to so many shell holes. We had advanced about 40 yards when I turned around to see if the second wave was coming. They had just got over the top and seemed to have a good line. The German barrage seemed to have just opened and was playing into the second wave, but I could not notice men dropping yet. Quite a number seemed to be advancing from shell hole to shell hole. Our own steady barrage seemed to be playing somewhere between 40 to 30 yards over the German line, and was not very effective in keeping the enemy down as they were standing ready, with bayonets fixed and bombs. . . .

"The first wave kept advancing with very few casualties till within 70 yards of the objective when the enemy opened fire with machine guns on the left, and with rifle fire all along our objective. At this moment I noticed quite a number of our men falling and the first wave became very weak and scattered. On my right I could see only an odd man going from shell hole to shell hole and bearing off a little too far to the right as the line appeared to be broken about the centre of the company. I, being on the left of the first wave, my object was to keep in touch with the 50th Battalion who seemed to be some 50 to 60 yards away to my left. I called to my men to make a partial incline so as to connect up with them but we had not gone many yards when we ran into very heavy rifle fire and it was at this point that most of the casualties occurred.

"On the right the advance seemed to be checked as I noticed only an odd man going forward, and they were shot down after advancing only a few yards, which left the first wave completely wiped out as I thought. The second wave did not come up, so, with so few men left in the first wave I realized the futility of entering the enemy's trench, and instead, we secured shelter in shell holes some 10 to 20 yards from our objective."

Although Lieutenant Gyles had no way of knowing it, the 50th's attacking party on the left had been badly cut up, and the 46th's second wave was all but wiped out. As they went over the parapet, the German barrage began. The line was soon ragged but the men pushed on regardless. Among the first killed was Lieutenant Guest who was to lead this wave.

The survivors sought shelter from the storm of steel in shell holes. Huddled in their shallow refuges with a driving sleet pelting them mercilessly, the men of the 46th, some of them badly wounded, were forced to lie almost motionless for fifteen hours or more. To show a head was to commit suicide, for the enemy were free to fire unhindered at every target which appeared. In the most forward positions life was even more precarious. The German trench was only a few yards away, and a well-placed "potato-masher" from there could wipe out the occupants of the nearer shell holes. Added to this inhuman ordeal was the constant shellfire. The only comfort against this was the widely held soldier's theory that no two shells ever fell in the same place.

For those who survived, there were sights and memories they would relive in sheer anguish the rest of their lives. "I caught up with about eight men from the 50th in a ditch," wrote one private, "and stayed with them for long hours. There was a stretcher bearer shaking like a leaf in a storm, tending the wounded less than one hundred yards from the enemy. I saw two of their snipers dodging here and there, seldom stopping in one place for even two minutes. One of them got the stretcher bearer in the head. He fell only a few feet from me. I crawled out and dragged him into our ditch when I heard him groaning. I pushed some brains which were oozing out, back into his head and bound him up. I must have been with that dying stretcher bearer for twelve hours or more. I took over his job and by four o'clock in the afternoon bound up several wounded men who had reached the ditch, and then got them safely away. The stretcher bearer never fully regained consciousness, but he raved on about his wife, Marg. At about two in the morning the rattles in his throat and his groans got too much for me.... I crept away, leaving him and his remaining bandages and bag with him. I don't care now. I never believed I could forget his name when I examined his identity disk."

Behind Regina Trench the casualty clearing station was swamped. "The doctors had been going on about as long as we had, about fourteen hours or so. I prefer not to describe what I saw," wrote one 46th veteran. "I will put it another way. You have seen a thousand-bushel pile of wheat surrounded by bales to prevent spreading. Well, the bodies lay stacked around the outside like bales. These were the dead, both ours and Fritz, who had died on the operating tables. The centre of the pile was made up of legs, arms, hands, and a few more bodies."

In no man's land the frightful hours dragged on. The shattered remnants of A Company and the supporting platoon still huddled in the foul shell holes, cold, wet, and terrified. Major McLean had been killed as had most of the NCOs. The only remaining officer was pinned down effectively by German fire. Each man was on his own in a pandemonium of death. As evening darkened into night, the survivors crept from their pathetic shelters and slipped quietly back to Regina Trench. Many came back wounded but unassisted. Most of those fortunate enough to escape serious injury dragged or carried less fortunate men with them.

Those on the right had been somewhat luckier than Lieutenant Gyles and others on the left. They had found a shallow sap running out from Regina Trench and had by mid-morning returned to their jumping-off point. This action was conducted by Sergeant Bowles. He then placed his men and himself under the command of the 44th Battalion. The men on the left trickled back after dark, and Lieutenant Gyles emerged from no man's land to resume command.

"When I got back into Regina Trench," he reported, "I was informed by Sergeant Bowles of the situation and of what he had done, which I considered to be satisfactory. As far as I know any men who left the lines were acting as Stretcher Carriers, and in one case, to take prisoners back. All that night I had parties carrying out wounded and working on the same until a Brigade runner informed me at 9 A.M. on the 19th instant, from the O.C. the 10th Brigade that all men who took part in the attack on the morning of the 18th instant must come out of the line at once, and that he wanted to speak to me. I ordered the men to put on equipment and get ready to fall out. There still being two wounded men left in the trench, I detailed men to take them out which left everything clear as far as I know, with the exception of one machine gun and crew which Captain Meckleham (44th Battalion) would not relieve.

"After returning to the Battalion Orderly Room at 114 Bapaume Road, Stretcher Bearer Hoskins informed me that he had found two more wounded men out close to the German line whom he had brought back to Regina Trench, and left in charge of Captain Meckleham who said he would make arrangements to evacuate them. These two men, I feel sure, were the last of the wounded left in 'No Man's Land.' "

A burning resentment welled up inside the troops despite their weariness. Another abortive attack—25 October all over again. When would the generals realize what the privates already knew?—that a successful attack needed to be well planned.

The killing went on. Death could be unusually gruesome on the Somme, but few incidents surpassed that which took place during those last days of November 1916.

Runners were now being sent in pairs in the hope of getting more messages through. On one black and dismal night two of these runners were heading from the front line to Battalion Headquarters at the Red Chateau, when, without warning, the incredible happened. Drummer Savage suddenly saw his partner, only a few feet from him, vanish. He stopped in the steaming mud but there was no sign of his chum. Then from deep within the earth he heard an agonized moan. He crept slowly towards the sound until he found himself on a slippery, hard surface. Before him yawned the black outline of a brick-walled well. The moaning was coming from deep below.

It was around midnight when Savage reached the Red Chateau and located Corporal George Tomlinson—"Old George" of the Medical Section. He and a small party made their way back toward the front and were able to locate the well. A rope was looped around Tomlinson and he was lowered into the abyss. It was then discovered that a much longer rope would be needed. The agonizing sounds from the inky pit told him that the man was in extreme pain. Abandoning caution, Corporal Tomlinson ran, full out, back to the lines of the Lahore Battery. Eventually enough rope was gathered to enable the weary corporal to begin the long, muddy run back.

It was nearly dawn when Tomlinson reached the bottom of the well, and the Germans had begun to shell the area quite heavily. He found the runner still alive but in terrible pain. The man's legs had been driven up into his abdomen. Working as gently as the cramped position would permit, Tomlinson tied the rope around the man's chest and watched as he was hauled away up the well. Overhead he could hear the exploding shells muffled by the sixty or so feet of earth above him.

As George Tomlinson waited his turn to be pulled up, he noted that the bottom of the well was not wet. There was not a foot of land on the surface that was this dry. He decided to light his pipe and relax his strained nerves. His first match went out. So did the second, and the third. Then it was that George realized there was so little oxygen in the well that he was having trouble breathing. He sat down and prayed that he would stay conscious long enough to tie the rope around himself when it was lowered again.

The oxygen held out, and Tomlinson was hauled up. As he clambered out, he discovered that it was broad daylight and the enemy was shelling his party determinedly. Having endured the ordeal of more than five hours at the bottom of the well, the unfortunate runner had died moments after being rescued. Tomlinson's men had already begun to bury him. The corporal ordered his men back to the Red Chateau before there were more casualties.

The next day Tomlinson, Savage, and a few others returned to string barbed wire around the well to prevent a recurrence of the tragedy. They took with them a cross, painted and lettered, to put over the soldier's grave, but a shell had already landed on the spot and no trace could be found of the runner.

By 23 November the 46th was back in the line. Casualties and sickness had so reduced the battalion that every available man, specialist or not, was brought up into the front line. Despite this, the battalion was woefully weak.

"Very few of us went into the line on November the twenty-third," recalled Jim Broomhead. "I don't believe there was more than one man for every ten yards. On the twenty-fourth someone sent me to find out how things were on the left. I bet I went along the trench for two hundred yards before I made contact with anybody. There was not enough men to take care of the parapet and it was all broken down. I was passing by one of these gaps when I was sniped. He got me through the chest. I didn't know where he was, but I later found he was sniping from the ruins of Pys. Next thing

I remember is the face of Lieutenant Cattell looking over me, then calling for volunteers to take me out. I will always believe that if it wasn't for Lieutenant Cattell I would have died in that trench."

Vic Syrett had his share of troubles that day as well. He was on duty as a runner and had almost reached the front line on the left side of the 46th's trench when he was hit. "The sniper was up on the hill above us, somewhere in the outskirts of the village of Pys. His first shot went through my neck, between the windpipe and jugular. He took off the end of my nose with a second shot before I gained the shelter of our front line. This was at noon on November 24. Just a few minutes earlier, the same sniper had hit Jim Broomhead with one shot, only he got it through the chest."

That night, 24 November, the 46th left the Somme front lines for good. By next morning the decimated battalion was resting at Tara Hill. Within twenty-four hours a draft of seventy-two men arrived to begin filling the gaps in the unit. At 11:45 in the morning the battalion was on the road leading to Varennes, heading north to join the rest of the Canadian Corps.

As the 46th marched away, many of the men wondered just what had been achieved as a result of their suffering. The suffering was evident enough—600,000 British and Empire casualties had been claimed at the Somme. Of these 24,029 had been Canadian. What had been gained?—A few acres of mud now freezing solid. Bob Brown summed it up: "It seemed so senseless to us that had to climb through all this just for the sake of sitting three hundred yards away from where we were the day before."[10]

Fifty miles behind the lines at Haig's headquarters, life continued in the manner of a minor court. The field marshal had isolated himself from the physical horrors of war with a barrier of yes men and luxury. He had not yet visited the front, but possibly one of these days he would have time to talk to his men and see the battlefields in terms of mud and blood rather than as neat lines on maps.

Why had Haig pressed on with the Somme "offensive"? From the first day of July, when it had been launched—drenched in the blood of sixty thousand British casualties before lunch—until the abortive attack on Desire Trench, the whole concept seemed insane. There was no strategic prize to be won, and even a long advance with few casualties would not have altered the situation to any degree. As Winston Churchill pointed out, "The French and British commanders had selected as the point for their offensive what was undoubtedly the strongest and most perfectly defended position in the world."[11]

It appeared that battles were to be won only by brute force. *Finesse* and *surprise* were not words used or understood by Allied generals. As one writer put it, "They applied themselves to the task of breaking the German line with the intelligence of a group of savages trying to extract a screw from a piece of wood."

CHAPTER SEVEN

Winter Below the Ridge

> *To us this business of military glory and arms means carrying parties, wiring fatigues, wet clothes, and cowering in a trench under shell-fire.*
> C. Y. Harrison, Generals Die in Bed

The 46th Canadians arrived at their destination, Chateau de la Haie, in a pouring rain. The chateau had been a stately mansion. Now its grounds were spotted with quonset huts, which looked grotesquely out of place amongst the towering trees and memorabilia of centuries. The chateau lay about three miles west of Vimy Ridge; as 10th Brigade Headquarters, it would soon become a familiar and welcome home to the 46th.

The battalion had spent a few days at Doullens, west of Albert, before moving to Bruay for two weeks. By 18 December the troops were ensconced in the huts at the chateau. It was a short stay. The Canadian Corps, united at last, held the western slopes of Vimy Ridge. The 46th was to relieve the 1st Battalion at the northern end of the ridge. The operation would be an unwelcome novelty—a daylight relief.

In the distance the men could see the ridge. It appeared to be rather low, although the northern tip rose four hundred feet or more. There was an abrupt break in the outline at that point and then the Lorette Spur continued on towards the north. Through the gap in the ashen-grey ridge ran the Souchez River, which was in reality a stream meandering through a marshy valley. On the

Lorette Spur could be seen the scars of old trenches from which the Germans had been driven by the French while the 46th was still at Sewell in Manitoba.

The western slope of the ridge was gradual and offered the deeply entrenched enemy a superb field of fire down towards the Canadian lines. Vimy's chief value was as a vantage point to observe the Allies' every move for miles behind the lines. Because the eastern slope was very steep, the Germans were able to bring supplies and artillery right up to their own doorstep with little danger of being seen or hit.

The daylight relief made the troops uneasy. It could become an overwhelming tragedy. Nevertheless, the next morning, the nineteenth day of December, the 46th marched out of the grounds of the chateau. The area through which the men marched was shattered and silent. The villages had been pounded into rubble, and dotted over the desolate landscape were abandoned farms. To men from the wheatlands of Saskatchewan, the most poignant sights were the shrapnel-torn binders sitting forlornly where they had been abandoned during the harvest of 1914—over two years earlier.

The road, normally hard, was covered with up to six inches of slime. Through Carency the 46th doggedly trudged. The ridge appeared in more detail. There were no signs of life visible on its grey slope. It was an eerie sight made more ominous by the many graves scattered haphazardly over the countryside. The men squelched on down the sunken road to the spot known as Hospital Corners, where an advanced dressing station had been set up.

At Hospital Corners a screen of sacking warned the men that they were now under close observation by the enemy. Ahead lay Zouave Valley, so named for the large numbers of French Zouaves who had died there assaulting the ridge in the early months of the war. Here the 46th filed into the sloppy communication trench known as 130th Alley. Shells began to "crump" the area, but the trench afforded the needed protection and no casualties were suffered. Eventually the men reached the invisible line where the shellfire could no longer hit them, due to the intervening ridge. Now they could study the ridge more closely. The jagged lips of craters were visible as were the outlines of a maze of trenches and shelters. The area below the crest resembled a long-abandoned city of cave dwellings. The column was led out of the valley into a large pit. It bore a name familiar to the veterans of the Somme—the Chalk Pit.

The Chalk Pit would serve the 46th as Battalion Headquarters and general base of front-line operations during the ensuing months. George Kentner, a replacement from the 196th Battalion, described one of the dugouts. "The entrance was abominable. It was so low we had to get on our knees, and so narrow that with equipment one had difficulty getting through. We were ushered into a repulsive tunnel-like structure. Bunks were arranged along the walls. The place was dimly lit by candles placed on bunks, mess tins, helmets, or shelves cut in the wall. The air was foul, the floor dirty and damp. Many of the bunks needed repair. Rats and mice scurried everywhere. But it was a place of warmth and safety!"

The front-line trenches straggled across the face of the ridge farther up. To reach these, the forward companies climbed a wooden stairway the last hundred yards to the firing line. Most of the men drew a sigh of relief—compared to the Somme these trenches were well made and wonderfully kept up.

The 46th had been assigned the corps's worst sector, overlooked as it was by the Pimple, a knoll rising 394 feet at the northern end of the ridge. The battalion's area also included the swamplands between the Pimple and the Lorette Spur. The Pimple was of no great prominence, but its field of fire made it deadly to those below. The Germans had fortified this hill with a view to permanent occupancy. The surface was a maze of well-built trenches, while below were numerous bomb-proof dugouts. Deep tunnels connected these strongpoints.

The men soon recognized what a delicate spot they had been given. The reporter, F. A. McKenzie, after visiting all along the front, wrote: "This left flank of our position on the Ridge was as unhealthy a spot as I have known. German snipers seemed to be able to get men at the most acute angles of the trench."[12]

On the rare occasion when one could look "up" no man's land, an unpleasant scene was revealed. "In front of us, perhaps two or three hundred yards from our front line lay the German forward positions," wrote Private George Kentner. "A dirty mass of shell-shattered mud, strewn with numberless tangles of barbed wire formed the forbidding reality of no man's land. Behind us at the foot of the ridge was Zouave Valley and away to the southwest we could see the broken tower of the church at Mont St. Eloi."

Almost directly beneath them in the gap between the two spurs of the ridge lay Souchez. Once the charming centre of a prosperous farming region, Souchez now lay in ruins. Its comfortable houses and dignified white stone churches were mere rubble. The remains of the village were completely surrounded by rolls of barbed wire.

Christmas was only a few days away when the battalion arrived at its new position. The longed-for mail arrived on the twenty-third, and Christmas Day found the 46th taking part in a midday relief, this time going the best way—back for a rest. Despite the mud, the heavy kit, and the bundles of Christmas parcels to be carried, there was no griping.

Throughout December, the 46th had received several drafts to fill its depleted ranks. Men from Saskatchewan units, such as the 188th, mingled with men from other provinces. One unusual battalion, which contributed a large number of fine soldiers to the 46th, was the 196th Western Universities Battalion made up of a company from each of the four western provinces. An exceptionally high portion of these men would become officers later on.

New officers had also joined the battalion. One who was already known to Moose Jaw and Regina men was "Handsome Bob" Boucher, the high-scoring winger of the Moose Jaw Maple Leafs. Many recalled that glorious night when Boucher had scored four times to lead the Leafs to their 14-6 drubbing over the Regina Vics. Another young lieutenant winced each time anyone recalled that night—he was Freddy McCulloch, the Vics' goalie.

The 46th underwent some internal reorganization at this time. The Canadian Corps had split up the Lewis gun section of each battalion. Now every company would have four of these light machine guns. Battalion Bombers was also to be split up in an attempt to make each company more self-contained. Behind the lines, corps schools were established to train the specialists from the front. Everyone looked forward to a week or so at one of those schools away from the shadow of the ridge.

The Vimy front was supposed to be a rest front, but the continual bombardment by both sides soon destroyed that illusion. "The life we led on Vimy was abominable—always cold and wet—keeping the trenches in bad condition," wrote one of the new men. "Our clothes and equipment were continually wet and caked with mud. Working parties of the most disagreeable nature were the order of the day. Night and day, in the most inclement weather these tasks were performed. Quite often during the night Fritz would send up red, orange, or green flares along with the never-ceasing white ones. This was usually the sign for an impending 'strafe.' Then shells of various sizes would shower our position. One instinctively hugged the side of the trench and almost shuddered at the terrific crashing of shells close by."

A veteran summed it up somewhat differently: "Although the Germans looked right down on us and gave us lots of mortar and machine gun fire, it was a vast improvement on the Somme."

Curry ("Spy") Spidell, a raw-boned homesteader from Mortlach who was now a bomber in the 46th, described a night both normal and memorable: "Three of us had spent the time as usual, crawling around no man's land. After spending the night out there crawling and lying in shell holes and almost getting ourselves killed under the German wire in an attempt to discover whether anything unusual was taking place in the German line—nothing was—we headed back to our own line at the first indication of dawn. We came in on D Company front and met its rum ration. We got a shot. We went through C Company and got another rum ration. Then we went to our bomber dugout—a small affair—and got our regular ration. We always got a double shot. In short order we were feeling on top of the world."

After breakfast Spy and his comrades found a dugout at the base of the ridge, in which to stretch out. It was the morgue. Men killed during the day were taken there before being carried out during the night.

When Spidell woke, it was four in the afternoon and his greatcoat was gone. "I sat up. The place was full of men—dead men, dying men, and wounded men. My greatcoat was covering a man on my right who was blowing bubbles of blood. I crawled to the door over the men and pushed the sandbag aside. I saw new shell holes, scores and scores of them. Most of them were half-filled with water. It had been raining, but the sun was shining now.

Right in front of me were two signallers mending telephone wires.

" 'Hey,' I asked, 'what happened?'

"They looked up wide-eyed. One of them asked, 'Where have you been?'

" 'In here asleep.'

" 'My God, you must have been asleep. You mean you haven't heard anything all day?'

" 'Nothing.'

"He shook his head. 'Why the Germans hit us today with everything they have. Our front line is a wreck. All communications cut. Do you really mean you didn't hear anything?'

" 'Right.'

"They looked at each other, and then at me. 'Look, fella, you were not asleep. You were dead.' "

The other night activity dreaded by every man was the work party. This could be either removing the soil taken from the tunnelling operations going on under the ridge, or carrying ammunition, barbed wire, trench mats, or rations to the front line. Pat Gleason, a newcomer from Yorkton, Saskatchewan, would always remember one work party. "Chris Smithson was an inveterate grouse. He was just ahead of me carrying two bags of coke on his right shoulder (fore and aft) and two bags of rations on his left. We had just about made it to the end of the duckwalk when, quite unexpectedly, there was a burst of machine gun fire. The bullets ripped the bottom out of one of the bags of coke letting it slither out into the mud, and of course the other bag went with it. Chris stopped dead in his tracks and stood shaking his fist at the enemy line and shouting in genuine anger, 'You goddamn sons a'bitches, you couldn't do that a mile back—you wait until I carry it all the way up here!' "

The main problem for the 46th Canadians was to control their unique front, from the swampy valley of the Souchez to the Pimple, almost four hundred feet above it. "We used to hold the Souchez Valley with a series of seven posts during the nighttime only," recalled Neil McLeod, a gangling farm boy from Turtleford. "During the day there was no one down there because it could be covered from up the ridge. There were four or five men in each post and they were connected by a wire. The first post would jerk once, the second post twice, and so on—signalling, in the event that anything happened. It was a wet slimy place and although you wore waders it was pretty uncomfortable. So they brought out hot cocoa at one or two in the morning in charge of the orderly officer and sergeant."

These posts had to be evacuated each morning before daylight, and as soon as the men at number one post left they jerked the wire, and so it went down the line. That meant that those in number seven post left last although they had the farthest to go. The men from the posts spent the day in the relative security of the Chalk Pit. "I mind one morning when we didn't get away early enough. If you started too soon there were too many of you exposed at once, so you had to wait till the others had time enough to get out. We were walking along beside the old trench system that was full of mud and water, when the Germans spotted us. We had to dive into it and two of our fellows were wounded. . . . The only way in after that was through the muck, crouched over till it was up to your neck."

Every six days the battalion changed positions. There would be six days in the front lines followed by six days in supports, and finally six days back at Chateau de la Haie. But even that was not free from danger. "At Chateau de la Haie during a prayer at Sunday morning service, a German plane dived at us," wrote Frank Taylor, a music teacher from Manitoba. "We all scattered, including the padre. All except one—Colonel Dawson. He looked thoroughly disgusted and was heard to remark that his men should not desert in this time of prayer."

January and February were unusually cold, but things changed for the better behind the front. The 10th Brigade received a new brigadier; St. Pierre Hughes was replaced by Brigadier-General Edward Hilliam, D.S.O. A new man was also assigned to lead the Canadian Corps. He was Julian Byng, a former British cavalry general noted for his efficiency and inventiveness. A new feeling began to sweep the corps. It was in the air—something big lay ahead.

One of the most obvious signs of this new energy was the

sudden interest in raids. For the 46th Battalion, the first raid of the new year took place on 28 January, resulting in no fatal casualties, although Curry Spidell, the homesteader from Mortlach, and five others received coveted Blighties. Then, on 12 February, a massive brigade raid was carried out, with each battalion in the 10th Brigade contributing 200 men—800 in all. On this raid the Germans lost 160 men killed to the brigade's 150 casualties, most of whom were only slightly wounded. Raids began to occur almost daily. On the morning of 19 February the 47th "put on a show," which unfortunately drew heavy retaliation in the form of mortars and shrapnel shells, causing the 46th to suffer several casualties. One of these was Victor Tallis of Borden. He was the second member of that musical family to die with the 46th. He would not be the last.

Later that day the 46th staged its own raid. Three officers and ninety-three men went over the top and encountered a lone machine gun, which they quickly silenced. Twelve dugouts were destroyed and at least ten Germans were killed by the raiders. Several of the dugouts contained enemy soldiers and a few more had been accounted for by the preliminary bombardment. The 46th suffered "only" thirteen wounded and two missing. Harold Emery, the one-time butcher, was wounded, though not seriously enough to get a Blighty. The only thing unique about the raid was that it took place in broad daylight, at 5:30 in the afternoon.

This daylight raid was just another part in the mosaic which was designed to make the enemy a prey to nervousness. The Germans on the Pimple knew that they could expect the Canadians in their trenches at any hour of the day—on any day. There was no such thing as a "rest front." Despite this activity, the Germans never retaliated with a raid of their own.

Several days after the raid, a death occurred which shook everyone. "Old George" Tomlinson was standing in the bay of a trench, talking to one of the men and a popular young officer, when their conversation was suddenly interrupted by the explosion of a shell. "The officer's head was blown to pieces," said Tomlinson. "It just disintegrated. I was left untouched, but brains and flesh were spattered all over the other man's face and upper body. He went insane—screeching and clawing at the mess. He scrambled out of the trench and ran shrieking towards the rear." Tomlinson and another man took after him and tackled the man. They dragged him back into the shelter of the trench. "He was taken out of the line for a while, but later they sent him back to the 46th."

The last night of February saw the launching of another massive raid. Fortunately for the men from Saskatchewan, the 10th Brigade was not involved. It was the 11th and 12th that combined in an elaborate operation involving 1,700 men. No bombardment was employed, as chlorine gas was to be used instead. Unfortunately it blew back on the attackers at the same time that the Bavarians opened a withering fire on them. Only 37 prisoners were captured, while the Canadians suffered 687 casualties.* During the next two days the Germans helped the Canadians to recover their dead. After this, small raids took place *every* night. The result—1,400 more casualties in two weeks.

By this time every Canadian on the ridge had figured something big was afoot. The constant raids to glean information, the nightly removal of subsoil from the tunnels at the foot of Vimy, and the ever-expanding network of light railways leading to the front—all indicated a big push. When a soldier was out of the lines it became even more obvious. Supply dumps were hidden everywhere. Artillery units were lined up row upon row. The slowest private in the Canadian army could read the signs. Had the Germans?

By 20 March the preliminary bombardment of the ridge had begun, although few realized it. Guns of all sizes were registering, but in small groups. The Machine Gun Corps had begun firing around the clock. Long-range indirect fire from their Vickers began falling on road intersections and lines of communication. The enemy trenches were now being pounded faster than they could be repaired.

On the night of 31 March the last big raid (in reality a reconnaissance in strength) was launched, the raiders being supplied from the 47th, the 50th, and 46th—two hundred men

*After the war it was discovered that three dugouts packed with men of the 11th Bavarian Regiment had been wiped out by the raiders who tossed in Stokes shells.

and five officers from each battalion. The raid was scheduled twice and cancelled twice, and the 46th received further cancellation orders at the last moment. These orders did not reach everyone, and Lieutenant Hall and about thirty men headed out on their own. Two of this party were killed and eleven more wounded before they made it back to the line. Of the 47th's raiding party, only one platoon was able to break into the enemy trenches. They brought back two prisoners but suffered six killed, forty-seven wounded, and eight missing. Meanwhile the 50th Battalion had been caught, like the 46th, still filing into position when the barrage opened. But they got away, against little opposition, and brought back two prisoners at a cost of twenty-four wounded. It was a frustrating night for the Canadians.

A few days later the 46th was back at Hersin-Coupigny, but not for long. By Easter Saturday the men were certain that they would shortly be "going in" and that it would not be a routine raid like the previous ones. Next day they turned in their packs, keeping only the few articles they wished to take with them. "It was Easter Sunday," noted George Kentner, "bright and pleasant. Shortly after dinner we left Hersin-Coupigny, once more facing towards Vimy Ridge. . . . The main road was unbelievably congested. All roads were crowded with various infantry battalions, limbers of all sorts, masses of motor lorries, and guns of all calibres. Everything imaginable was streaming towards the front."

The following day would be Easter Monday, 9 April 1917. For the first time the four Canadian divisions would advance on the enemy together.

CHAPTER EIGHT

The Battle of Vimy Ridge

> *They [Canada and the colonies] can be completely ignored so far as concerns any European theatre of war.*
>
> General Friedrich von Bernhardi

"As the first grey streaks of dawn shot across the sky, I was alive with interest," wrote George Kentner, "curious as to what I was about to behold. It was a disagreeable morning—cold with a drizzling rain."

Zero hour was at 5:30 A.M., and with but four seconds to go there was a sudden silence—not a sound was heard. Then, at precisely 5:30, all hell broke loose. Every gun on the twelve-mile front opened up. The three tunnels leading up to the German lines were blown.

"It was a sight I shall always remember," wrote Private Laurence Colpitts, a Maritimer serving with the 46th. "About 5:30 every gun behind us cut loose and the German trenches became a line of bursting shells, falling so close together you could scarcely see between the flashes. It was a continuous wall of flame and mud."[13]

Bugler Vic Syrett watched spellbound. "Being on a slope, the infantry could see the flashes of the guns behind them, then turn and watch the arrival of the shells. The machine guns opened up and from the tunnels came the infantry. What a joy it was to find that the artillery had done its stuff, and the wire was cut."

As the battle opened, the 46th Battalion remained in three support trenches—Arras Alley, Music Hall, and Bajolle—which lay south of their normal sector in front of the Pimple. The battalion was temporarily attached to the 12th Brigade, and two companies were to be used if elements of the 12th ran into trouble with their attack on a series of craters on Hill 145. And trouble there was.

Although the situation on the right of the battalion seemed satisfactory, it was discovered that the Germans still held several of the craters. From these, they had begun working down Basin Trench until contact between the 11th and 12th brigades was severed. By early afternoon the 72nd Battalion reported that the enemy was massing for a counterattack. The time had arrived to move the 46th across Zouave Valley and place it in readiness to advance on the crater.

A and B Company were detailed to carry out the attack. B was to take craters 1, 2, and 3, while on the right A Company was to extend the line and make contact with the 11th Brigade. At 5:45 that afternoon the men climbed out of the jumping-off trenches and advanced over the unfamiliar ground. In moments they were lost from view.

No more was heard from these two companies for eight hours. Colonel Dawson's face remained expressionless, although he, like everyone else at Battalion Headquarters, was desperately anxious. Eventually, at 1:40 the next morning, Lieutenant Gyles's laconic message arrived: " 'A' Company and one platoon of 'C' Company [which was temporarily attached to 'A'] occupy line about 300 yards to crater #2 which is occupied by the 85th and 87th. 85th in crater #3. Will be dug in by morning. Enemy shelling not severe. Some of our 4.5's a little short. Patrols are out in front."

The eight-hour period between the signal to advance and the receipt of this message had not been uneventful. "We went through a long tunnel, deployed, and struggled through the mud without a supporting barrage, trying to avoid water-filled shell holes as best we could," wrote Bob Tingley, a private in B Company. "We faced machine gun fire and scattered overhead shrapnel, but my section made it to the far lip of a gigantic crater which was our objective, joining up with the 38th Battalion.

We had a shorter distance to travel than some of our boys, and looking to the right we could see our line of troops moving forward with little groups of Germans working towards the rear by short dashes from shell hole to shell hole. We blazed away at them, but I don't think I caused many German widows to mourn that day."

The 12th Brigade report recorded that the 46th's advance was "carried out splendidly. About 150 enemy encountered in vicinity of #3 crater and dispersed." A machine gun and several prisoners were taken in this area. The objectives were taken with few casualties to the 46th. With their positions secured, the two companies then remained under intermittent fire from "whizbangs."

Although the men of A and B companies did not realize it, they had been sent into the critical spot on Vimy. The entire attack by the 4th Division had faltered. On the left of the 11th Brigade, the 87th Battalion had run into heavy fire from a section of the German trench that had been left untouched by the artillery at the request of "the infantry, who proposed to use it afterwards," as the 4th Division's *Report on Operations* states.[14] As a result, the German defenders were able to pour a devastating flank fire upon the successful units to each side. The divisional commander chose to throw the nearest reinforcements in to clear up the situation. These were the 85th Battalion from Nova Scotia, newly arrived in France, plus the 46th's two companies.

Meanwhile, the other three Canadian divisions had been entirely successful in gaining all their objectives on 9 April. Many of the original 46th men served with distinction in their adopted units. Certainly none behaved more heroically than Private William Johnstone Milne, a lad from Moose Jaw. Now wearing the kilt of the 16th Canadian Scottish, Bill Milne twice stalked and bombed German machine gun posts which had held up the advance. Milne did not live to see Moose Jaw again for he was killed later that day. For his gallantry on 9 April 1917, he was posthumously awarded the Victoria Cross.

With dawn on 10 April, the 4th Division's well-laid plans had to be modified considerably, for the 11th Brigade had not been able to hold Hill 145, the highest point on Vimy Ridge. Without Hill 145, the Canadians could not hope to retain the remainder of the ridge, for the Germans could direct fire over the newly gained ground along its length. The original attacking troops from the 11th Brigade were now so exhausted that two uncommitted battalions of the 10th Brigade, the 44th and 50th, were ordered to storm Hill 145. This meant that the assault on the Pimple, the final objective, would be delayed.

On the morning of Tuesday the tenth, Colonel Dawson received orders that A and B companies, the two that were already in the crater below Hill 145, were to advance in conjunction with the two other 10th Brigade battalions. The attack, originally set for noon, was changed to 3:15 P.M., but the cancellation order did not reach the 46th in time. When a small barrage opened up to the right of the target, the two attacking platoons went over the top and established outposts in Basin and Cyanide trenches as ordered. Three and a quarter hours later the remainder of the brigade attacked, and the 46th's two platoons advanced even farther along Basin and Cyanide. For the rest of that day and Wednesday, A and B companies clung to their new positions under constant heavy machine gun and artillery fire.

Wednesday, 11 April, was relatively quiet in that no assaults were launched. The C Company platoon, which had been loaned to A, rejoined C and D in Blue Bull and Vincent tunnels. Canadians and Germans both prepared for the climactic battle, the attack on the Pimple. This was the prominent knoll atop the northern end of the ridge and was the 46th's normal sector. The original plan was that it would be attacked by British troops, and it was not until four days before the attack that the Canadians learned that they would be responsible for clearing the Pimple. It was obvious to both sides that they must attack promptly.

The 10th Brigade was assigned the job, but the necessity of deploying it elsewhere required the postponement of the attack until Thursday, 12 April. The Germans had taken advantage of this delay to bring up fresh troops to take over the Pimple. The elite of the German army, six-foot Prussians from the 5th Guard Grenadier Regiment now held the fortress on the northern tip of Vimy Ridge.

The weather deteriorated as the men of C and D companies moved up to their old front-line positions below the Pimple.

Private Kentner of D Company was there: "We spent the night in a crowded dugout and tried to get a little sleep. We were awakened about two o'clock and given a drink of hot soup and some biscuits. We then filed out in the order in which we were to 'go over.' They issued us with picks and shovels, which we carried on our backs stuck down behind our equipment. It was a cold night with a mass of flying clouds, behind which the moon shone occasionally. Artillery activity had subsided though one could still hear the crash of a bursting 'minnie' or the dull roar of our heavies.

"The trenches were so pounded we were compelled to walk on top. At Kings Cross we entered the old familiar trench leading to the Chalk Pit. This we passed through, and proceeded out into the open by our old isolation posts. It was damnably hard work—making our way through that mud and water. Then the enemy detected us! Up went his flares lighting everything about us. His rifles and machine guns opened up, and his persistent but ill-directed fire forced us to take cover in the mire of the shell holes. The clouds overhead had now become dense, and snow was beating down upon us. For half an hour we lay shivering in the mud and water, but this wait caused the enemy to relax his fear. Conditions soon became normal, permitting us to rise from our damp and repulsive shelters and proceed to our jumping-off positions.

"Just as morning began to break we heard the rattle of many machine guns and the swish of thousands of bullets over our head. A moment later we saw the horizon in our rear lit by the instantaneous flash of many batteries, heard the crashing roar of the guns, and almost felt the screaming of the shells over our heads. At once we stepped forward toward that crashing wall of bursting explosives which was our barrage on the enemy front position. Almost at the same instant the snow storm increased in intensity. Great huge flakes were beating down upon us and directly into the faces of the enemy."

Another of the attackers, Private Allan ("Spike") Smith from Saskatoon, noted, "That snowstorm was the best barrage we ever had." The squall saved many lives, for the supporting barrage had been less effective than usual, due to the enemy's dispersal among shell holes in front of the Pimple.

Nevertheless, the leading waves were met by intense fire. Neil McLeod, the gangling farm boy from Turtleford, was part of a rifle-grenade team. "We hadn't gone three or four steps when the little fellow who loaded the rifle grenades for me had his head blown off. I was looking right at him and all of a sudden his head just vanished. I had bits of his brains splattered all over my tunic."

George Kentner wrote: "We had scarcely started when we began to have casualties. A man on my right dropped—another close by on my left went down—another barely three paces away let out a fearful yell and went sprawling in the mud. As we neared their front line, we were greeted by stick-bombs which took effect but didn't stop us. In a moment we were in the front line. The bay I jumped into was occupied by four Germans—all dead."

Slowly but deliberately, the troops advanced. Although the fire had been heavy as the 46th moved up to the Pimple, it intensified as the men swept over the top. On the rearward slope the hail of fire was even worse, for the main defensive line had been established there. If it had not been for the snowstorm, the men of the 46th would have made a fine target as they crested the peak. But the storm had also caused some confusion, and although it was not realized at the time, D Company's attack had angled off somewhat from its objective.

To the right, the 50th and the 44th were making easier progress, and before long the Germans were in retreat. "In about half an hour they were completely broken up," the Maritimer, Laurence Colpitts, recorded. "Some of them would throw down their rifles, and with hands up, come running across to us begging for mercy with comical gestures. Small groups could be seen running for safety toward their own lines. I was firing on these as fast as I could work my magazine and take aim when a sniper on our right got me in the shoulder."[15]

At seven in the morning, two hours after the barrage had opened up, a proud Colonel Dawson reported that his flank on the Pimple was secure. Except for a determined post of Germans between the 44th and the 73rd battalions, the ridge was in Canadian hands. Within twenty-four hours this small nest of Germans pulled back.

The Pimple had cost the 46th one hundred and eight good men.

The Butterworth brothers were split up: Jim stayed with his company but Dick was going to England with a Blighty. Frank Taylor, the former music teacher, was carried down from the Pimple badly wounded. Laurence Colpitts had been hit by a sniper. Chris Smithson, famous throughout his company as a champion griper, had a Blighty—though he did not grouse about it. His chum, Pat Gleason from Yorkton, had stepped over the bodies of four of his pals only to be hit in turn. He was lucky—assisted by a wounded Japanese Canadian, by a Canadian general, and by the good old "Sally Ann," Gleason lived to fight another day.

As soon as the Pimple had been cleared of the enemy, the troops were ordered to dig in. D Company, which had ended up in the wrong position, was shifted farther to the north and the entire area was left in the hands of the 46th, although one company of the 47th and one of the 102nd were loaned to Colonel Dawson for support.

Heavy counterattacks were expected any moment, and sniping and shelling took their toll as the men worked, digging a new line of trenches. But 13 April dawned with no signs of the expected German counterattack and at 4:00 P.M. orders were received to advance a new line along Can-Can and Clanish trenches. "To go over without a barrage in broad daylight seemed sheer madness," wrote George Kentner, "and we despaired of success. Everything was quiet, not a shot was fired. Zero hour came and with it the order to advance. Cautiously, but without hesitation, we struck out in the open."

"When we jumped off at five, we were stretched out for one hundred yards or so," Lieutenant John Copp later recalled. He had been transferred to D Company, and found himself in command. "I jumped out first at about the middle of the line and the company followed behind me. When we got halfway across I looked behind me and found that I was all alone, about forty yards ahead of the line. I slowed up and we approached the German line together. I had a Mills bomb in my right hand with the pin drawn—ready to throw it at the first German I saw. There was a dugout right where I jumped into the trench. I called down to see if there were any Germans. Then I got rid of the bomb by throwing it down the dugout. Colonel Dawson told me afterwards that from his vantage point he could see the Germans scuttling along their communication trenches to the rear."

"To our surprise we were not fired upon and we became bolder," wrote George Kentner. "Even reckless exposure did not draw fire. As we proceeded, it became evident that Fritz was gone. Down through the trench system so lately occupied by Fritz we stole our way to the outskirts of the town."

They had advanced to the edge of the village of Angres. While the company dug in, Copp and the company sergeant-major crept into the village through the silent ruins. At each step they expected to hear the crack of a sniper's rifle or a burst of machine gun fire, but Angres was deserted. At 9:30 that evening an English company relieved D and the 46th went into reserve.

The Battle of Vimy Ridge was over. For the Canadian Corps it was a great achievement, although the victory had not been won easily. Canada had suffered 10,602 casualties—3,598 of them fatal. Still, even this toll of misery was considered relatively mild after taking an "impregnable position." The defenders had been badly mauled. The number of Germans killed was never fully calculated, but over 4,000 were made prisoner.

The 46th had suffered 200 casualties. Of the 108 that occurred attacking the Pimple, 26 had been fatal. A and B companies had suffered 92 casualties, including 26 killed and 2 missing.

Lance-Corporal Neil McLeod, newly promoted, helped with the burials. "It was kind of a tough one too—burying some of your own fellows. But you just buried him where he was. You put his blanket over him and covered him with about eight inches of earth. He had a little cross and you took off the dog-tags and put them on the cross. That way you could spot them all over the place. I never realized there were so many."

Shortly after the battle, the Pioneers under Sergeant Nick Bretherton constructed two large white crosses made of wood salvaged from the village of Ecurie. One cross bore the names of the dead of 9 April; the other, those of 12 April. They were dedicated by the chaplain, Captain Cumming-Ching, at a short memorial service. The crosses were placed in position on the Pimple and were destined to remain there for years, silent sentinels over the final resting place of so many young men.

Was the victory worth it? At the time, Private Bill Musgrove, one of the 46th's New Brunswickers, did not think so. "After the Vimy attack, I said that it was a mistake. For the amount of men and material we lost and the amount of ground taken, it wasn't worth it. However, one time a little later I came out of the line and struck across country. I landed in the old German front line on the Pimple. There was an old periscope left there. I took a look through it for curiosity and almost flipped. You could see into our old front line, communication trenches, and for miles back of the line! I changed my mind quick about Vimy being a mistake."

CHAPTER NINE

The Summer of '17

Days of unendurable monotony and moments of indescribable fear.

Lt. Reginald Bateman, 46th Battalion

The same day that the 46th came out of the line they met a lieutenant-colonel who was being temporarily attached to the battalion. The new man was instantly recognized by the few remaining originals—he was Herbert Snell, the 46th's first commanding officer. He had been sent to the battalion as part of a scheme to give more senior officers experience at the front. These temporary attachments became known as "Cook's tours." On the whole, the plan was not successful, although for the 46th it probably worked better than in most cases.

Despite the big Canadian victory at Vimy, war weariness had set in. France had suffered terribly—over one million casualties and the loss of her northeastern provinces. General Nivelle's vaunted offensive in Champagne had failed miserably. In the weeks that lay ahead at least fifty-five mutinies were to take place in the French army. Fortunately for the Allied cause, these mutinies were hushed up so successfully that neither the enemy nor the general public learned about them until after the war. The men of the 46th knew nothing about this calamity, though they were aware that a revolution had begun in Russia.

Even the good news of taking the ridge had a sour side. The victory at Vimy seemed to have taken the British High Command by surprise, and they had not exploited it. The Germans had simply withdrawn to a new line just west of Lens. Once again they were allowed the choice of battlefield; the Allies would have another hard nut to crack.

There were many new men arriving to replace the casualties incurred at Vimy. Two such were Percy Hellings, a wiry bantam from Moose Jaw, and his constant partner, Ernie Harris, an amateur heavyweight boxer who had been trying his hand at farming south of Swift Current when the war broke out. It was a bewildering world they had stepped into.

One newcomer, Don McKerchar, a schoolboy from Strathclair, Manitoba, lost all his illusions of glory when he arrived. "The first parade I was ever on with the 46th was a grim affair. We were all paraded—the whole battalion—and a prisoner was marched on with an escort. Then they read out that the fellow had been sentenced to death for desertion in the face of the enemy. He had run away during an attack and they had found him somewhere behind the lines. Anyway, they commuted his penalty to ten years penal servitude after the war and put him back into the line. He seemed like a good lad. He tried to make up for it all the time. You couldn't have found a better soldier. The sergeant seemed to like him, and after an action recommended him for the M.M. or the D.C.M. Of course, he knew he'd never get it, but it might help cut a few years off his sentence. I figure he had just made a bad mistake at the wrong time and he had to live with it. Ten years penal servitude after the war—what a thing to look forward to! He never had to serve his ten years—he was killed at Passchendaele."

On 22 April the battalion marched out of Chateau de la Haie, where the men had been resting up, and back along the old familiar roads to Vimy. One day was spent in the Chalk Pit before going into the new line. "It was with a feeling of curiosity we struck out that evening. We were going through towns and covering ground which we'd never seen and which had but lately been captured from the enemy," wrote Private Kentner in his journal.

The new front line was vastly different from anything the 46th had experienced before. It stretched across a level plain. In front lay the ruined suburbs of Lens. Famous for its coal mines, Lens was surrounded by the rubble of small, company-built towns which had once housed the thousands of miners who had laboured in the pits below. A maze of railway tracks which had been used to remove the coal now lay as barriers in all directions. Here, there were fewer trenches as the railway embankments formed natural parapets. Large slagheaps, known as "fosses," loomed everywhere. Most, if not all, were infested with enemy machine gunners and snipers. Across the front, running diagonally from the southwest towards Lens, stood an ordered row of stately trees. These lined the Lens-Arras Road. On the right lay the ruins of La Coulotte. The front faced a German strongpoint known as the Triangle, while to the left the sluggish Souchez River meandered eastward.

As the Canadian Corps explored the area recently captured from the Germans, word circulated of some of their remarkable accommodations. Certainly nothing impressed the men of the 46th as much as the discovery of Piano Dugout. This was a very deep dugout on the communication trench known as Prescott Road at the southern edge of the battalion's sector. The dugout received its name from the grand piano that it contained. The enemy artillery officers who had once occupied the rooms had been men of refined taste; the walls were lined with the finest of wood panelling. No luxury was too extravagant for these spacious quarters. Few of the soldiers had ever seen such luxury before—certainly none had ever seen a "bivvy" to compare.

The war weariness that had set in seemed to affect both sides, for there were numerous German prisoners captured and invariably they were far from dejected. "They annoyed me in their gladness to be taken prisoner," Lance-Corporal Harold Emery remarked. "Our machine gun section had just been decimated and I was the only survivor. I was so smothered in blood that I was taken to a medical post, stripped and examined before I was declared unwounded. My head was ringing and I staggered and fell several times. Now you can understand me, watching these German prisoners laughing and talking—I felt like killing them."

German snipers seemed to be everywhere and they took a large toll of Canadians in this sector, but the Canadians had also mastered this deadly trade. Jim Butterworth, the bomber from Coleville, described one of the 46th's best snipers. "Cox the Fox was a tall, thin chap with blond hair and a small waxed moustache, an almost round face, very keen eyes, and a continuous grin. To me, his facial expression was that of a weasel. He was the keenest rifle shot I ever knew. He used Fritz's sniper rifle with its exceptionally good telescopic sight. Fritz tried every dirty trick in his bag of dirty tricks to pull a fast one on us, and the Fox was sly enough to catch him with his pants down on several occasions. One Fritz would carry a Red Cross flag followed by two more carrying a stretcher. On the stretcher was the relief sniper. They would stop by the sniper's pit in no man's land. The Fox held his fire but called in machine guns for Fritz's next change-over. When the change-over came it was just one b-r-r-r-r and exit five Fritz."

On 5 May the 46th received orders to seize the Triangle, the heavily fortified enemy trench formation immediately to the front. One of those who took part in this attack was Private Don McKerchar, the new schoolboy recruit from Strathclair, Manitoba. It was an unnerving experience for a greenhorn. "The sergeant in charge of the platoon at that time was Sergeant Stevenson, an old North West Mounted Policeman. Everybody thought the world of that man. Every young fellow has a hero and he was mine. I thought, now, if I do everything Stevie does, I'll be okay. They had dug a jumping-off trench forty or so yards in front of our line. I purposely got right behind Stevie. We were crowded—very crowded—and I was right up against him. I was nervous and it was a nice night and I wanted to talk to someone so I said to Stevie, 'It's a nice night, isn't it?' 'Yep.' So I said, 'Pretty quiet, isn't it?' 'Yep—but you wait till the barrage starts. They know we're coming and they'll give us plenty.' And I thought I could feel him trembling. Here was my hero. If he was afraid, it was time for me to get afraid too, and it worried me.

"We sat there for four hours and by that time he was really excited. Then the barrage opens up and Stevie says, 'Come on boys,' and he climbed out of that trench. You'd have thought he was walking down the street, everything was as normal as could be. I was following behind him and we were going up in file. So far, I had never seen a man killed. We hadn't gone far till I see Stevie fall forward on his face. I stood there. I didn't know what to do. Then he looked up and yelled 'Get out of here! The barrage will get you in a moment.'

"That scared me and I started to run and only one man kept up with me. We were absolutely lost and didn't know what we were doing. We ran into our own barrage and a shell landed between this fellow and me, and he was killed. I ran, and first thing I knew I jumped into a trench. It was Fritzie's front line.

"Someone had given me a bag of Mills bombs and a pair of wire cutters. I stood there. The noise was terrific and I didn't know what to do. So I started down this trench to see where I was. I came around a corner and right in front of me was a German soldier—I could see his helmet. I dropped my bag of bombs and got my wire clippers round his throat when someone behind him yelled, 'Leave him alone! He's my prisoner.' Some of our boys had gotten in the trench down further."

The remainder of the day was a thriller. Having taken the Triangle, the 46th had stirred up the German hornet's nest severely and the enemy reacted violently. Fire and steel rained down upon all three sides of the Triangle as the Canadians prepared to repel the inevitable German counterattack. But there was a pleasant surprise for young Don McKerchar: "About eight in the morning Stevie came along. 'By God, I thought you were dead,' I said. 'No, I just got caught in some barbed wire.' I was never so glad to see anyone as I was to see Sergeant Stevenson that morning."

During the day, Company Sergeant-Major Nick Bretherton, the former Pioneer sergeant, discovered that the Germans had left behind three "fishtail" guns and quantities of ammunition. He trained a squad to fire them, and for the rest of the day the Germans were able to study at first hand the marvellous efficiency of their own equipment.

The Germans counterattacked at least three times. During the afternoon they moved in under cover of machine gun and artillery fire but were driven back without setting foot in the Triangle. As darkness again approached, their persistence increased and the roar of the guns rose in a gradual crescendo of hate.

"It was the wildest night I saw," Bill Musgrove, the New Brunswicker, wrote many years later. "Nobody knew what would happen, and no man knew if he could live through it. By the time daylight arrived the excitement had died down. A white flag was seen in the German line and word was passed among us not to fire. A German officer came out halfway into no man's land and said that he wanted a conference with one of our officers. An officer went out and an armistice for our front was called for the day. Both sides began dressing and picking up the wounded and dead. It was an act I shall always remember. To see a little humanity among all that hate and misery."

Morley Timberlake of A Company was one of those who took part. "We and the Germans left our shell holes and trenches and visited each other, exchanging cigarettes, etcetera. This went on for some time and the skylarks were singing merrily overhead. Eventually both sides had the casualties cleared and we all returned to our respective holes and trenches. The artillery, rifle, and machine gun fire started again, and the skylarks' singing was drowned out."

The 46th was withdrawn soon afterwards and did not move back into the front line again till the last week in May. Then, at midnight on 31 May/1 June, poison gas was projected at the enemy lines. "The wind blew the gas back on us," wrote Private George Fountain, "and we had our gas masks on for endless hours. In retaliation we got back a German barrage that shook the embankment. I remember a tough old corporal, who happened to be in our slot and who boasted all the time of being an atheist, getting down to pray."

The next morning six young officers joined the 46th: Lieutenants Armes, Dixon, Elliot, Gunning, Kennedy, and Leroy. Theirs was a violent welcome, but it was a glimpse of the future. Within five months all would be casualties.

A couple of days later the 10th Brigade was ordered to attack the enemy line between the Souchez River and La Coulotte. This assault was to be made by the 44th and 50th battalions, with the 46th supplying one platoon to capture a cement machine-gun emplacement located in a railway subway. Although the operation was accomplished successfully early on 3 June, heavy counterattacks forced the two battalions to withdraw, and by seven in the evening it was obvious to Lieutenant Tubby Reid of the 46th that his platoon was isolated and almost out of ammunition. The order was passed to retire.

During the withdrawal, Private Hugh Cairns was an outstanding figure. He had led his Lewis gun crew forward at a critical moment to supply covering fire for a battalion falling back on the 46th's flank. He recovered two of this unit's guns and brought them into action as well. Although he was wounded at this time, he kept up a constant fire. "Cairns saw some of the Germans coming out of their trench trying to cut our men off at the flank," wrote Bill Musgrove, the New Brunswicker. "He lined his gun on them and drove them back. His two helpers on the gun were casualties. He grabbed two men from the retreating battalion and put them loading the ammunition drums. While his back was turned those two beat it. Boy, Hughie was mad."

The next morning Hughie Cairns described their behaviour— in his own colourful fashion—to their adjutant. As a result, Cairns was recommended for a court martial, but Colonel Dawson, after giving him a lecture on respect for officers, recommended him instead for the Distinguished Conduct Medal.

The days that followed were quiet. Behind the lines the battalion occupied itself with drill, inspections, battle training, and of course the detested carrying parties. On the night of 24 June, Jock Rankin led a raid that met with no opposition whatever. That was a milestone.

Despite the lull in enemy activity, the Canadian tradition of constant night raiding and patrolling continued at its normal pace. Patrols generally included four scouts—one fore, one aft, and one to each side. Movement was slow and stealthy. When a flare shot up from the enemy line, the prowlers froze and searched their eerie surroundings for movement. After the flare had flickered out, the patrol crept silently forward once more.

One night the bantam-weight Percy Hellings and three companions surprised a German patrol of seven men, whom they quietly disarmed and motioned into a shell hole. One of Hellings's companions spoke German, and the two groups discussed their homes, the war, and life in general. It ended with an exchange of cigarettes and a suggestion from the Germans that they meet again the next night. "We let them go back unarmed," recalled Percy. "It was our duty to take them prisoner, but you see you'd have to stand up there and walk them back. If either of you made the least noise you were as liable to get killed as them." The suggested meeting next night did not take place.

The 46th missed out on the fierce fighting at Eleu dit Leuvette and Avion. It was a spectacular fight with flame throwers and bayonets, but the 46th Canadians were at Chateau de la Haie, content to stay indoors out of the rain. Optimism was reviving and the illegal diary of a Manitoba boy, L.W. ("Pat") Burns, recorded for 29 June: "War outlook better. Free betting that war over in August."

In July the 4th Division spent most of its time in training and sports. The highlight was the Brigade Sports Meet held on Dominion Day. It was a great day for the men of the 46th: they were the overall winners, bringing five trophies back to camp. These trophies may still be seen at the Armoury in Moose Jaw. The 46th won other awards during these weeks: the machine gun and rifle championships, best wiring section, best turned-out transport, and best turned-out platoon (Lieutenant E.M. Johnston's No. 6 Platoon). The popular battalion nine lost only one ball game all that summer.

During these halcyon days there was more time for the men to catch up on their letter writing. One recently arrived replacement, Private Dick Greves, probably summed up the interests and feelings when he wrote: "The crops here are pretty good.... We are having a pretty easy time just now as the battalion is having a month's rest. After this is over I expect we will be getting all we want in the way of excitement. We are not very far from the front lines as we hear the guns quite plainly.... We get better fed here than I expected we should, and the hours of drill are not quite so long.... I don't think there is any need for Bob or you to enlist as I feel sure that the farm needs attention and I don't see how old Heinie can hold out so very much longer.... If you can get the time off, take a run up and look at the crop will you." Greves had been farming near the village of Tugaske when he enlisted and his letters to his brother were always full of concern for the crops and his beloved horses.

By 31 July when he wrote his second letter from the 46th, he had had his first taste of action. "I have not been up to the front line yet as we were only in reserve the last time but I saw enough even there. It doesn't give you a very pleasant feeling when you hear the shells whistling overhead and see a few poor beggars being carried out on stretchers. Anybody who has never actually been through it can have no conception of what the life is like. I take off my hat to those heroes who have been through it for so long and remain just as cheerful as ever. I have got with a fine bunch of boys and once you get acquainted they will do anything for you. We have to look on the bright side of things or we should go nutty. I shall certainly be quite contented with batching in the west again if I pull through this alright. If I should meet with any accident I leave it to you, old kid, to look after mother and see that the two girls get a decent chance. I have left everything to mother. . . . Don't forget to write once in a while, letters mean quite a bit to a fellow out here."

While Greves was adjusting to life at the front, His Majesty, King George V had visited the Canadian Corps—on 11 July—to confer a knighthood upon Arthur Currie, the new corps commander. A former school teacher, insurance salesman, and a real estate broker from Vancouver, Currie had joined the militia in 1897 as a private. When the war broke out he had been a 39-year-old lieutenant-colonel. Now he was in command of the Canadian Corps. This was good news to all, for Sir Arthur was known for his organizational ability, his attention to detail, and his concern for the front line soldier. A feeling of optimism swept the corps.

CHAPTER TEN

Aconite Trench

War is the business of barbarians.
Napoleon

After those placid July days the 10th Brigade moved north of Avion and took over a sector of the line in the suburbs of Lens. This was a new experience for the 46th. "First time we were ever right in a city," Neil McLeod, now a corporal, commented. "The buildings were half shot down and practically obliterated. There'd be the odd one still standing with the roof shot off. The German snipers used a system of sniping from these particular posts to try to hold us up. If you tried to go down a street, look out. You had to go down through the basements—one basement to another. You know how these houses were in the Old Country— just one long block of them. You'd bust a hole from one basement to the next. Then you'd come up every so often. If you got behind a German sniper and he spotted you behind him he got out pretty fast. But we lost a lot of men that way."

Several weeks earlier Sir Douglas Haig had ordered the Canadian Corps to push its lines up to the Mericourt-Lens railway south of Lens. Results were not really important; the assault was simply a holding attack to induce the Germans not to send troops to the Ypres Salient where Haig's "masterpiece," a plan for clearing the Channel ports, had already begun. The Canadian Corps's new commander, Sir Arthur Currie, strongly protested the choice of battlefield, and eventually it was agreed that the

Canadians would instead attack Hill 70 just north of Lens. This position, if captured, would at least be defensible and would have some strategic value. Nevertheless, Hill 70 would not be taken easily. In September 1915 the British had grasped it briefly but had been driven out by strong German counterattacks. The Germans had not moved from it since.

At 4:25 A.M. on 15 August, the 1st and 2nd Canadian divisions launched their attack on Hill 70. On their right the 4th Division sent the 11th and the 12th Brigade towards the city of Lens. The 4th Division's attack was really a ploy to draw enemy fire away from the main attack. The diversion worked well. The 12th Brigade came under heavier retaliatory fire than did the attackers from the 1st or 2nd Division.

The 46th arrived in the front line two days after this attack and relieved the 102nd Battalion. The position they took over was actually a series of unconnected posts along Bell Street facing Aconite Trench. Contact between the front company posts was maintained by patrols. Before the battalion had been in the line a day, patrols had been across no man's land and had entered the enemy's trench. The Germans abandoned that section, and the 46th established posts there.

The next days were spent duelling with the enemy for possession of a row of houses and a strongpoint known as the School House. Patrols went across, drove out the Germans, established posts, and in turn were driven out by hostile artillery fire. The 46th was then ordered to turn its position in front of the School House over to the 50th Battalion, since, in conjunction with the 47th and 50th, it would be mounting a full-scale attack towards Lens in the morning.

The attack was to begin at 4:35 A.M. on 21 August. Three companies would lead the advance—B on the left, D in the centre, and C on the right. At about two o'clock that morning Colonel Dawson received the tragic news that all the officers of B Company had become casualties when a solitary shell had hit the hole in which they had gathered in advance of their platoons. Major Baker and Lieutenant Gunning were dead, and Lieutenant Gilpin was wounded. Major Gyles, Lieutenant Armes, and Lieutenant Walker went forward to hold together the company, which had begun to suffer heavy casualties from shellfire.

At long last 4:35 A.M. came and with it the Canadian barrage. The men climbed out of their jumping-off trenches and shell holes. Percy Hellings, the bantam scout from Moose Jaw, was with D Company in the centre of the advance: "It was pretty hard to keep track of everybody because it was dark. The only time you could see was when the Germans sent up flares. In the meantime between the flares and the dark you didn't know where you were going. In our company the sergeant got knocked out, the corporal got knocked out, and I was on the lead so I says 'All right boys, I guess we've got to go without 'em,' and away we went. They were shelling us pretty hard and we just kept dwindling back behind—some of them getting knocked out, but a few of us kept going until we hit a railway embankment. I said, 'We've gone too far,' and we wasn't long finding out. By the time we got halfway up that embankment the old machine guns really opened up on us. We thought there must have been a million of them—boy, the noise and the racket! It was just good luck that some of us got back and hid behind a piece of wall, and worked our way back. By this time it was starting to get daylight. But we got back and started digging in and that was it. It was quite an experience, I'll tell you."

On the right, C Company had eliminated a German machine gun crew attempting to escape from Aconite Trench. "Artillery pounded Aconite Trench," recalled Hartley Hea, a private from Lang, Saskatchewan. "We moved in close. The firing stopped and we rushed the trench. A German hand grenade landed in front of me. Too late, I thought, to throw it back. When I came to, I looked around to see if I was in heaven or hell. It was hell, but I rushed forward and reached the trench. We continued on. There were many dead bodies, Nova Scotia boys and Germans. Next—through a house, across a wide, open space, then up an alley about half a mile. We started to dig in, when the officer in charge ordered me to leave (without my pack) and run back to locate the company on our left."

At this point an Aeroplane Contact Patrol flew over and called for flares. These were lighted but had the disastrous effect of bringing down a barrage of "friendly" fire. Two of the 46th were killed and two more wounded. The men of C Company were ordered to withdraw leaving their two dead comrades behind.

Meanwhile, Private Hea had located D Company on the left and was returning. "I met our company racing out. I went to look for my pack, but a bullet by my ear sent me back. I never saw the company again." Private Hea spent the remainder of the day with an outpost of the 47th.

On the battalion's left conditions were becoming serious. The officers who knew the ground were all casualties. Within a few yards of the jumping-off trench Lieutenant Walker and several NCOs were hit. The men advanced regardless, but there were gaps in the line and one platoon eventually dug in on the edge of Great Peter Street. This left B Company almost isolated, and in trouble.

In the centre, D Company had begun to regroup as scattered remnants spotted one another in the daylight. Things were almost peaceful for a few moments, and Ernie Harris and his chum, Percy Hellings, had time to watch one of the stretcher bearers bandaging a wounded prisoner. But then, as Hellings described, "All at once a German popped up—right out of the ground it seemed—and shot the stretcher bearer. There was lots of us with rifles, but the poor stretcher bearer had nothing, and the German turned and shot the stretcher bearer. I had a bomb so I just pulled the pin and let him have it. Because why didn't he shoot one of us who had a gun? It was the only bomb I ever threw outside of practice."

By this time C Company on the right had begun digging in along Brockle Bank, an embankment named after one of the 46th's officers, Stanley Howson Brocklebank. The company had sent back three prisoners for interrogation.

The adjutant, Major Hope, was sent forward to the isolated B Company to report on the situation. When he arrived he found the depleted platoons in possession of Aconite Trench. The official *Summary of Operations* described what followed: "In company with No. 781559 Sgt. W.E.A. Best and three others, he moved up Amalgam (Trench), and near where this trench crosses Great Peter Street, ran into a party of Germans getting out of a dugout. These Germans held up their hands in token of surrender, but one of them threw a bomb. They were accounted for."

Gradually, all the trenches in the neighbourhood were cleared of Germans and consolidation was quickly under way. Numerous prisoners were escorted to the rear, and a disheartening number of wounded 46th men continued to stream past.

The wounded included an officer and three men from the 87th Battalion (Canadian Grenadier Guards) who had taken part in the opening battle on 15 August. They had remained in no man's land ever since with their wounds unattended. Two had lain in a shell hole in the front of Aconite Trench for six days. During one of the nights of their ordeal, a German had crawled out and given them each a drink of water. The officer and the other man were found in a ruined house where they had secreted themselves from the surrounding enemy.

Despite heavy casualties, all three attacking companies were firmly established in their new positions before evening on 21 August. During the night of 21/22 August both sides sent out numerous patrols, but the 46th was fortunate in coming out ahead. Two German patrols were badly shot up and suffered seven known casualties. The 46th's patrols all returned unharmed.

Like many others that night, L. W. ("Pat") Burns was employed in bringing out the wounded. "We had gone to Absalom Trench which was only a 'half trench.' Your body was exposed from the waist up. We heard this shell coming and we ducked in the trench and put the stretcher down. Then we heard a thud. I said to the other guy, 'Oh, hell, it's just a dud.' So we picked the stretcher up and started to walk. Then we smelled gas and we stepped in the phosphorus which kind of flamed up. We put the respirator on the wounded man, then we put them on ourselves. But it was too late for us and too late for the wounded man for we had all inhaled the gas. We finally got him in and laid him down. Then we both collapsed."

The next two days were occupied in consolidating the positions captured. The Battle of Hill 70 and the push into Lens was finished. The Canadian Corps had been entirely successful in taking the hill but was not able to make any great gains towards Lens. As usual, the cost had been high. The 46th had suffered 278 casualties taking and holding Aconite Trench. Of the six young officers who had arrived on 1 June, three—Major Roy Gunning,

Lieutenant Armes, and Lieutenant Dixon—were gone. Gunning had been killed after less than two months with the battalion.

By 26 August, the 10th Brigade was back at Chateau de la Haie. Here it stayed until the thirtieth, and as usual the days were taken up with drill, training, and the inevitable work parties—this time digging trenches on Vimy Ridge. These trenches were an insurance against future German onslaughts and were known as the Red Line.

From 30 August to 27 September the battalion was either in support or back of the line. It was a period in limbo, punctuated by such diverse events as a Dumbell concert, several gas attacks, the capture of a spy near the Red Line, short rations, a bombing attack by enemy planes, being "CB'd" (confined to barracks), ball games and an address by the chaplain general.

On the night of 27 September it was back to the front line. Several casualties occurred while going in. The next few days were typical trench days—gas, shrapnel, rats, lice, filth, and boredom. (One highlight was seeing a German plane shoot down two observation balloons.) The nights were spent patrolling no man's land.

Vic Syrett, company runner and bugler, was now serving with the forward sections of B Company. "I was in an outpost continuously which necessitated a patrol by one man only, up a deserted trench for some one hundred and fifty yards to what had been a railway level crossing. In the hours of darkness your heart was in your mouth as you rounded the corner of the trench into the next bay, not knowing who was lying in wait for you there. Then, too, seeing the lighted fuse on the big minnenwerfers as they were up and losing sight of them as they reached the peak of their trajectory added to your uneasiness as you waited for them to explode on impact—that's when I missed having a companion the most."

During all this period there was an air of expectation. Hill 70 had been taken in a dramatically efficient manner reminiscent of Vimy Ridge—two striking victories in a row. To the southeast of Lens lay Sallaumines Hill, the twin of Hill 70. With this in the hands of the Canadian Corps, the foe would be forced to withdraw completely from Lens. Now with Currie in command, the Canadians felt assured of a third big victory. Sallaumines would be next—or so they thought.

The troops by this time were completely exhausted. "The last two nights in the lines the men were going to sleep standing up," recalled Ernie Harris, the former boxer. "This was an offence, and they detailed fellows to go up and down the bays to wake the boys up." At last, on 4 October, the battalion straggled back to Chateau de la Haie, and two days later the men were billeted in Hersin-Coupigny. Here, they rested and refitted for six days.

For the rest of his life Ernie Harris would remember one small incident from this period. "There was a runner went up to our headquarters. He was an Imperial from the Worcesters. Curiosity got the best of me and I went up to the runner and said,'You'll excuse me asking, but you brought a message down here, didn't you?' and he said, 'Yes.' And naturally I asked, 'What was it?' So he said, 'You're going to get moved.' 'Where are we going to get moved to?' And he said, 'A place called Passchendaele.' "

CHAPTER ELEVEN

Passchendaele

Impossible orders issued by generals who had no idea what the execution of their commands really meant.

Lloyd George, commenting on Passchendaele

Private Gordon Brown was enthralled. Just seventeen and a farm-labourer-cum-soldier from Redvers, Saskatchewan, he was now approaching the front for the first time. Gordon was in D Company and they were crossing a heavily shelled corner in the ruins of Ypres.

"The enemy were sending over big shells, about one every two minutes or so. You could hear them coming. . . . All the traffic approaching would come to a stop, but those caught at or near the corner sure done their damndest to get out of there. As soon as that shell burst, out came the sentry and got everything moving again—at the double. The first casualty I saw was at the corner. It was a rider on horseback. He had been up the line and was coming through with a message or something. This shell just caught him square in the head and the horse too, and both toppled over. We were in single file about fifteen or twenty yards from him at the time."

The battalion moved on through the traffic and the shellfire, past the famous Cloth Hall, and onto a damaged bridge over a canal. "I saw just to the right a pair of white swans swimming as though they had not a care in the world," Brown noted. "Then we were led off to the right-hand side of the road. 'From here to there is your billets,' an NCO told us. It was just a wide open, shell-ridden place on the bank of the canal.... One C Company sergeant, a veteran of several battles, was heard to gasp in disbelief and say, 'My God, will we ever see civilization again?' "

The next few hours in their muddy billets allowed the men of the 46th to look back over the happier days since they had left the Lens front. An eternity ago—12 October to be exact—they had marched through Coupigny headed by their band. Next had come a series of bus rides and route-marches interspersed with wet, uncomfortable nights. There had been strange sights—armoured cars and, of all things, Lancers. Two days stood out—one because it was payday and the rain stopped, the other because they had been inspected by General Currie.

"I never seen a battalion look so smart in all my life," declared Pat Burns, a Manitoba boy. "Buttons polished, rifles cleaned, all equipment in order—a perfect, perfect, perfect battalion if there ever was one. When Currie came on we all had to fix bayonets and 'present arms.' He spoke to us man-to-man. Currie was a wonderful leader."

And now, two days later—under pouring rain—the men huddled in the pathetic shelters they had scraped together from bits of tin and groundsheets. Conversations varied. For the new drafts it was to marvel at the sea of mud and the deluge of rain that never seemed to stop. The veterans were apprehensive. "I never felt it before, but something has just struck me," big Ernie Harris told his closest friend, Percy Hellings. "This is my last trip in the line. I don't know whether I'll get wounded or whether I'll get killed, but this is going to be my last trip."

Glumly, Percy replied, "Well, I don't know what it is, but something's going to happen to me on this trip—I can't figure it out." Then he laughed, "We're a bright pair to get in a spot like this."

The next day the 46th moved into close support in a row of shell holes. The 50th was to hold the front line, such as it was, with the 44th and the 47th in the rear. Out through the ruins of Ypres they marched, passing the Menin gate and onto a plank roadway built on top of the original road now under inches of oozing mud.

Shattered and discarded equipment littered the area. Smaller items had vanished in the mire, but trucks, artillery pieces, and tanks lay partially submerged on all sides. Into this vast sea of slime enemy shells plunged and sank before exploding with a muffled roar and a shower of mud and filth.

As night fell, the men marched into new horrors. They left the road and headed cross-country on duckboard walks which twisted across the miles of swamp. With every step the duckboards swayed drunkenly. On all sides lay the unburied dead who would eventually sink into unknown graves. The enemy had long since ranged in on every foot of this treacherous boardwalk. Shells fell regularly, and those which did not simply "plop" into the mud uselessly took a high toll of mules and men.

"If you stepped off the duckwalk you were in trouble," Percy Hellings emphasized. "There'd be a piece blown out, you see. Well, if one or two of you could get across, maybe they could push the duckwalks back a bit, but it was all in the dark. Trying to space them a bit so you could jump across was terrible. Me being small, I didn't step far enough. I went up to my waist—just right down and that was that, but I grabbed a piece of duckwalk. They pulled me out, but the first thing you know there's another guy in there. It was pretty slow progress."

Eventually the battalion arrived at its destination, where it took over from an Australian battalion. "The Australians we relieved were very white and walked and looked like zombies," Vic Syrett noted.

There were no trenches to take over. There were in fact no visible signs of defensive works except for two battered pillboxes captured weeks earlier. The pillboxes were used as headquarters, and the men were scattered about, ostensibly in shell-hole posts. However, every shell hole was filled to the lip with slimy water, below which lurked bloated and decaying bodies, and a few feet of liquid mud. "We'd try to get a higher spot where there wasn't so much water and you'd dig down a little bit," said Percy Hellings. "Then you'd have to dig a deeper one to the side of it so the water would run down into the deeper one instead of soaking you. All you had was your blankets and groundsheet to try and keep yourself warm."

When morning came, incredibly pale and watery, the men stared about them aghast. How could anyone have sent them to fight in such an impossible place? The few who tried to write a description of the scene soon gave up. Probably the best attempt ever made to portray this hell on earth was made by an Englishman, R. A. Colwell, who served there months later, long after the Battle of Passchendaele had ended:

"For miles and miles there was not a sign of life of any sort. Not a tree, save for a few dead stumps which looked strange in the moonlight. Not a bird, not even a rat or a blade of grass. Nature was as dead as those Canadians whose bodies remained where they had fallen the previous autumn. Death was written large everywhere. Where there had been farms there was not a stick or stone to show. You only knew them because they were marked on the map. The earth had been churned and re-churned. It was simply a soft, sloppy mess, into which you sank up to the neck if you slipped from the duckboard tracks—and the enemy had the range of those slippery ways. Shell hole cut across shell hole. Pits of earth, like simmering fat, brimful of water and slimy mud, mile after mile as far as the eye could see. It is not possible to set down the things that could be written of the Salient. They would haunt your dreams."[16]

During the first four days the men were kept at the demoralizing labour of work parties. They saw sights they would never have believed possible—mules loaded down with ammunition floundering into the mud to disappear forever; stretcher cases requiring sixteen to half-carry, half-float them out; light railways sunk so deep that only the tops of the little locomotives still showed. The worst of all was the plight of the artillery, for their failure could result in catastrophe for the infantry.

"We were trying to get artillery closer," said Gordon Brown. "We had ropes tied onto the wheels and they had these big wooden cleats fastened on to stop them from sinking. I'd venture to say there was two hundred and fifty, maybe three hundred men on one gun trying to pull it up. We might get a hundred yards or so." These guns positions somehow had to be shored up and made solid. Every shot the gun fired drove it deeper into the quagmire and caused the next round to fall short. In some places tons of bully-beef tins were used to provide a foundation, all to little avail.

Vic Syrett summed up the soldier's feelings: "Before we could even start an attack, the poor infantryman was organized into big work parties to manhandle all of the guns into positions from which they would be of some use. And believe me, that was exhausting work, particularly on the skimpy rations we were getting—and mostly cold at that. The infantry became so exhausted—not a good way to be when it was your turn to take over the front line."

In an attempt to alleviate a situation that it had no means to control, Battalion Headquarters brought a cooking unit up with much labour, and it provided hot tea and soup continually. But by the time the weary soldier had slithered and churned his way back to his own hole, the liquid had been diluted by rain and thickened by mud. Worse yet, it was cold.

Another attempt was to provide warm underclothes for the men. "They brought up some underwear—long johns," recalled Percy Hellings. "Boy, did they ever feel good, I'm telling you. It was just pull your clothes off and pull 'em on. All these guys in the mud and under fire trying to find a dry spot so you could get your feet out of the mud. You'd get on a groundsheet so you wouldn't get mud all through your underwear. It would be funny if someone were taking a picture I guess, but we didn't think nothing about it. We were often glad of that underwear. By golly it was cold."

Dry socks and whale oil were also issued, to prevent trench foot. "One can well imagine the time we had trying to get our puttees off after standing in that mud up to our knees for days," wrote Gordon Brown. "As it was still raining, there was nothing for it but to sit in the mud and go to it. What a job that was to get those wet, muddy socks off, our feet rubbed with that oil, and our new wet socks on, and then try to put our boots back on, then the muddy puttees. Needless to say, that many of us gave up after we had the first foot done."

In the meantime, Battalion Headquarters had received orders to prepare to attack on 26 October. Haig, still miles and miles behind the lines, had decided that Passchendaele would be the place where "we shall be attacking the enemy on a front where he cannot refuse to fight, and where, therefore, our purpose of wearing him down can be given effect to."[17]

The Third Battle of Ypres, as it was officially designated, had begun triumphantly in June with the Battle of Messines engineered by "Daddy" Plumer, the British general in command of the Second Army. After this opening round, the battle was entrusted to the usually unsuccessful General Gough and his Fifth Army staff—an unpopular and glib combination. The offensive had now lasted more than five months and had obviously run down. Nevertheless, it was decreed that Passchendaele Ridge must be taken before "bad weather" set in. The Canadian Corps had now been called up. The 3rd and 4th divisions were to attack side by side, the 4th attacking with a spearhead of only one battalion—the 46th.

The 46th would encounter an exceptionally effective system of defence when it went over the top, for the German line was not a trench line to be held doggedly until the final collapse. It was a series of concrete pillboxes, which sheltered the infantry during shelling and served as deadly strongpoints when attacked. The occupants poured out when the shelling ceased and manned the numerous shell holes in the area. Thus it was simply a matter of them moving from shell hole to shell hole or manning a machine gun in an all but indestructible pillbox. Moreover, the Germans who occupied these pillboxes were not riflemen but machine gunners, "a handpicked collection of hard, murderous veterans."[18]

In addition, the British High Command had contributed immeasurably to the German's defence by clinging to the theory of preliminary bombardment. Three years of shelling had turned the normally marshy plain of Flanders into a vast mud pudding. After each German "defeat," the British inherited the quagmire that the shelling had created. To this ghastly situation was added a grim jest of nature—rain. Five times the normal amount of rain fell during the autumn of 1917—157mm., as against 29mm. the previous year.

The Canadian plan of attack was simplicity itself. On the left the 3rd Division would attack on a front three battalions wide. On the right the 46th alone, as the spearhead of the 4th Division, would attack the first objective, the crest of a low rise 600 yards in front of the Canadian line. The divisions were completely separated by the Ravebeek, formerly a small stream, now a wide water-filled depression. To the right of the 4th Division were the Australians. The boundary line was a destroyed railroad, once connecting Roulers with Ypres. The 46th's front was crossed diagonally by the Zonnebeek-Passchendaele Road. The extreme right was dominated by Decline Copse, a German stronghold. Having taken the rise in front of the Canadian line, the 46th was to occupy this copse. Then the remainder of the 10th Brigade would take over.

The 10th Brigade at this time was not an efficient organization. "Friction . . . develops between the Brigade command and the units," records the official history of the 44th. "As an instance of the policy which gives rise to this feeling—the customary individual reconnaissance prior to offensive operations is, at Passchendaele, taken away from battalions and conducted by Brigade. The result would be amusing—if not so tragic in its consequences. Battalion commanders, all thoroughly experienced in forward reconnaissance, are conducted by a Brigade staff officer comparatively unused to conditions in the forward area. Battalion scout officers, expert in reconnaissance, are likewise led forward by equally inexperienced mentors. Net results are: irritation to all concerned; nothing of value to units in the brigade."[19]

To the men in the line the resulting orders seemed anything but thorough. As Harold Emery wrote, "An officer pointed vaguely in a northeastern direction over some ground and mud. No one seemed to know anything, and all directions seemed to be by pointing someplace. If there was a plan of attack I never heard of it."

The 46th Canadians had already suffered many casualties during their four days at Passchendaele, although they had not yet seen a German—not a live one at least. Forty-two replacements arrived on 25 October, and they were incredulous when they saw the soupy battlefield. These reinforcements brought the battalion up to a strength of 600 men. Each of the four companies was at an average strength of 135 all ranks. The balance included Headquarters, runners, signallers, and cooks.

The day before the attack was recorded in Private Pat Burns's diary. "October 25: Great artillery duels all day. Dugout continually caving in. 'Some time!' At dusk battalion moved up to no man's land and took shelter in shell holes ready for advance. Talked with Major Hope. Rained all night."

That night Lieutenant A.J. Elliott of D Company led a patrol out into no man's land. "We met another 46th party out for the same purpose. Shorty MacNab suggested we should try to make less noise, which was good advice. Soon we sensed the presence of an enemy patrol. We heard a voice speaking in English with a distinct German accent. To make a long story short, we disarmed them and took them in to Battalion Headquarters where after a brief examination they admitted knowledge of our plans. Although this was suspected, it corroborated this important point."

The men could not believe that they were expected to attack in such appalling conditions. "I never prayed so hard in all my life," said Pat Burns. "I got down on my knees in the mud and I prayed to God to bring me through. My whole life went before me and I couldn't see any future. I really prayed, believe me."

Inevitably zero hour arrived—5:40 A.M.—and the attack began. "In the early grey dawn of the morning our guns all opened up, laying down a barrage for us fellows," wrote Private Gordon Brown, the new recruit. "We were on the move forward. I had not gone far till I was hit on the back of the head by a fragment off one of our own shells. I believe there were as many casualties, if not more, caused by our own guns as was caused by enemy fire."

"We didn't go far," recalled Percy Hellings. "Our own guns were in this sloppy muck and they couldn't keep the range and they dropped short. The Germans were using overhead stuff. We were right in the middle of it—getting shelled from both sides—a pretty rough situation. They were coming down just like rain. ...I don't think I went twenty feet and there was dozens like me. When I was hit, the sergeant alongside of me got his shoulder shot off with a piece of shrapnel."

Hellings's boxer chum, Ernie Harris, carried on through the quagmire. Within thirty yards he found himself alone, the only survivor of the first wave. He waited for the second wave and continued the advance with them. Again, he was the only one left when he reached the low ridge which was the 46th's first objective. There were still two German pillboxes spitting machine gun fire. Somehow Harris struggled to them, one after another, and slipped Mills bombs into their gun ports. Then he was called back by Captain Leroy, who had gathered a pitiful handful of men together. The din was indescribable. Leroy passed his orders by shouting in Harris's ear and pointing. The little group was to advance to the knocked-out pillboxes. Harris had taken about two paces towards the pillboxes when a shell came. "It exploded there—a good-sized shell—and blew the seven of us up, and the last I remember I was about the height of a one-and-a-half storey house. I remember going up but I don't remember coming down."

Meanwhile Harold Emery and his Lewis gun section kept to the low spots, muddy as they were. Eventually an officer on higher ground ordered Emery and his crew to join him. "He stuck out like a sore thumb, silhouetted against the fast-brightening daylight. The whole lot of us lasted about ten minutes. I believe a whole battery of small guns opened up on us. The officer and his men just melted away. I got my men into a shell hole. It was not deep and we were hit twice. Poor Penny screamed and I saw blood flooding out of his belly. Young Jerry Grimes was hit and lay still. I now got hit—in two places. My artery in my thigh spurted blood and I rammed a field dressing into the hole. I next took off my puttees and bound them as tight as I could, but still I was very wet with blood." Emery crawled back, passing through a shell hole full of men. He had just left it behind when a shell obliterated it. Not a sound came from the men who had sheltered there. A few yards farther and Emery passed out.

By this time Gordon Brown, who had been concussed by the shell fragment that had hit him, had regained consciousness. The seventeen-year-old rookie from Redvers struggled forward and rejoined his comrades near the basement of a shattered building. Apparently it still contained Germans. "They didn't seem to want to come out too willingly so we tossed a Mills bomb down there and then they came out. One poor devil came out with his guts in his hands—a fragment had ripped him right across the stomach."

It was almost daylight as Brown's badly depleted platoon set off for the crest of the ridge. Somewhere in the gloom a German machine gun opened up in bursts, picking a man off each time. Soon there were very few left. "Finally," recounted Brown, "one of the boys discovered the bullets were coming from down in the swamp to the very left of the advance. We had by-passed him on our way up in the morning. He was well hidden—almost impossible to get a shot at him with a rifle—and one shot at a time was all we could get out of our rifles without cleaning the bolt by pouring water or urinating on them.

"There was a young fellow with me by the name of Donald Dickin from Manor, Saskatchewan. He had poor eyesight and wore thick-lensed glasses. He was in the rifle-grenade section and said, 'Show me the blighter, Brownie, and I'll get him.' When I pointed out where this gunner was, Dickin said he was out of range; he'd have to get closer. So us fellows covered him the best we could with our rifles while he made a dash to get within range of the machine-gunner. When Dickin got into a shell hole I took after him and joined him, and again pointed out where this enemy gunner was. Dickin thought he could get him with a long range rifle grenade, so he got what he thought was the right angle on it, and pressed the trigger. I watched that grenade go up in the air, turn, and come straight down beside the enemy gunner. As soon as the grenade exploded I was on the run to get him before he could get his wits about him. But I need not have been in a hurry. Dickin was as good as his word—he had got him. Dickin came over to see how good a job he had done. After taking a better look we saw that the poor devil was chained to his gun! We then went back to the three other fellows in the shell hole by the hedge."

By this stage, those of the 46th who had survived the advance were in position on the crest of the ridge. "I went over with I think it was fifteen men in the machine gun section," recalled Pat Burns, temporarily an ammunition carrier, "and every man was hit beside me. A fellow by the name of Piercey and I were the only two survivors who got to the objective. We jumped into a big hole, and I had the machine gun, which I knew nothing about, all the ammunition we could carry, and there we were—holding the front line. We were standing in the hole looking over no man's land and we were on the top of the ridge of course." From their position on the ridge, the survivors could look through a battered hedge into

German territory. It was green and pleasantly rolling, and in the distance hundreds of figures in field grey were swarming like angry hornets.

Colonel Dawson knew that an enemy counterattack could be expected at any time. Desperately he attempted to get information on the situation and dispatch his few reserves to the most critical points. B Company had already been inserted into the line, so he began taking platoons, then companies, from the 50th Battalion, which was to support the 46th. At 4:00 P.M. time ran out.

On the ridge Pat Burns and Piercey, the two survivors of an entire Lewis gun section, steeled themselves to repel the German counterattack. Pat Burns would never forget those moments. "You could see them jumping up out of the trenches and coming towards us, and here was I trying to fire the machine gun. I got it going, but it stuck and I didn't know what to do. Captain Kennedy was sitting on a little knoll back a bit—about twenty-five yards or so—and he sent up a sergeant to help me out. Just before he arrived I heard a 'crack' and Piercey was hit right through the eye and he fell down in the bottom of the hole, and the last words he says was, 'Carry on, Pat.' That was all he said then he was gone. This sergeant jumped into the hole and he jumped on Piercey and that made me mad. He got the gun working as the enemy were advancing and he really got a lot of them. He mowed quite a few of them down before the gun stuck. And then the shells started bursting around the hole so he said, 'Let's get the hell out of here.' He jumped out of the hole and he hadn't gone any more than ten feet when a whiz-bang got him right in the back. He went one way and the gun went another way, and that was it. Brother, was I ever scared. That was it. Captain Kennedy by this time was waving at us to retire. So we started back."

While all this was happening, seventeen-year-old Gordon Brown was still in his shell hole by the hedge on the ridge. Although that morning he had gone "over the top" for the first time, he was already a veteran, taking pot shots at the Germans as they advanced. "Until they were in range they were in mass formation and getting closer by the minute, and we were helpless to do anything about it. When they were within ten yards of the hedge the lance-corporal said, 'Anyone got a grenade?' Like a darn fool I said I had one. 'Throw it then!' he said. Some of them were already starting to climb through the hedge a little down from us. So I get's this grenade unsnapped off my harness, got the pin pulled, and turned around to throw it. And when I turned around I sees I'm all alone—nobody's there. Here I am with this grenade with the pin pulled. If I drop it, I'm out of luck; if I toss it over it will kill a few but make the rest pretty mad, I thought. I didn't know what to do for a second. All these things went through my mind in just a flash. So I tossed it. Boy oh boy, bullets were flying! I could see bullets hitting the ground all around me. One of my puttees was cut off, there were bullets through my pant-legs, bullets through my uniform here and there, but none of them touched me."

Meanwhile the German shelling had knocked out a Lewis gun post in front of the position of Lance-Corporal Walter Henstridge, who was in charge of a rifle section. Oblivious of the heavy fire sweeping the area, Henstridge ran forward to take over the Lewis gun. It was jammed. Under a hail of bullets, he cleared the stoppage and opened fire on the swarms of enemy in front. Their attack faltered and scores of field-grey figures scattered to seek shelter from the chattering Lewis gun.

Suddenly the steady fire ceased—another stoppage. The Germans, sensing their opportunity, rose and swept forward. The lance-corporal calmly opened the breech, found the stoppage, and resumed firing. Once more the German advance faltered. Their impetus lost, they scattered. Henstridge had broken the enemy attack.

At that moment a shell exploded next to his shell hole and the gun ceased firing. Witnesses from the support line could see Henstridge desperately trying to carry out repairs, for he did not seem to be injured, despite the near miss of the shell. Germans appeared on the crest of the hill, but still he struggled with the damaged Lewis gun. At the last moment, seizing the weapon, he leapt out of the shell hole and retreated. Bullets spurted around the feet of the lone khaki figure as he sped across the open. Suddenly a shell exploded and he went down. He died there in the mud in front of the support line. Henstridge was recommended for the Victoria Cross, but higher authorities reduced this to a Mention in Dispatches.

At this point in the battle the situation had become critical. The line of outposts had been overrun and the enemy now held the ridge along the hedge in great strength, forcing the Canadians to withdraw. In the confusion, orders were either not received or were misunderstood. The withdrawal, though in general orderly, did not halt at the new support line. When the 46th men arrived, they found the supporting troops had retired also. The withdrawal continued. For some, panic took over.

"You'd never believe how scared a person can be," one man recalled. "I didn't know anything, I couldn't see anything—just run, run, run—I never stopped running till I got back to support when an officer stuck his revolver in my face and said, 'Halt!' I stopped then. He said, 'What are you running for?' I tried to tell him, but—?"

"The sight of the men streaming back indicated that it might be a serious condition of affairs," wrote Colonel Dawson in his report. "The 46th Battalion Headquarters, consisting of runners, signallers, orderly room staff, and batmen, were ordered to stand to, and the crowd of men falling back, who proved to be carrying parties and stretcher bearer parties, were ordered to turn about. One Company of the 47th Battalion was found in shelter trenches near Battalion Headquarters and I gave the order for all to advance. The whole of this body of men at once advanced under Lieutenants Lett, Martin, McLean, and an officer of the 47th Battalion, and were preceded by Major Hope who went forward to discover the situation."

Private Pat Burns recorded with amazement Major Hope's arrival: "Dressed immaculately—you'd think he'd just stepped out of a band-box!"

Lieutenant Phillips and Captain Kennedy had already rallied the remnants of the forward companies, but it was Major Hope who turned the tide. "He said, 'We can't lose that place. The 46th has never lost an inch of ground yet!'" recalled Don McKerchar. "About five o'clock that evening he got out in front of us with his revolver in his hand and he led us across there again without a barrage. We retook the place."

By now, the Germans seemed to have had enough. They put up little resistance—possibly because their normal leavening of machine-gunners were no longer alive. A number of prisoners were taken, but the majority retreated to safer positions, and the hedge on top of the ridge was once again in Canadian hands. However, the line was thinly held, for the 46th had suffered such enormous casualties that it could barely form one understrength company. Some of the original supports from the 50th Battalion were intermingled with it as were the recent arrivals from the 47th. It was decided that the 46th would be relieved at once by the 47th. And so the men pulled out.

"All Companies came out very weak," reported Colonel Dawson. "Of those that went into the attack, the losses were; Headquarters; 1 officer wounded.—15 other ranks wounded. 'A' Company; 1 officer killed, 1 wounded.—11 other ranks killed, 49 wounded, 16 missing. 'B' Company; 4 officers wounded.—7 other ranks killed, 73 wounded, 6 missing. 'C' Company; 1 officer killed, 3 wounded.—17 other ranks killed, 74 wounded, 16 missing. 'D' Company; 2 officers wounded.— 16 other ranks killed, 65 wounded, 25 missing."

The battalion had been shattered. Of the 600 men who had made up the 46th South Saskatchewan Battalion that morning, 403 were now casualties. Despite these ghastly statistics, the spirit of the survivors was unchanged. Private McKerchar unwittingly summed up the feelings of everyone. "There were sixteen men and one lance-corporal out of our whole company, Lance-Corporal Shove. The rest of us were just ordinary soldiers and every one of us had been hit a little bit, but we were staying in."

No sooner had the men taken stock of the gaps in their ranks than a new urgency impelled them back into the maelstrom of horror. "There were too many poor devils who got wounded," said Gordon Brown. "They were lying in shell holes and whatnot and got stiffened up and were in awful shape. I and Dickin and whoever was able to, went back and carried in as many as we could, but still there were fellows pleading with us to come back and get them. I made trip after trip that night and the next day."

Harold Emery was one of those found—unconscious but still breathing. He was brought in just before dark. And in front of the two knocked-out pillboxes lay the former boxer, Ernie Harris, who could remember being blown up but not coming down. "When

I came to (I don't know how long I'd been out), I looked, but I couldn't move. I thought my left arm was shot off and I could see quite a hole in my abdomen. I could use my right arm still so I unbuckled my belt and I could see where I was wounded badly through the abdomen. And I got one in the back of the right shoulder, two in the leg, and one in the head and I couldn't move that left arm. When I saw all of this I said, 'Well, your fighting days are over, Ernie,' and I lay there. Then the OC happened to cough and I said, 'Is that you, sir?' He said, 'Yes. Is that you Harris?' I said, 'Yes. How do you feel?' 'I feel damned tough. How do you feel?' I said, 'I feel just the same way too.' Then Captain Leroy passed away and I was the only one left of the seven that had been hit by that shell." Ernie was eventually discovered and carried in.

Don McKerchar was one of the searchers who squelched through the sea of mud that night. "We heard somebody splashing in one of the holes. It was a little fellow by the name of Smith. He told me he was fifty-three years old and I don't know why he was ever there at that age. Anyway, I tried to pull him out, but he was stuck solid in there and I couldn't get him out. Eventually I slipped in with him, but I got out all right. Finally I did get him out, but when I did, he just collapsed. He couldn't get up at all. Shells were dropping all over the place and we still had a long way to go. I got my arm around his waist and he put his arm around my shoulder and I helped him out. He told me, 'It's a good job you came. I'd been in there hours and I didn't think I'd ever get out. I was just going to go under and drown.'"

When the terrible task was at last accomplished, the weary men fell into instant oblivion knowing that it would not last for long. "We went back to a German dugout, one of those real deep dugouts they had built out of concrete," recalled Pat Burns. "What got me the most was that all around this dugout were piles of 46th dead. We went down into the bottom of the dugout. Captain Kennedy survived and we got into the company rum. So he just dished it out by the cupfuls. You had one cupful and then you just passed out like a light."

The following day, 27 October, was spent bringing in more of the wounded who had been missed the night before. Too often all that remained was a thin red stain on a slime-filled shell hole—another 46th man who would be forever "Missing in Action." The lucky ones had died instantly. For others, it had been a matter of slowly bleeding to death or suffocating in the remorseless grip of the Passchendaele mud. Not a few of the wounded had been gassed to death as they lay helpless during the previous night's barrage.

Eventually the long day drew to an end. The 46th was withdrawn from the line that night, and guides were sent up the duckwalks to meet the weary infantrymen. Bandsman George Johnson would always remember that night. It was the most exciting and most heartbreaking of the war for him. Sent up to guide some of the 46th in, his journey through that ghastly landscape, laced with bursting shrapnel, was one to remember. Through the darkness he spotted Colonel Dawson followed by a few men straggling along the duckboards. "I asked the colonel where the battalion was. He said they were all there except a few that were coming by another route."

The guide for the other party was Neil McLeod. Several weeks earlier he had been chosen to attend an NCO's course. Now a brand-new sergeant, he had arrived at Potijze, the battalion's base camp, in time to meet Sergeant-Major Gillings. "The old sergeant-major was standing there. 'Boy,' he says, 'are you lucky. The battalion is pretty near wiped out. But there's Lance-Corporal Shove and sixteen men left in D Company. So you take this rum jug and go to the end of K Track and wait there till they come, and then bring them back in.' They had tents set up for them and it was raining like a bastard."

It was about two o'clock in the morning before the men of D Company came out and were met by Neil McLeod. "I could hear Shove talking—a little short cockney. You could hear him a mile away too; he had a voice like a bull. Boy, they're talking pretty loud, I thought. I guess we're a long way from the enemy. So I stopped them. 'I'm Sergeant McLeod. I'm here to show you in.' 'Oh,' he says politely, 'that's grand.' 'I'm supposed to give you fellows a drink of rum right now.' 'Don't you dare,' he says. 'They've all got more rum than they can drink—every one of them's got his water bottle half-full of rum.' Their rum ration had come up, you see, and their casualties had been so heavy they had divided it up among themselves. They didn't want any anyway. There wasn't a one of them would have taken another drink. We had to go about another mile. Little Shove and I were walking along and he says, 'You're the luckiest fellow in the world. It was terrible. It's the worst thing we ever got into—all mud and corruption. Half our wounded are drowned in the mud—just drowned in the mud.' "

In spite of their appalling experiences, next morning the remnants of the battalion were called out for the routine inspection. "We lined up there and the adjutant had the unit," recalled Don McKerchar. "Colonel Dawson came out and he turned the unit over to him. The colonel said, 'Where's the rest of them?' The adjutant says, 'That's all you have, sir. There are no more left.' Colonel Dawson broke down and cried. 'Take them away and dismiss them,' he said."

Although the battalion was cut up and the survivors exhausted beyond belief, work parties were still required. Those left out of action as specialists, those who were slightly wounded, those returning from leave—all were pressed into service. Neil McLeod, the battalion's newest sergeant, was one of the latter. He took a work party forward with sections of duckboards. He was aghast. "You couldn't see a damn thing—only mud, mud, mud, mud. You'd see the odd dead man, but the most of them at Passchendaele were under the mud. Slime!—not just half-water and half-mud that we call slime here. It was terrible! Who in blazes?—Somebody ought to have his bloody head knocked off that ever thought up that. Every battle we ever went into we had to do in mud."

The following evening the 46th was withdrawn to Ypres. "Everyone was given a good dish of hot stew and an extra large ration of rum," George Kentner recorded. "The next morning we packed up and marched to the railway station where we entrained for a little town some distance in the rear. I remember the colonel watching us as we passed by. He too was pale and haggard, and aged beyond belief."

Several days out of the line followed, but still the 46th could not escape the "grim reaper." A Gotha plane bombed the battalion's billets and the cooking section was badly hit. Soon the remnants of the battalion were sent back into the lines, as a massive work party had been organized by Brigade.

Don McKerchar had by this time discovered that his hands were badly blistered from mustard gas, and his arm had been put in a sling by the medical officer. "That night some brigade major decided he was going to take up a working party to dig a trench in the front line. Well, we had just come from there and we knew that you couldn't dig a trench." McKerchar also knew that he couldn't dig with only one arm but was advised by the major, "You can carry a shovel for someone else." It was an abortive exercise, as everyone had known it would be. Not only was it impossible to dig the trench but more casualties were suffered in the attempt.

That was the 4th Division's last day on the Passchendaele front. The men were withdrawn to Hazebrouck. But for an enormous number of young Canadians there was no withdrawal: they would remain forever under the mud of Passchendaele ridge. The twenty-sixth of October had been one of the most tragic days in the Canadian Corps's history. A mere five hundred yards of the vilest terrain in Europe had been taken at a cost of 1,558 Canadian casualties.

The struggle continued until 10 November, by which time the village of Passchendaele had been captured and a salient pushed even farther into the lion's mouth. By 14 November, when the Canadians withdrew, the corps had suffered a total of 15,654 battle casualties. Within six months the Germans were to retake all the ground that the Allies had so dearly paid for.

Before the Canadians had been thrown into Passchendaele there had been three possible alternatives as to their employment. Firstly, they could have been used as expected—to capture Sallaumines Hill flanking Lens. This would have necessitated a German withdrawal from Lens. The second alternative would have been to commit the corps to the spectacular breakthrough at Cambrai. The attack there was to take place on 20 November with dramatic results. Unfortunately, Byng's follow-up action was hampered by a shortage of reserves, and it ended in near-disaster. The Canadians might well have made the difference here.

The third alternative was Passchendaele, but weather conditions alone made it most impractical. Nevertheless, it had been chosen for the "decisive blow." General "Fighting Frank" Worthington, the founder of the Royal Canadian Armoured Corps, served there as a private with the Canadian Machine Gun Corps, and his verdict on Haig's choice was clear: "I can forgive the Somme, but I cannot forgive Passchendaele, because the same mistakes were made over again, in a more exaggerated form, and Passchendaele had no value strategically in the over-all picture of the war. None whatsoever. They laid the blame on the French, who demanded that they attack there to relieve Verdun. Well now, I don't think that that holds water, because when you are going to commit an army you fight where you are going to win. You don't fight where you are not going to win. And that was not a place to win."[20]

Haig had as yet not visited any of his troops at the front. Nor had any of his staff. Now, after three years of warfare, one of his staff officers came to view the scenes of victory. For Lieutenant-General Sir Launcelot Kiggel, 17 November 1917 was to be a day of triumph: he was about to visit Passchendaele, the long sought-after prize of Sir Douglas Haig and his staff. "As his staff car lurched through the swampland and neared the battleground he became more and more agitated. Finally he burst into tears and muttered, 'Good God, did we really send men to fight in that?'"[21]

CHAPTER TWELVE

The Second Winter

Oh, it's a lovely war.
What do we care for eggs and ham
When we have plum and apple jam?
Quick march, right turn.
What do we do with the money we earn?
Oh, oh, oh, it's a lovely war.
From a popular song of the war

On a soggy, grassy field just outside Bruay, D Company of the 46th Canadian Infantry Battalion was going through the motions of drilling. "Right turn!—A-bout turn!—Left, right, left, right." The commands rang out and the company marched back and forth. "Then along came a little old lady with a cane," Gordon Brown recalled. "She shook this at the company commander and he halted the company. He says, 'We have to vamoose out of here. The old lady won't allow it.' He felt kind of hurt, but we were sure making a mess of that grassy field. I could see the old girl's point. So she put the run on the whole bunch of us and that was the end of the parade for that day."

Since leaving the Passchendaele area the battalion had been billeted in houses in Bruay. Vic Syrett summed up everybody's feelings. "It was good to be in clean quarters in Bruay once again, to renew civilian acquaintances and meet the new men who had been assigned to us." There were certainly a great many of the latter—men from Saskatchewan battalions such as the 128th, the

210th, and the 229th (all from Moose Jaw), and the 217th, raised from small towns along the CPR mainline in the eastern part of the province.

By this time, men dispatched to battalions in the field were given no choice of unit. When possible they were sent to a battalion from their own area, but as there were four battalions from Saskatchewan, reinforcements never knew where they might end up. Private Jack Huckerby described the emotions of the newly arrived. "I was quite pleased with the 46th, but when we found out it was the Suicide Battalion it kind of changed our picture a bit. We wasn't there long till we found that out and found out why they had that name. But it gave us some consolation to know that we belonged to one of the better units, one of the more famous units, you know, with a famous name."

For each batch of newcomers the welcome was the same as that experienced by another Jack—Jack Featherstone, a sniper: "The first night I remember lying there on the floor and I said, 'By golly, I must have the itch or something.' We were sleeping with this old fellow who'd just come back from the line. 'You're lousy,' he said. 'I've never been lousy in my life,' I said. 'Well, you are now.' From then on we were ALL lousy—the officers—EVERYBODY! They used to have a steam outfit they put clothes through. You could get brand-new clean underwear that was just as lousy as what you had on."

Along with the new drafts came men returning to the battalion after recovering from wounds received in earlier actions. One such man was Lieutenant Reg Bateman, considered one of the most popular officers in the 46th. The first professor of English at the new University of Saskatchewan, Bateman had enlisted as a private in the 28th (Northwest) Battalion at the outbreak of war. He had eventually been wounded, then commissioned and sent back to Canada to raise a company of the 196th (Western Universities) Battalion. Promoted to the rank of major, Reg Bateman realized that he was destined to spend the rest of the war as one of the "drones" in England. So he asked to be reverted to the rank of lieutenant and was sent to the 46th. He had arrived in June 1917 and had been wounded at Aconite Trench. Now that he was back, the men declared, they would soon be in the thick of things.

But in the meantime the soldiers were quite content to "rest" in

Bruay. This meant drill, battle practice, firing at the ranges, inspections, and aerial piquet in the town. "Bruay at that time was just about the same as Moose Jaw—a nice little city," remarked more than one plainsman. In the evening there were sometimes concerts by the 4th Division's Maple Leaves or the famous Dumbells. As always, the *estaminets* beckoned successfully to many of the men each evening. "They were lovely inside, just like an English pub. You could drink the stuff there all right, but you were drunk all that night and the next day. I've seen us come out of this *estaminet* and there were fellows lying along the sidewalk— both sides, you know. My chum, we dragged him home—one under each shoulder—and dragged him home to camp, otherwise he'd get pinched. You had to get them into camp so the guards couldn't see them."

On one occasion the 46th was called upon to provide the Brigade Guard. For this honour, the tallest and smartest soldiers were selected and marched off under Sergeant Neil McLeod. Led by the pipe band, they swung proudly down the road to Divisional Headquarters, four miles away.

"I stopped the guard out in front," said McLeod. "The brigade major came out. I drew up my guard and 'presented arms' to him. So he started his inspection, but he inspected the sergeant first! He pulled a clip of my ammunition out and said, 'Oh, what a filthy condition! Your guard, Sergeant, is in filthy condition. My compliments to Colonel Dawson. Take your guard back home.' So we turned around and I paraded them back. The pipe major saw us so the band waited for us to catch up, and we were piped back to our headquarters. Then the sergeant-major spotted us and I thought, man, here's where I really get it."

McLeod was then paraded before Colonel Dawson. "The colonel looked up and said, 'Explain to me what happened.' So I told him and gave him my clip of ammunition. Then I waited a few moments before he looked up. 'I'm sorry that this had to happen,' he said. He called his batman and one or two over and they polished the ammunition right there and he says, 'Now you parade your guard back there and give the brigade major MY compliments.'"

So the guard marched back, this time with the pipe major cursing. "The brigade major came to the door and never looked out at anybody. 'Just post your guard, Sergeant,' he said."

On 21 December the battalion left Bruay for the front near Lens. It was generally felt that if one had to be at the front, the Lens area was a good place to go. After all, it was now relatively quiet and it had an abundance of luxuries. These included captured German dugouts—deep, ventilated, and on occasion even tastefully furnished. There was coal lying everywhere, and the ruined suburbs provided ample furniture for cosy "bivvies."

During this period there were continual work parties. "Rumours were current of an expected push by the enemy," wrote George Kentner. "Large stretches of barbed wire entanglements were being constructed in the Vimy sector." This was the Red Line, a defensive system modelled on the Germans' defense in depth, studied at such enormous cost at Passchendaele. Vimy Ridge was being fortified mightily. It was even arranged to flood, by means of dams, the Souchez Valley between the Lorette Spur and the Pimple. This would inundate the 46th's old battlefield.

Everyone knew what to expect. With the Americans in the war, their enormous manpower could be anticipated within a year. But Russia had collapsed. This would give the Germans one last chance to deliver a knockout blow, freed as they were on the Eastern Front. But when and where would the blow fall? Not before Christmas, that at least was certain.

Christmas Day 1917 was one remembered by most soldiers. Pat Burns's diary recorded: "Xmas Day in France. Had dinner at 12:30—potatoes, carrots, beef, pork, tea, bread, pudding, beer, cigarettes and nuts. Working party at night." Gordon Brown remembered it for a different reason. "All I can remember is waking up in the morning without my shoe laces. I had leather shoe laces and they were all chewed up as far as my puttees. Rats had chewed up both of them and I had to go the rest of the day without laces."

Soon the 46th moved into the support line. For a time their quarters were the celebrated Piano Dugout, noted for its artistic decor. There were few casualties but the weather was misery enough. Severe cold was followed by a two-day blizzard which ended on 9 January. This was topped off by a thaw.

"We had a lot of rain. Sometimes we had some snow—it would

snow at night and melt the next day," recalled Bob Stevenson, a Lewis-gunner from Gravelbourg. "It created a sea of mud in no man's land and everywhere else. There wasn't much chance of either side attacking because you couldn't get across no man's land. The trench was about half caved in. It was just a ditch full of mud. They had issued us with hip rubber boots. You needed that to walk up and down the trench. When we were relieved I can remember getting stuck fast in the trench and someone having to pull me out."

During the night of 17 January a strong battle patrol was sent out into the soupy expanse of no man's land, but heavy wire entanglements and an unexpected trip wire frustrated the mission, and the raiders had to retire—though without suffering any casualties. Another raid, early in February, was more successful and drew considerable attention.

"They organized this principally to give us fellows that hadn't had any actual experience in attacking a trench something to do, I guess," Bob Stevenson, the new Lewis-gunner, surmised. "One thing that really impressed me was the barrage. I'd never seen one, and it was something else again. They were hitting every ten feet of that line with a shell about every thirty seconds. The noise of that going over your head was something again, too."

The attackers had been divided into two groups, and the right-hand party under Lieutenant Steel experienced difficulties from uncut wire, enemy machine gun fire, and from their own bombardment which was off the mark. Jack Featherstone was scandalized. "A bunch of us got hit. Our own shells was falling too short. Gee! I got knocked over a bunch of wire, and little Watson he got it right on the side—pitched him up in the air—higher than the ceiling by one of our own shells."

The *War Diary* reported: "The left party (under Lieutenant Simpson) advanced under an excellent barrage and made its way through the wire. This presented no difficulty whatever.... Here some machine gun fire was encountered from a gun firing from... fifty yards behind the bank. Sgt. Bourton gallantly led his squad round behind this gun, found a cement gun emplacement containing three men with a gun and captured the party. Two members of the crew attempted to escape up the railway embankment but were captured by the squad on top." Two of the men from this crew were brought back as prisoners.

Another prisoner was taken by this party before the raiders' time limit expired. Lieutenant Simpson fired up the red flare to indicate a withdrawal, and the men of both parties retired to their front line, bringing their wounded and prisoners with them. The latter numbered four, as Lieutenant Steel's party had also captured a Prussian.

Colonel Dawson's report went to Brigade Headquarters, where it was rewritten and proudly forwarded to Divisional Headquarters. Its report, sent to Corps Headquarters, positively glowed. A good example of this polishing process can be seen in the comments regarding the supporting mortar barrage. Private Jack Featherstone's indignant remarks have already been recorded. Lieutenant-Colonel Dawson wrote: "The right party experienced some difficulty from the 4.5's or Stokes falling short, and after the barrage lifted, not clearing to the right sufficiently." Major General Watson's *Division Intelligence Report* stated blandly: "Our barrage was very good."[22]

The subject of casualties underwent a similar metamorphosis. Dawson's report stated: "The operation cost two men missing, one severely wounded, and two slightly wounded." General Watson summarized this as, "Our casualties were very light."[23] But this was merely a beginning. Sir Douglas Haig liked the corps's report so much that he submitted his own to the papers to bolster the wavering Home Front morale during these dull but brutal days. The *Daily Mail* reported:

> Second Day Raid at Lens
> Canadians Again Successful
> from Sir Douglas Haig, France, Thursday 9 A.M.

Early this morning the enemy's trenches near Lens were again raided successfully by Canadian troops. A number of Germans were killed and a few prisoners and two machine guns were captured. Our raiding party returned to our lines without loss.[24]

Someone back there was so pleased with the raid that they

awarded the company commander the Military Cross. This, despite the fact that he was on leave in England at the time.

While all these refinements were being made for the benefit of "higher ups," history, and the general public, the raiders were celebrating. "After we got back," said Bob Stevenson, "we went back to the reserve line in a big dugout there. We got a double issue of rum, and like somebody said afterwards, 'You'd have thought they captured the whole German Army.' Everybody got telling how many he'd killed and captured and there were considerably more than four."

CHAPTER THIRTEEN

The Spring of '18

For what we are about to receive, may the Lord make us truly thankful.
    Customary pleasantry before going over the top

By the spring of 1918 everyone was on tenterhooks. All realized that the Germans must gamble, and that they must do so soon if they were to win the war. Now that weather conditions had improved and they had been able to bring their troops from Russia to the Western Front, they would certainly launch something big. The only riddles were Where? and When?

The Allies had lost the advantage and strategic initiative of 1917. Passchendaele and other offensives had cost 400,000 British Empire casualties. The French army was a brittle weapon since the mutinies of 1917. Italy's gigantic defeat at Caporetto had forced her western allies to send reinforcements—two corps—from their already tiny reserve. The United States had also been a disappointment so far; only four and a half divisions had arrived, and their government would not commit them. Like the Canadians, the Americans wanted their troops to serve as an independent force.

As a result of these factors the Empire troops had taken over a larger portion of the line, despite their decreasing numbers. On New Year's Day the Canadian Corps alone held 13,000 yards of front. A Cabinet subcommittee, brushing aside advice from the army, had reduced the establishment of each British division by one quarter. This was achieved simply by cutting each brigade to three battalions. The "surplus" battalions were formed into new divisions.

Fortunately for the Allied cause, the Canadians and Australians were not affected by these measures. In fact, the practice of overposting began in the Canadian Corps at this time. Overposting meant the attachment of one hundred extra men to each battalion. These men were generally rotated into the line, leaving a surplus of trained soldiers, twelve hundred strong, for each division. The men were drawn from the ill-fated 5th Canadian Division which had been training in England for nearly a year.

By February on the crucial British sector, fifty-nine slim divisions faced eighty-nine German divisions. Farther south one United States and ninety-nine French divisions were opposed to only seventy-one German. It was obvious against whom the big push would be launched. For the man in the trenches, however, none of these figures were available. He could only soldier on and hope for the best.

The day after their much-publicized raid the 46th men went back into support in the cellars of Lievin, and the next three weeks were taken up with the inevitable march from camp to camp, with inspections, drill, and training. The days were pleasant. The baseball season had begun and the 46th continued the previous season's winning ways. Nevertheless, the constant rumble of guns in the distance kept everyone alert. Each day the bombardment seemed to increase in volume and tempo.

Then, in a misty dawn on 21 March, the Germans attacked the Fifth and Third armies farther south. Their tactics included infiltration by crack "storm troops," and this worked magnificently: the thin British front was shattered and the most desperate phase of the war began. For the Canadians it was two days before the news came: "They've broken through on a fifty-mile front, five miles deep!"

The 46th was promptly moved to a line north of Loos, and before dawn on the twenty-eighth a new weapon was unleashed on the Germans. It was all very hush-hush, but for the men on the work parties it was thrilling and laborious. A new system of projecting gas was to be tested. A light railway was laid that night and hundreds of steel cylinders were brought up close to the front line. Ranges and angles had already been determined, for the cylinders would fire their gas like mortars. The firing would be done electrically by a single switch.

Private Gordon Brown worked through the night. "Six or more cars like little coal cars were brought up to near the front line by a gas locomotive, then were pulled and pushed by manpower the rest of the way so as not to make too much noise. When the cars were in position they were tilted to the proper angle to point toward the enemy front line. Our men were all taken out of the front line except for a few outposts and they had to have their gas masks on. The wires were all hooked up to a power unit and at a given time the switch was turned on, and with a loud roar those gas cylinders went hurtling towards the enemy line a few hundred yards away."

The whole operation was so secret that the troops in general knew nothing about it. Some heard the two salvos fired but did not realize anything unusual was afoot until pandemonium broke out in the German lines. Gas alarms sounded frantically for several minutes. Then all fell silent. Word came out that the gas was no mere poison gas; it also had corrosive effects on metals, leather, and many other substances. For several days hardly a shot was heard from the enemy line.

"Things were fairly quiet all that day," Gordon Brown wrote. "Early the following morning I was with a scouting party sent out into the enemy lines to see what damage was done. There was no life anywhere we went, and I only saw a few dead enemy. Their leather gas masks were all shrivelled up like they had been in a fire. They were mostly older men or quite young ones."

Brown also took part in the cleaning-up operation. "A working party wearing gas masks was sent on ahead with large fan-shaped shovels to scoop the gas out of the trenches and dugouts. It seems this gas was heavier than air and it would settle in low spots so we had to shovel it out. It looked so foolish to me at the time, but it really worked. You lower the shovel down edgeways, give it a half turn, and lift it up. The fellow next to you does the same thing. That way you got the swing of it and just pass the gas along from one to the other until it is out in the open, the same as you would so much dirt."

While the Germans near Loos were suffering from this new gas, their forces near Oppy had launched a heavy attack on the 56th Imperial Division, and further attacks were expected. The 4th Division was therefore temporarily detached from the Canadian Corps and ordered to the Oppy front. The 46th marched there along roads crowded with motors and lorries, general service wagons, field ambulances, the occasional staff cars, and columns and columns of infantry. The march ended near Roclincourt, a short distance from Arras, where the men camped out in the open, camouflaged as well as possible by screens.

Those with time to check the calendar realized that this was Easter Monday. On the last Easter Monday some of these same men had gone over the top at Vimy. That night, as they looked northwest to the southern flank of the ridge outlined in the dark by a long flickering line of gun flashes, they wondered if they were about to take part in another famous battle.

It was on the night of 4 April that the battalion moved into the front line at Oppy, a night remembered for many different reasons. "We had to bury a whole bundle of Scotties and Germans," Private Jack Featherstone recalled. "We had to dig holes out in no man's land. There were a few Germans all puffed up and lying in the support trench. We'd have to cover them up and bury these Scotties and do it under this overhead shellfire. And the preacher, by golly, he took his tin hat off during the service."

The Lewis-gunner, Bob Stevenson, had a similarly macabre memory: "There were a lot of bodies lying out in front there. I was in charge of a burial party and we went out as it was getting dusk. The little padre, really a prince of a fellow, left word that he was going to be up to say a service. So we had quite a number of these fellows gathered up, and kind of levelled out a big shell hole and laid them in there. When the padre got up it was black dark, really black dark. We got out in front and we couldn't find the shell hole. After we'd investigated about half a dozen of them I said to one of the boys with me, 'We're not going up and down here half the night looking for shell holes. We'll probably find a shell instead. Check the next one and tell him it's the one so we can get out of here.' The next one turned out to be the right one as luck would have it. So the padre had his service and we got back to our line okay."

When the men were able to peep out into no man's land they were surprised by its width. One thousand desolate yards separated them from the enemy's front line. Directly in front lay Oppy Wood. It was a wood in name only, but its stark, skeletal trees masked the village of Oppy which lay behind it. The sheer size of no man's land made one fact obvious to all—there would be plenty of patrol work.

"That Oppy front was a big salient," recalled Pat Gleason, now recovered from his Vimy wound. "At night you'd see their Very lights—they really used a lot of them. You could see them almost all around us except for a little place at the back where there were no lights. That was our only possible exit. If they'd closed in they'd have us surrounded."

During the weeks that followed, the battalion stayed constantly in the lines—seven days in front, seven in support, seven in reserve, and then back to the front line again. For the men there were no longer dates. All days were the same. The only landmarks in time were the patrols and the occasional nighttime raids.

It was during this long stay at the front that an officer was charged with "desertion in face of the enemy." One of his men wrote: "Knowing the man as I did, and I was in his platoon when he was merely a lance-corporal, I know he didn't have a cowardly bone in his body and he most emphatically had no intention of deserting. Somehow or other, he got hold of too much liquor up the line, and when that happened he went a bit wild and did whatever entered his mind. This time he came back to the transport lines, ordered the captain's horse to be saddled and brought to him, and took off for Hersin-Coupigny. He proceeded to get more drink, ran out of money, sold the captain's horse and complete outfit, and proceeded to *really* tie one on."

He did not attempt to go any farther and was soon apprehended. He offered to repay the captain, resign his commission and revert back to private as long as he could remain with the battalion. Nevertheless, he was court-martialled and sentenced to be shot. This sentence was commuted a few days later, but he was ordered to be cashiered. "I saw him once more after that," recalled a friend, "and he was really down in the mouth. He said, 'I wish to God they had shot me. I just *can't* face my folks at home after this.' Well, I don't know how he worked it, as I've never seen him since, but not long after I heard he was back in France as a private in another unit. I sincerely hope he had the opportunity to demonstrate that he was certainly no coward."

During the last days of April a new threat began to be felt. An influenza epidemic had been sweeping the world, and now the Western Front was beginning to feel its weight. Pat Burns's diary for 26 April states: "Took sick with disease prevailing in Battalion. Nearly 100 cases."

Facilities for flu victims were primitive. "You lay right on the blooming old boards with one groundsheet and a blanket," said Private Featherstone, the sniper. "It was just like an old granary and we were there several days." Influenza played an important role on the Western Front. Records show that sixteen percent of all British casualties during this period were from the flu. The Germans suffered even more heavily due to their poorer food situation.

On 6 May, after more than a month in the line, the 46th was relieved by the 6th Battalion, Seaforth Highlanders of the famous 51st Highland Division. The crucial spring was over. The troops soon heard what had been happening during the last forty-odd days. Three huge bulges had been punched in the Allied line, though the breakthrough had not occurred. There were tears of frustration in the eyes of many veterans when they heard of two of the places that had fallen so quickly after having been won at such enormous cost in earlier days—the Somme and Passchendaele, now back in German hands.

Allied losses in men and material had been serious. The French, who had been only partially involved, had lost 90,000 men. The British Empire had lost 236,300 men including an unheard-of 70,000 as prisoners of war. It was estimated that German losses were even higher. Only one Empire corps was left intact—the Canadian Corps. It would be the spearhead for the victory campaign.

CHAPTER FOURTEEN

Something in the Air

> *The Canadian Corps, magnificently equipped and highly trained in storm tactics, may be expected to appear shortly in offensive operations.*
>
> From captured German documents marked "Secret"

There was something in the air, a sort of suppressed excitement, a conviction that great events lay ahead. On the surface there appeared to be little reason for this thrill of optimism; the Allies were still on the defensive. In fact, on 27 May the Germans had unleashed an offensive upon the French along the Chemin des Dames. The result was an immediate ten-mile advance—the longest since the advent of trench warfare.

The Canadian Corps had been withdrawn from the line at a time when troops were urgently needed to fill gaps along the Western Front. The 46th had been out since 6 May, and all indications were that it would stay out, even though the brigade had been designated as a "mobile reserve." This meant that early any morning it could be called upon to move to the front at an hour's notice. At other times the battalions would be given four hours' notice. But no excitement ever came of this, and at Marqueffles Farm, just outside Bouvigny, the glorious summer days succeeded one another.

Marqueffles Farm was really just another camp. It was situated to the east of Vimy Ridge, at the northernmost end where the Lorette Spur dwindled away into Bouvigny Wood. "It was just a low place on the ridge front. There were no buildings, but there was a pub—right on the corner of the parade ground," recalled Charlie Skeates, a former barber.

As always, there were rumours. Curry Spidell, the Mortlach farmer, had returned to the 46th, and he recorded the rumours for posterity. "One rumour was that we were part of the shock troops to be used in case of another attempt by the Germans to capture the Channel ports. The other rumour was that we were there to receive training to take part in some major operation which was to take place later on."

Intense training was carried out at Marqueffles Farm. The emphasis seemed to be on fitness, marksmanship, and mobility. Day after day it continued: drill, march, dig, exercise, and fire—over and over.

One way to make training more interesting was to stage competitions. There were contests for everything—bayonet fighting, musketry, Lewis guns, rifle grenades, and so on. Contests started at company level and sometimes worked right up to corps level. The 46th won the Army Rifle Association Platoon Meet for the 10th Brigade and on 3 July won the Divisional Championship at Houdaine. This emphasis on competition soon spread into all fields and there were sports days at every level.

"We won the football championship," wrote George Kentner. "After two fierce overtime struggles. Sergeant Lord of my company scored the only goal of both games. Jimmy was carried home by our boys and the team was met by our band and battalion *en masse*."

"We had a good football club," admitted Jinx Jenner. "All except the goalkeeper—that was me. Playing the 47th and 50th and 44th, we got by with maybe one or two goals scored on us. A travelling Imperial club came around. They scored nine goals. They took me, ball and all, back into the net. Oh boy, could they instep a ball in there! I thought I was a goalkeeper until then!"

Most evenings were free. "If you were close enough to an *estaminet* you'd go down there for a few drinks. Wherever the French could get in with a beer parlour they'd do it," commented Shorty Bond, a strict Methodist. "But I never saw a drunk on active service or behind the line."

Crown and Anchor was the ruling passion of many soldiers. Charlie Skeates, the barber from Swift Current, had ventured into the field by purchasing a cloth Crown and Anchor board. "Every time we'd go into a pub we'd pull it out, or when we were on a route-march, soon as we'd stop for a rest we'd pull the cloth out right on the road. They always wanted to play too. I always had a fair amount of money on me. Some of the guys said, 'By God, when we go over the top I'm going to grab that money.' " Charlie soon became comparatively wealthy. "You'd have a good run, and lots of times you made around five hundred francs. But when we went out on rest I used to spend it on the fellows."

Not every soldier spent his evenings so innocently. "There was the odd case where a guy stepped out," Shorty Bond noted. "I remember one man packing up his kit and putting on his pack and he says, 'Well, boys, I'm going to leave you.' 'Where are you going?' 'Oh, I've got to go to Pecker Hill.' He'd got a dose. They'd give him the best of medical treatment for that particular ailment I'd suppose. It was nothing more or less than a bad cold to some of them. There was always a flock of women, prostitutes and that, following the troops, especially in the rest areas."

Eventually this idyllic period had to end. On 7 July the 46th went back into the line, relieving a Highland regiment. Corporal Curry Spidell was in the advance party and he was concerned to notice three ten-inch artillery shells lying in the trench he was to take over. Someone had removed the nose cap from one without blowing himself up, and cordite littered the floor of the trench. The Highlanders walked over it unconcernedly. When Spidell mentioned this to the sergeant in charge, he was told that they had always meant to sweep it up but had never got around to it. Then the sergeant set about shaving in preparation for being relieved.

"He had just lathered his face," wrote Spidell, "and had his razor in his hand when we heard a 'puff,' saw a ball of flame, and heard a yell on our right. We ran over and there was a man with a smoking kilt in his hand doing the Highland Fling." He had dropped a cigarette butt. The sergeant's only comments were, "Dinna ye ken enough to rub oot a butt 'afore ye drap it? How do ye expect tae go oot o' here tonight in yer bare arse?"

"The man did not reply," wrote Spy. "He looked at his legs. They were somewhat scorched. He stopped and picked up his kilt, shook it, looked at it, and put it back on. One side was partly gone, but it still served its purpose. The sergeant watched him go. Then he said 'Ach, weel, he got rid o' the cordite for ye.' "

When the Canadian Corps went back into the line there was a changed air about the men. In recent days they had heard about the German air raids on their undefended hospitals. Nurses and patients had been killed in cold blood. For most, this news brought a touch of personal hatred for the enemy. A few days earlier word had also been received of the sinking of the *Llandovery Castle*, a hospital ship that was returning from Canada. Only 24 people were rescued out of a total of 258. Those who died included fourteen Canadian nursing sisters. One was Mae Sampson, a Regina girl. As the 46th filed into its new positions, the men looked grimmer than usual and their slogan was often heard: "Remember the *Llandovery Castle*."

The front was unusually quiet for a time but the soldiers were soon brought back to harsh reality. For Shorty Bond it happened on 25 July. On that date a stray shell dropped in a trench held by the 46th, and Bond's brother Billy was killed. "I found out about it within an hour or so. I was permitted to see him, but then he was sent back and buried. Outside of that there was nothing—this was warfare."

The next night the 46th Battalion raided the German line. Two officers and sixty men crossed no man's land with the object of taking prisoners and knocking out several reported enemy posts. A covering party of eight scouts under Lieutenant Bobby Crowe prepared the way beforehand and protected the raiders during their assembly.

The assembly was the trickiest part of the whole operation, for the assembly point was one thousand yards in front of the Canadian line, and the raiders had to slip forward at 9:30 P.M.— five and a half hours before zero hour. It was a long tense night made more dreary by frequent heavy showers. However, all went reasonably well once zero hour arrived. Two prisoners were taken, a handful of Germans killed, and the raiders returned, except for one man reported missing. Four raiders were wounded. As raids went, this one was a success.

By and large, the nights after this were very quiet, but by this stage in the war there were men in every battalion who had had the fight knocked out of them. They had had enough. Stan Colbeck, a recent arrival from Llewelyn, Saskatchewan, met one of these his first day in the line. "The sergeant sent myself and another little fellow back to get water. We had just gone a little way when a Jerry shell exploded about half a mile away. Well, this fellow with me shouted, 'They've got us!' and dived into a bunch of willows. I stood there; I couldn't believe what I had seen. I didn't know that he was shellshocked—he was the first I had seen. When he came out of the willows he was shaking like a leaf and was white as a sheet. The poor little guy should never have been there. Three years in the front line and he never got a scratch! He told me that every time they went over the top or into the line he prayed that he would get hit."

Another new man, Donald MacKay had a similar experience. "One member of the Signallers was assigned the task of caring for the pigeons—usually a long-service man who would be relieved of other duties. He was always referred to as Pigeons. I remember the night I went with Pigeons for a fresh set of birds. Coming back, there was periodic shellfire. Every time one would explode nearby, Pigeons would throw himself flat in a shell hole. He would lie there panting for a long time before he would venture forward."

One other man had also had enough. At this time the 46th held a deserter under guard. He was one of the "old men" of the battalion and he had already escaped twice. His latest had been on the pretext of going to the latrine, but he had vanished into the dark once he was outside. His hapless guards took his place in "the jail" for several days thereafter.

Eventually he was recaptured. Desertion was punishable by death. While everyone waited to see what would happen, he was kept in the battalion guard room. "I was given three men to go and guard him," recalled Don McKerchar, now a sergeant. "The guard room we had was simply four posts driven into the ground with chicken wire around that and tar paper on the outside of that. It had a bit of a roof on it too. I decided I was *not* going to jail over this fellow and he was not going to get away from us, so I got a set of handcuffs and put them on him behind his back. I caught him once. He had rolled over beside the wire and had started working on the wire and I kicked him back into the centre and told him to stay there. Well, then he told me he had to go to the latrine, and you had to take a man to the latrine when he has to go. So I had to get his handcuffs off so he could get his pants undone and I put them back on in front of him. I loaded my gun and says, 'My bayonet is right behind you, and don't try to get away because I'm mad, and I'll shoot if you try.' Anyway, he didn't try to get away and I brought him back. The police picked him up about eight in the morning. He was quite a character."

During these weeks of summer many changes had taken place. Several new officers had arrived, including one with a familiar face. E. D. ("Mac") McDonald was back, but as a lieutenant in charge of No. 10 Platoon. Since being wounded and tipping over a stove in the aid post to the rear of Regina Trench, Mac had been cooling his heels in Blighty. When he returned he saw few faces he recognized. There was one, though. His lifelong chum, Hugh Rising, was also back and in charge of a platoon.

On the last night of July, the 46th was relieved. The next day it set out for Gouves, east of Arras. The day was hot and the troops enjoyed marching through the pleasant farmlands. The next afternoon they moved by bus north to Tinques where they entrained in the evening. By this time the rumours had spread: "We're going north to the Ypres Salient." The train headed northwards, but after much manoeuvring in the dark it disgorged its confused occupants at Pont Remy *southwest* of where they had started. The time was two-thirty in the morning and a six-mile march lay ahead through pretty rural towns and forested hills. By five the companies were billeted at Caumont and Limeux.

Realizing how tired the troops were, Tubby Reid, one of the company commanders, decided the following night that he would march with them instead of riding on horseback. "That evening," related Bob Stevenson, "he lined us up and said, 'I know how hard it is on you boys marching. I'm going to walk right with you tonight,' and he gave his orderly the horse. That was the last night he gave his orderly the horse, I'll tell you. We were straggling into this place they'd picked out for the bivouac next morning, and the RSM was up at the front trying to get us into line a bit. Old Tubby was staggering worse than the rest of us, and he says to the sergeant-major, 'Leave the men alone! Leave the men alone!'" Captain Reid had chosen a poor night to be "one of the boys"—the march from Caumont to Crouy had been eighteen miles long.

It was at Crouy that a number of the men were detached. They included the members of the pipe band, various other volunteers, and Lieutenants Rising and Steel. The word was that they were to attend "tank school."

More long, weary nights of marching followed, until on the night of 7 August the battalion finally approached its destination—Gentelles Woods, near Amiens. The twelve-mile hike that night was carried out under strict time-scheduling, and smoking was prohibited. There were frequent encounters with army control posts. It was obvious to the men that they were in the midst of a vast array of might. Closely massed rows of artillery loomed on all sides, their barrels pointing menacingly towards the east, their crews quietly readying for action or sleeping beside them. Everywhere infantry columns were moving up—each as silent as a host of spirits. At 2:00 A.M. the men were in position just west of Gentelles Woods. There they settled down for a few hours' sleep. It would be their last for some time because it was now 8 August 1918. The Last Hundred Days had begun.

CHAPTER FIFTEEN

Amiens

> *August 8th was the black day of the German army in the history of the war.*
>
> General Erich von Ludendorff

"We rolled into our blankets there among the guns," wrote Curry Spidell, "but at 4:20 Ack Emma, the world exploded. Those guns all let loose at once. I think I bounced a foot off the ground. The earth did not tremble, it jumped, and we jumped with it. It was wonderful to see the whole bush light up with flashes from hundreds of guns hidden in there."

Two hours later the 46th began to advance across open fields. The battalion was the rearmost in the Canadian Corps. In front, the first three divisions were advancing. The 4th Division followed up in Reserve. The 10th Brigade was in turn in Divisional Reserve and the 46th brought up the rear of the 10th Brigade.

Although the common soldier did not realize it, the Canadian Corps had become the most powerful striking force in the world. Built up to almost army strength and intensively trained for open warfare and pursuit, it was a powerful weapon in the hands of a dynamic leader. The fact that the corps had been rested and husbanded for this offensive had led other overworked units to refer to the Canadians as "Foch's pets." Now the corps had been committed and there would be no rest for a long time to come.

The enemy defences consisted mainly of hidden machine gun nests. To overcome these, one hundred tanks had been allotted to the Canadians. The overwhelming power of the attack completely demoralized German forces in their path. As a result, Canadian artillery began to limber up and move forward. From their position in the rear, the 46th men watched fascinated.

"It wasn't long before the main road on our immediate right became a river of traffic—everything from horse-drawn vehicles to observation balloons, yes, observation balloons being hauled along on their motor lorries. Very soon afterward wounded started coming back. They were all in very high spirits and told that the attack had gone very well," Lieutenant McDonald recalled.

All morning the 46th advanced in lines of sections, two platoons strung out rearward in each line. This type of formation and this steady advance was something new to veterans of the war. All was peaceful and there was nothing to do but plod forward and look at the sights. "Sometimes from a hilltop we would see the battle line miles in front of us with shells bursting from horizon to horizon. There we were always halted to rest and to view the spectacle," wrote Curry Spidell. "We really had a very enjoyable day."

It was indeed a thrilling day for Canadians. The attack's success was obvious. In the distance the odd tank or a wave of advancing khaki could be seen. Signs of enemy panic were everywhere. Equipment lay abandoned and prisoners streamed back, but it was the little things that impressed Gordon Brown. "We had the enemy pretty well on the run. In fact, one little village we come to, they were just eating breakfast—porridge and everything was there on the table—everything. In fact, we captured one nurse there. It was the first nurse I ever saw, a German nurse."

It was ten minutes before noon when the 46th finished passing through the town of Hangard where they crossed the River Luce. Lunch was served, and as the cheery men joked and relaxed, a sight the like of which they had never seen (and would never see again) appeared on the horizon to the rear.

Lewis-Gunner Bob Stevenson couldn't believe his eyes. "The guy beside me says, 'Look behind, Stevie.' I thought the Germans were behind me or something, and I wheeled around. Over the hill behind us our cavalry was coming in a solid line about five feet apart just as far as you could see right or left—for about a half a mile I guess we could see. A solid line of horses coming at the lope there! To see that line of cavalry coming was quite a sight. They went right on through us, of course."

All that afternoon the men passed signs of heavy fighting, and always, from far to the front, came the faint sounds of battle. At five o'clock they arrived before Perrone Wood. Here they came upon many of the cavalry which had so impressed them earlier in the day. Said Acting Unpaid Lance-Corporal Stevenson, "The Germans were in this little wood, and they really knocked them horses down coming up that slope. But the cavalry split and went around them, and they got those Germans too, 'cause they never had a chance to get out. But they really knocked them pretty bad going up there. There was dead horses all over that slope, and a lot of dead men too."

"Horses, we saw more dead horses—new saddles on a lot of them—lying there all shot in the head. They'd been wounded and they had to shoot 'em all," Jack Featherstone remarked sadly.

The men were impressed when they entered Perrone Wood. "There were some guns in there that never had the covers off," Private Featherstone later recalled. "Big guns hidden in that wood and never got time to fire. There was also a pump and everybody rushed there and they yelled, 'Don't drink it! We've got to test it first. It might be poisoned!' But somebody said, 'We're so doggone dry we don't care if it is poisoned,' and we filled our water bottles."

The 46th prepared to bivouac for the night. Outposts were sent out and the men relaxed after their long walk. They had advanced approximately six miles that day. There was excitement in the air. The eighth of August had been the greatest day in the war, they agreed. Now, what would the days ahead bring? In the meantime, "make the best of it" was the attitude, and some did just that. "My platoon and I found a lovely billet at a place where the Germans had dammed a little stream and made shower baths," said Mac McDonald. "And we all had a shower—a warm shower. There was coal or coke or something there to warm the water. We all had a lovely shower and we felt clean and relaxed."

Not everyone was so lucky. There were still a few men hard

at work. Like the other runners, Vic Syrett was kept busy all day carrying messages back and forth. "It was well into the dusk of the long summer evening. I had delivered a message to a tank unit. We were near Le Quesnel at the time. I was on my way back to Battalion H.Q. when I was hit in the left arm by a machine gun burst although they probably weren't firing at me." Thus Vic Syrett, one of the last originals, had his Blighty.

That evening many of the men wondered out loud about their absent comrades who had been sent to the so-called tank school. "Well, they sure missed a helluva day," was the attitude. Nothing could have been further from the truth, for the men who had been detached several days earlier at Crouy "to attend tank school" had been in the thick of the fighting all day long. They had been assembled into Lewis gun teams which had been thrown into battle in a most unusual way. One hundred new Mark V tanks had been set aside, each of which carried, along with its crew, one infantry officer, a scout, two Lewis gun teams, and a Vickers team. A bold plan had been conceived to send these monsters forward eight miles beyond the start line. There they would disgorge their passengers to hold positions and harass the enemy until the infantry came up. The Lewis gun crews had been made up from various infantry battalions plus one company from the Canadian Machine Gun Corps.

Lieutenant McDonald's chum, Hugh Rising, was one of the 46th's officers detached for this scheme. "Rising told me that— one, the tank got lost; two, the tank broke down; three, that his men got pitched about and got sick with the motion and fumes. He had quite a dreadful time. In any event his foray was not very successful."

Rising's experiences were common. The fumes from the unventilated tanks made their unseasoned passengers ill. Some got out and walked behind while others even had to be evacuated. Many tanks were hit or broke down and few reached the "dotted blue line" on the map.

The 46th suffered several casualties from this venture. Lieutenant R. J. Steel, the former Cape Town Highlander, and his crew were all wounded. His crew included pipers Baggett, McGeachin, and Smith, all members of the 46th's pipe band.

"Archie Smith told us about his experiences afterwards,"

Sergeant McLeod recalled. "He said it was stinking hot, there wasn't much room, and you couldn't see very much. All you done was sit in there and when you got to a certain objective the tank officer would open the doors and let you out. Archie was quite pleased. He came back boasting, 'I'm a tank man now. When I go into battle I ride a steed. You fellows got to do the foot-slogging.' That was the joke after about three drinks."

The next morning saw the advance resume, and at eight o'clock the battalion moved off. The 46th was to relieve the 72nd Battalion and establish a support position. The advance was a repeat of the previous day, although the marchers now veered north of the Amiens-Roye Road towards the centre of the corps. As the lines of troops snaked through the fields of ripened wheat, memories of harvests in the prairies flooded back.

By evening the 72nd had been relieved and supper was served. At 9:25, a new twist—orders were received to *stop* working and to *rest* instead. Things were indeed looking up. Meanwhile Battalion Headquarters burned the midnight oil. Orders had just arrived— the 46th would attack next morning.

Lieutenant McDonald, the one-time bank clerk from Moose Jaw, recalled the early hours of 10 August. "The officers of the 10th Brigade were called together and were told what we had to do that day. This was reasonably early in the morning and it was quite an extraordinary sight. Brigadier-General Hayter was there on his horse, we were around him, and there were a few 18-pounder guns scattered about without any emplacements."

By six in the morning the 46th and 44th were en route to their jumping-off place. The attack would go in at eight, and their jump-off would take place along the Rouvroy-Vrely Road which ran at right angles to the line of attack. On the left the 12th Brigade was to attack, while to the immediate right the 44th would advance towards Fouquescourt. The 46th's objective was the village of Maucourt and the area south of it.

The companies were in position by 7:00 A.M. To the right was A Company followed by C. The left of the line was occupied by B, with D in support. The men lay down in the fields of wheat to wait. It was a longer wait than anticipated, for the attack was postponed until the tanks could get into position.

At last, at 10:15, the order finally came to advance. The men stood up and moved forward through the wheat. The manoeuvre was routine; it had been practised over and over at Marqueffles Farm. Following just behind the small handful of tanks was a thin screen of scouts and snipers. Next came two waves in extended order, a hundred and fifty yards apart. The support companies followed two hundred yards behind in line of sections in file.

"The first part of the advance, which was something like two thousand yards, was reasonably uneventful," Mac McDonald observed. "We were supported by a very sketchy barrage fired by a few 18-pounders. There didn't seem to be any heavy guns helping us."

Not everyone would have agreed with his assessment. Sniper Jack Featherstone was one of the "chosen," infiltrating the German line behind the tanks. "They put two snipers behind the tank, but they didn't have enough snipers so they sent me with a rifleman. We were supposed to follow a hundred yards behind the tank and if they missed anybody you were supposed to pick them off before the first wave came up. Our tank got put out of action. He went sideways in one of these long communication trenches. His tracks were thrashing away and neither one of them could catch. So they put the yellow flag up—that's 'Out of Action.' I says, 'Let's carry on,' and the other fellow says, 'I'm not going!' I says, 'I ought to shoot you, you son of a gun.' But he says, 'I'm not going!' So he lay there.

"They sent another guy up, a fellow named Tooke. We carried on. Here we are, all by ourselves in the open prairie. Then there was this little old town. We just came up and these Germans were coming out of a dugout there. We got the drop on them. We just happened to see them and get our rifles up there ready. If we'd passed by, they'd have got us in the back.

"One old fellow there with a big moustache, he had a red handkerchief in his hand. I kept pointing at that, and he'd point at his mouth. I said, 'Open it up! Untie it!' (They tell you, 'Don't take a chance on nothing; they might have a bomb in there.') He untied it and it was a bunch of that doggone old black bread they used. We held him there till the first wave come up and then the officer took over. All of a sudden a machine gun started up. The officer in charge says, 'Jack, see if you can get that fellow.' I started across the road and that's the last I remember. One of those whiz-bangs landed right on the road."

For most it was an exhilarating morning—watching the Germans taking to their heels and running as fast as they could. But the 46th's advance began to draw more fire, and artillery began to lash the area. Nevertheless, the battalion pressed steadily onward, and soon the advancing troops came upon something more ominous than anything they had seen in weeks. Before them stretched hundreds of crumbling, weed-covered trenches. The 46th men were back where they had started. These were the long-abandoned trenches of the 1916 battles of the Somme. A fatalistic despondency settled upon the men.

"Never had a shell lit anywhere near us till we got up to the old Somme trench system," Sergeant McLeod related. "By golly, then there was just one trench after another. They were overgrown to some extent. You'd just step out of one trench, and in two or three steps you were down into another one."

"Suddenly Fritz landed a wall of bursting shells in front of us, and I mean a *wall*," wrote Curry Spidell. "The advance stopped. The barrage slackened and we moved again, but not very far. The Germans shortened the range and put another wall down in front of us. Gaps began to appear in the wall, and the line moved. A gap appeared right in front of Sergeant Jack Scott and me, and we made a dash for it. Just as we got there, it closed. At the explosion I swung sideways to the blast, and yelled, 'Look out, Jack!' As I did so, a small shell splinter came through my right cheek, cut off two teeth, and went out through my open mouth. Along with that I got three others in my right shoulder. My arm dropped. I was on the edge of an old trench and I spun around and tumbled into it. Jack jumped in beside me.

"I had been carrying two water bottles full of rum, and a two-quart carton of Wagstaff's Strawberry Jam. (We had not seen strawberry jam for months.) I had the jam slung on my back in a rope carrier I had made. I tried to tell Jack to take the jam, but could not move my jaw to speak. I motioned to Jack to take the jam, and he took it. He left the trench, found our stretcher bearer,

Robinson, and sent him to me. Robinson bandaged me. I gave him the rum and started back to the forward dressing station."

Enemy resistance had stiffened all at once. "You could see heads popping up as you advanced and you had to watch you didn't put yourself too much in view," said Shorty Bond, a runner for C Company. Shorty knew what he was talking about, for he had put himself into view and a bullet had gone right through him just a quarter of an inch above his heart. He was carried back to cover by his company commander, Captain Gyles.

The German defences, though makeshift, had been well manned by fresh troops thrown in after the disasters of the first two days, and the stream of prisoners had slowed to a trickle. But the Canadians were in a deadly mood; the *Llandovery Castle* had not been forgotten. "I took this German officer—arrogant bugger. Next thing he was ordering ME around. Things had gotten pretty hot, so I just stepped back and let him have it. He had this Iron Cross ribbon on his coat, so I frisked him, and sure enough, he had his damned Iron Cross in his pocket. He had a picture of him and his wife too. I still got that picture."

On the left, the 46th's first wave had arrived in front of the village of Maucourt, and there a dramatic episode unfolded. "We ran into a battery of Fritzie guns up on a hill," said Sergeant Don McKerchar. "We had to take those, and to do so we had to take them by sectional rushes. It was the first time I'd been in a sectional rush and it was quite interesting. Eight or ten men would rush ahead; all the time they were running everybody else was lying on their stomachs and we were firing everything we could into the battery of guns to keep them from shooting. But they were still shooting shells directly into us. That was a matter of a couple of hundred yards away. As that section advanced twenty or thirty feet, the next one would go past them, and so on."

"They kept shelling us till we were almost on top of them," recalled Bob Stevenson, "and then they ran their horses out from behind and tried to hitch on to these guns and pull them out. Of course it was an absolute lost cause, that, because they couldn't possibly pull that off. One of the scouts was telling me afterwards he counted the bullet holes in one of the lead horses and there was one hundred and sixty."

The German gunners were all killed or captured and the 46th had the two guns which had, only moments before, been fired at them over open sights. One of the horses survived and Charlie Russell, the company runner, pressed it into service for its new masters. During the rest of the day the troops became used to seeing a grinning Russell galloping about the field bearing messages in the style of the Old West. Heavy fire was still coming from the village of Maucourt. "The unit on the Left Flank had not kept pace with our advance and had deviated from their Right Boundary," recorded the *War Diary*. " 'B' Company, leading the attack, were therefore compelled to swing into Maucourt village where they encountered strong machine gun nests, which were dealt with promptly and with great dash, Corporal Camm of 'B' Company doing particularly gallant work against these posts. Here, also, Captain Reid displayed splendid initiative and daring leadership in directing the advance of attack and mopping up of the village."

At last, at 1:25, the 46th was able to notify Brigade Headquarters that it had reached its objectives. As ordered, the battalion held the southern edge of Maucourt and a line running more or less south along the old Somme trenches. Unfortunately, the units on the left flank had still not come up.

The afternoon dragged on unpleasantly. Sergeant Neil McLeod had brought his platoon to ground in the maze of trenches to the right of Maucourt. There was no trace of the platoon on his left, so McLeod left George Kentner in charge and started out towards the left to locate the vanished platoon. To enable him to find his own platoon again he had one of the men stick his rifle and bayonet above the trench. Having found the neighbouring platoon, he was heading back to his own when "a great big 'coal box' come in and shot out a bunch of black smoke. I thought, 'You damned fool! It's landed right on top of your platoon for sure!' I jumped into the trench and was lucky enough to find them all right. Everybody was hunched up, and I just got back into the trench when these two legs and torso came out of the air. You'd have sworn somebody just cut him in two. Poor fellow, the rest of him had disappeared and we couldn't find a trace of him."

With the 46th now on its objectives, the immediate task was

to dig in. "We built a block on the trench which ran towards the Germans," said Mac McDonald, "and waited for the inevitable counterattack. By this time a few of our tanks appeared on the scene and had started operating in front of us. They were all destroyed—*All!* I think there was three of them. They were all set alight and the poor fellows in the tanks—those of them who managed to get out—were killed as they got out of the tank."

The enemy counterattack that McDonald expected did not take long to materialize. "Along the trench to our block came a party of German soldiers, headed by an officer who was promptly shot. One of the men on duty and myself got on top of the trench and went forward and bombed the rest of the party, but they got away. A machine gun opened up from somewhere, and we had to get back down into the trench."

By evening the situation had stabilized. The 50th Battalion had leapfrogged and had reached a railway line after heavy casualties. The 46th, with three companies now in the line, sent out three battle patrols to protect the 50th's flanks. No contact was made with the enemy, and the night was spent more or less quietly.

Although the men did not know it, 10 August 1918 had been a memorable day—Field Marshal Douglas Haig had made his *first* visit to the front. He was struck by the difficulty of moving through the old Somme battleground and he returned to his chateau determined to bring an end to the offensive in this area. But orders take a long time to filter down to battalion level.

The next morning the 46th was alerted to make a further advance. As the runners went to notify the companies, the enemy put down a heavy barrage. This was between ten and eleven o'clock. All the runners were hit, and at the same time word was received that the enemy was attacking the 50th in front. A tragedy was averted only by the quick action of Colonel Dawson. The 50th was signalling desperately for artillery support but there was no reply, so the colonel ran to a battery of field guns and advised the gunners of the crisis. Artillery fire came down just in time. Nevertheless, the 50th was driven back on top of the 46th.

Colonel Dawson immediately came forward to carry out his own reconnaissance, and Lance-Corporal Herbert Butterworth took a patrol out to the left to attempt to link up with elements of the 12th Brigade near Chilly. At the same time it was discovered that a serious breach had occurred in the front line. Between the 50th and the 47th a stretch of over five hundred yards had been strongly occupied by the enemy.

C Company under Captain Gyles was ordered to clear out the Germans and occupy this pocket. The captain led two platoons forward over a badly exposed stretch of no man's land. A series of short rushes, and the Canadians had infiltrated the enemy defences, using bombs, Lewis gun and rifle fire to drive out the Germans, who left behind fifteen dead and two machine guns. The 46th suffered no casualties. Captain Gyles graciously turned over part of the captured pocket to the 47th Battalion. The remainder stayed under C Company's care.

The following evening is best described by the *Report on Operations:* "At 5:00 P.M. orders were received from Brigade to relieve the 50th Battalion and establish front line in the old German system of trenches; relief to start at 8:00 o'clock. Relief took a very long time owing to the failure of guides, and darkness, and to the uncertainty of the line held. The line taken over from the 50th Battalion failed to agree with the line reported to be held and ordered to be taken over." Major Hope then went forward to reconnoitre and establish a true picture of the forward line.

The remainder of 12 August was spent waiting for relief. Both sides sniped and shelled each other, and it was amply evident that the Germans had reinforced their line with fresh troops. Despite this, the whole corps realized that they had knocked the Germans for their biggest loss of the war. Because of the confusion caused by the lack of maps showing the old trench lines, guides were unable to bring in relieving troops. So the 46th waited out another day. Finally, on the night of 13/14 August, the men made their way back to support positions.

The withdrawal was not without incident, thanks to the arrival of German planes. They dropped their bombs, which fortunately missed all living targets but were close enough to frighten some French artillery horses that were passing the 46th at that moment. "They crowded to their left and crowded a bunch of us fellows into the canal," declared Gordon Brown. "It was no laughing matter at the time. Some who could swim, swam across to the other side, but most of us started climbing out on our side. Two or three times I got just about out and someone would grab me trying to get out himself, and we would both go back in again. We finally made it out but I lost my rifle in that canal. The next morning when we went for breakfast there was no field kitchen for D Company as it had been crowded into the canal along with twenty-four hours' rations."

And so ended the Battle of Amiens. It had cost the 46th eight killed and a hundred and two wounded, two of whom later died. Four men were missing. Also on the casualty list was Lieutenant-Colonel Dawson who had eventually succumbed to the flu on the second-last night. A fighter all the way, he stayed in until he had to be carried out unconscious on a stretcher.

In total 11,362 Canadians had become casualties. This was the equivalent of half a division. Another side effect was the appalling loss in tanks. Never again would the Allies have as many as they had on 8 August, "the black day of the German army."

The Battle of Amiens was the beginning of the end for Germany. The Canadian Corps had thoroughly defeated ten German divisions plus elements of others. More than 9,000 prisoners, 190 guns, and 1,000 machine guns and mortars had been captured. The enemy line had been penetrated to a depth of fourteen miles. Despite all this, it was the moral effect which was most decisive. In the first two days, Germans surrendered in thousands. Their will to win had been smashed.

The battle provided material for thousands of letters home, but perhaps the most poignant was that written by Private Dick Greves to his brother in Tugaske, Saskatchewan. "Just a word or two so that you will know that I'm still safe and sound, well and happy," it began. Before his brother received this letter, Dick had been killed in action near a village called Dury.

CHAPTER SIXTEEN

The Drocourt-Queant Line

> *In that last hundred days we only had one really rough time, and that was taking the Drocourt-Queant Line.*
>
> Ross Cameron, 46th Battalion. Interviewed by the CBC

"We could see on our right a small wood being heavily shelled by Fritz," wrote George Kentner. "On our left was the dark outline of a ridge of ground. Out front all was quiet save for the odd burst of machine gun fire or an exploding shell." It was nearly five o'clock on the morning of 2 September and Kentner was waiting for zero hour. In a few minutes the 46th would attempt to smash the Drocourt-Queant Line.

The Drocourt-Queant Line was the first of a series of defensive positions, known collectively to the common soldier as the Hindenburg Line. One of the most powerful and well-organized defence systems in the world, the "D-Q" consisted of front and support trenches, both provided with numerous concrete shelters and machine gun posts, all of which were protected by dense masses of barbed wire. It was intended to be absolutely impregnable.

The men waiting to go over on that September morning were tired men. The 4th Division had come up from Amiens by train after the rest of the corps had already begun preliminary attacks. The 4th Imperial Division, which was more or less standing in for the 4th Canadian Division, had expended itself on these preliminary attacks and had declared itself unable to carry out all of its next assignment. Thus the 10th Brigade had been rushed into position after a ten-mile night march.

The 46th was temporarily commanded by the popular Jock Rankin. Less than four days earlier Jock had returned from a course at Aldershot, only to be rushed to the front with an advance party to get a glimpse of the area. Dury, a shattered village and the centre of the German support line, was the 46th Battalion's objective. The front line was to be breached by the 50th and 47th. Then the 46th would pass through them and take Dury. The battalion would have a 1,000-yard frontage and the expected penetration would be 1,300 yards.

Zero hour came and the advance went according to plan, as George Kentner's journal recorded: "Before we reached the Drocourt-Queant Line, we were abreast of the 50th and had become practically one wave. Here the barrage was scheduled to play for some time so we took what shelter we could. We were as close to the roaring barrage as we could possibly approach. Presently it lifted and we went forward preceded by a few tanks. It was next to impossible to crawl through the wire so we had to use paths which the enemy had left for his own convenience. Many were shot by machine gun and snipers as we passed through, but we retaliated in the same way. A number of them tried to run back. Of course, they had to use paths so they were huddled together. One of our machine-gunners dropped with his gun and opened fire. They went down in a heap, all but one. He turned and surrendered."

Once the front line had been taken, the 46th passed through to take the village of Dury, less than half a mile ahead. The tanks turned away and the infantry advanced alone as enemy fire intensified.

"We began our advance and were surprised at the slight resistance offered," wrote Kentner. "Entering the town and chalk pits we found large numbers of troops who quickly obeyed our orders to come out. Never had I seen so many prisoners taken in such a manner." Amongst the prisoners was the area commandant and his assistant.

But this was on the left flank. Things were not going so well on the right where C Company under Captain Blair was attempting to gain possession of the southwest corner of Dury. Here the advance had stalled under a continuous hail of machine gun and rifle fire from the sunken road.

Captain Bob Brown, following up with A Company, saw the situation and acted decisively. A volunteer was called for to return and find one of the tanks. Private Red Campbell, formerly a road foreman from Mortlach, Saskatchewan, raced back under heavy fire and presently reappeared leading a tank across the open ground. That would settle their hash, thought every man. Then there was a loud groan—the tank had broken down.

Captain Brown promptly ordered Sergeant Parker to take two sections through the village to outflank the enemy machine-gunners. Morley Timberlake was one of these men. "Our party of about twelve men took off under artillery fire and machine gun fire from the enemy. After a while we came to the right of the village and got onto a sunken road. Over to the right was a bunch of Heinies beating it from an old windmill. We potted at them with rifles and machine guns and caused some casualties. Advancing along the sunken road, we completely surprised and outflanked two machine gun posts simply swarming with men. After we fired a few shots we took the whole bunch prisoners, about a hundred to a hundred and fifty of them. Proceeding up the sunken road to help with the prisoners, I happened to look over to my left. I saw there another thickly manned machine gun post of Heinies shooting over to the left from an embankment. I dropped down on the bank of this sunken road and fired at the man operating the machine gun. He fell over backwards and the machine gun with him. Some more of the boys arrived and joined in the firing. We got many others but soon the remainder put up their hands to surrender."

By this time Captain Bob Brown had led the remainder of A Company in a frontal attack, and by 7:45 A.M. the south side of Dury was captured. Nine machine guns and 120 prisoners had been taken. Meanwhile, on the left, Lieutenant Rising and D Company had penetrated the northeastern end of Dury and had advanced beyond into the enemy's support line. There had been many casualties, including the gangling farm boy, now a handsome sergeant, Neil McLeod. "One of those round shrapnel balls, a nice wound, no bones broken," he said with evident satisfaction.

Several advance posts were then established east of Dury and the men waited in relative peace, alert for the inevitable counterattack. It came at noon with a tremendous barrage of artillery and machine gun fire. Soon the outposts became untenable. George Kentner was in one of these advance positions: "Evidently our machine gun post on our right had been overrun as the Hun seemed rather close to us. We saw a couple of our men run madly back to the bush. One was struck on the leg and fell in a shell hole. He reappeared in a moment, less equipment, and completed his dash. We were entirely alone with only our grenade section in view. Our only escape was over open ground which was now being swept by machine gun fire." The men dodged back in pairs. Some never made it to safety. The last two back appear to have been Gordon Brown and George Kentner.

By now the news received by Jock Rankin at Battalion Headquarters was not encouraging. Everywhere the outposts had been driven in and Sergeant Sturley's appeared to have been wiped out. The companies were suffering heavy casualties and were barely hanging on. An order was sent advising everyone of the critical situation and ordering the men to hold Dury at all costs.

Jock Rankin rushed forward and deployed his remaining platoons to seal the holes and provide flank cover. Now came the moment of truth. There would be no time to arrange artillery support. The lost ground would have to be retaken with the bayonet. "I was personally convinced that we would never succeed in reaching and capturing the position," wrote George Kentner. "We worked our way up and waited for the signal. Finally it came. There was a short pause at the end of the third whistle blast and then Corporal McVeety shouted, 'Come on, boys!' and leaped over the top. In an instant we were all over, racing forward, yelling and screeching and cursing as wildly as men ever did. One element in our favour was surprise. The sight of us charging across the open ground, with fixed bayonets, and our weird, wild, almost insane cries disheartened Fritz. His front posts ran back to their machine guns, but here they stayed. Seconds later the whole ground was swept by machine gun fire and men began to drop. McVeety was among the first to be killed. Never have I faced such a terrific storm of machine gun bullets."

"I don't suppose Mr. Rising got fifty feet before he was hit in the head with a bullet," Bob Stevenson recalled. "The small arms fire was terrific. A bullet hit me right on the belt and knocked me right down." Stevenson found his belt buckle doubled up, but otherwise he was all right, so he got up and charged again.

Suddenly whole swaths of the enemy could be seen going down in heaps. Well in front of the ragged, screaming line of khaki, Lewis gun fire had erupted unexpectedly to supplement that coming from the flanks. It was Sergeant Sturley's lost outpost. By now an irresistible fighting madness had overtaken everyone, including George Kentner. "We piled into his first line of posts, and those who had not run back remained there forever. . . . The enemy's nerve was broken. They began to run but our bullets were cutting them down. We were bent on their destruction and had no thought of mercy. Some threw down their rifles and rushed towards us trembling. In all, we took perhaps a dozen prisoners. Only a few escaped to their lines. The ground about the posts was fairly strewn with their dead bodies, with numbers of badly wounded lying about them. It was an awesome sight to look back over the ground where we had attacked. It was strewn with khaki and grey-clad bodies."

The situation had been restored. The enemy gave up Dury as a lost cause but continued heavy shelling and machine gun fire. By this time there were men from all companies in the front line, digging for all they were worth.

Mac McDonald had recently been appointed battalion Lewis-gun officer, so he had spent the day at Battalion Headquarters. At the first opportunity, along with Corporal Ewart Brown, he came forward to visit his lifelong friend, Lieutenant Hugh Rising. "There were one or two officers standing about in a rifle pit, not very deep. I said, 'Where's Rising?' and the company commander said, 'He's there.' Rising was lying dead under a groundsheet on the edge of the rifle pit. I had no idea he was dead. I couldn't possibly have pulled the groundsheet off him and looked at him. If I had done, I'd have cried. Of course, infantry lieutenants in the

Canadian Corps didn't cry. He was my dearest friend."

Badly shaken, Mac and Corporal Ewart Brown made their way back to Headquarters as German shelling intensified. "We were going along when Corporal Brown said, 'I think I'm hit in the back.' I had a look and couldn't see anything. All of a sudden, he sort of half collapsed and a pale pink froth started coming out of his mouth. I examined his back more closely and saw that there was a slight hole in his tunic where, it was obvious, a piece of shrapnel had penetrated through to his lungs. I got him down with an effort to the battalion dressing station. He was practically unconscious. The doctor in charge examined him and told me there was no hope. So Corporal Brown died."

On another part of the battlefield the 10th Battalion had taken its objective on Buissy Switch Line. This was in large part due to the actions of one of the original 46th men, Sergeant Arthur Knight from Regina. In the words of the London *Times*, he "showed extraordinary courage as an individual fighter." Knight had dashed forward alone and bayoneted several machine-gunners and a trench mortar crew. When the rest fled he had cut them down. Next, he had entered a tunnel alone, where he killed an officer and two NCOs, and captured twenty men. Eventually he had been mortally wounded after having routed another German party single-handedly. Knight was the second former member of the 46th to be posthumously awarded the Victoria Cross.

The following day saw the 46th moving forward in a general advance which extended across the entire corps front. The objective was a line on the map labelled the Green Line. It would overlook the Canal du Nord. The unit advanced in artillery formation, led by Jock Rankin, Lieutenant Tickler Scott (formerly a sergeant, now intelligence officer), and several scouts. Soon the battalion was experiencing heavy shellfire.

"It was the section on our right that was the first to suffer," George Kentner wrote. "A shell dropped on the first two men. One dropped and committed those awful, horrible struggles that men do when in the grips of death. It was terrible to witness one of our own comrades in such an awful way. But death kindly ended his sufferings."

The Green Line was eventually reached and everyone dug in to await events and attempt to find safety from the incessant shelling and raking by machine guns. Headquarters was established in a quarry lined with dugouts. It was 5:20 P.M. when Mac McDonald returned from his rounds. He was about to enter the Battalion Headquarters dugout when Captain Hepburn, the signals officer, waved a bottle of whisky from a neighbouring "bivvy." "This indeed was manna from heaven," said Mac. "I did a sharp right turn, and as I did, a shell dropped in the entrance of the shelter where Battalion Headquarters had been established. If I hadn't seen this bottle of whisky I would have been at the place where the shell burst because it was only about two or three yards farther on. Major Hope, second in command of the battalion, was pretty severely injured about the face. He was bleeding like a stuck pig from his nose, and altogether it was an extremely unpleasant sight."

Also in the dugout at the time was Lieutenant (Acting Captain) Reg Bateman, the former major who had reverted to lieutenant so that he could return to the front. He was killed instantly, and the University of Saskatchewan lost its first professor of English. Jock Rankin was also slightly wounded but remained on duty. Seldom had one shell hit a battalion so hard.

There were many casualties on 3 September. One of them, surprisingly enough, was the deserter who had been held under such close guard by Sergeant McKerchar. Many legends surrounded the case, but the 46th's deserter went into the line with the rest of the battalion on the third. Everyone knew what that meant: if a man on charge was sent back into action, all charges had to be dropped—there would be no court martial. No one today knows whether it was Rankin or Dawson who gave the man one final chance to redeem himself, but what is known is that the colonel held off proceedings for an inordinately long time and that Rankin was in command when the deserter went over the top with his comrades. There must have been a sigh of relief when the culprit picked up his third, and last, Blighty of the war.

After a night of accurate bombing by Gotha planes, which caused more casualties, Major Rankin received orders to send out two patrols next day at noon. One was to scout the village of Palluel and one to capture the bridges across the Canal du Nord. This meant advances of well over four thousand yards through the village of Ecourt St. Quentin and some marshes. Neither patrol stood much chance of success, and both were soon pinned down by snipers and machine gun fire. After several men had been hit, the patrols extricated themselves with difficulty and returned.

Meanwhile the rest of the battalion had been hard hit by shelling. Gordon Brown was one of the lucky ones. A slight wound in the arm put him out of action for three weeks.

That evening the 46th was relieved by the 116th, and after a long march with many halts the men were back at Vis-en-Artois, their jumping-off place only three days earlier. The next afternoon they marched back to Arras.

"Alongside the road a great amount of graves had been dug and men were engaged in digging more," wrote George Kentner. "Close by, lay rows of dead bodies awaiting burial. As we passed we knew that amongst them were some of the men who had chatted by our sides when we had travelled that road before."

The Suicide Battalion had suffered, but the fight at Dury had equalled anything in its brief history. The 46th had inflicted a crushing defeat upon the enemy. The number of prisoners taken was over four hundred and the number killed would never be known. The battalion had captured a field gun, an anti-tank gun, fifteen machine guns, an area headquarters, and an invaluable haul in secret documents.

Yet there were some melancholy moments ahead. Letters would have to be written to the next of kin of beloved comrades. Mac had to compose one. "I wrote Rising's mother and with an absolutely clear conscience was able to say that death had been instantaneous. We always used to say that of course. We didn't want anyone to think that their sons or husbands or brothers or fiances had died, as some of them had died, terrible deaths. It was always 'painless and instantaneous.' "

There would be many of these letters. The 46th had suffered 310 casualties in cracking the Drocourt-Queant Line. Fifty had been killed and there were twenty-four "missing in action." This nearly always meant "killed in action." Among the dead were Dick Greves, who would never again see his farm or his beloved horses; Reg Bateman, whose students would mourn him; Hugh Rising, the third of four brothers killed in action; Arnold Tallis, the third of that musical family to die with the 46th. There were seventy similar tragedies. Other familiar faces had gone too: the wounded included Major Hope, Sergeant Neil McLeod, Corporal Abbie Cairns, and Privates Gordon Brown, Spike Smith, and Charlie Skeates.

It made a young soldier think. Mac did. "I went, on the next Sunday, to a voluntary church parade, and for the first time in my life I took Communion. I prayed, I suppose, as sincerely as I have ever prayed in my life, for Rising, Corporal Brown, and all the others I knew who had been killed."

CHAPTER SEVENTEEN

The Canal du Nord

If anybody can do it, the Canadians can.
General Julian Byng, regarding the proposed
attack across the Canal du Nord

The column of fours swung along jauntily. No one wore kit or carried a rifle. It was the 46th returning from bath parade. It felt great to be clean and almost free of lice, with the whole evening in an *estaminet* to look forward to. The time was late in the afternoon on 25 September. The men swung into the town of Bullecourt where they passed the *estaminet* which they would pack that evening. Bob Stevenson, the former farm boy from Gravelbourg, decided not to wait until evening: "Tommy Meeres was in the section of fours ahead of me. 'What's the use of marching up the road and coming back again?' he says. 'Let's stop here.' So when they made a turn around one of the corners in town, we dropped out, and about half a dozen or so other fellows too."

But, unexpectedly, they were not joined by their companions later in the evening. "Some fellows from another battalion came into this *estaminet* and one of them says, 'What are you fellows doing here?' We promptly told him it was none of his business. He says, 'You know your battalion's moving off?' That kind of changed our tune and we decided we'd better get back." They did so, fortunately arriving a scant five minutes before the roll was called and only about ten minutes before the battalion moved off.

The 46th moved up to the front in the darkness, passing through lines of artillery—a massive concentration of 18-pounders standing wheel to wheel—and before long the men found themselves in the front line near the village of Inchy facing the Canal du Nord. Here they took up their position in a set of former German trenches that had been reversed and rewired.

The battalion had hardly settled in when Lieutenant Coates led a party of seven men, including Sergeant J. E. Sturley, into no man's land. Sturley was to establish a post far in advance of the front line to prevent the enemy from infiltrating up to the Canadian line, for Fritz must on no account learn of the massive build-up taking place so close to him. The NCO and his six men established their position and held on tenaciously for over twenty-four hours under constant machine gun and rifle fire. John Sturley was soon wounded, but no Germans passed this post alive.

If any German patrols had succeeded in penetrating the 46th's line they would have been shocked, for spread out behind the 46th lay the entire Canadian Corps, poised for what General Julian Byng called "the most difficult operation of the war."[25] He should have known, for he was the man behind the dramatically successful attack on Vimy Ridge eighteen months earlier.

During the next day the men were able to familiarize themselves with the area. It was obvious that the 46th would be leading an assault shortly, but no one realized what an enormous gamble it would be. The Canal du Nord had been under construction when the war broke out. It was forty-four feet wide at the bottom and widened to sixty-four at the top. The bottom in front of the 46th was actually at ground level, so its banks had been built up to a considerable height on each side. The canal had been flooded from the north to a point just north of the Canadian Corps's boundary, and there were constant fears that the Germans would be able to flood it whenever they suspected an imminent attack.

Corps Intelligence had reported an almost unbelievable system of German defences. First, there was the canal itself with its thin line of defenders on the west side. Next lay the Canal du Nord Line on the east side, parallel to the canal. This consisted of two lines of trenches protected by several belts of very strong wire. "Deep dugouts were situated in this Line, which, owing to the gradual slope from the Canal (upwards) to Bourlon Wood, had an absolute command of the Canal du Nord."[26] After this major obstacle lay an area developed for the Germans' patented machine-gun post defence. This area included Bourlon Wood and the town of Bourlon. Only after these obstacles had somehow been overcome would the attackers reach the Main Line of Resistance, the Marquion Line. This last line had everything the defender could ask. It held many well-sited, deep dugouts and covered machine-gun posts. In front there lay wide swaths of wire. To protect against tanks, numerous artillery batteries lay concealed behind the reverse slope. Finally, there was another vast network of strongpoints and machine-gun posts which spread out behind the Marquion Line. Together, these defences completed the famous Hindenburg Line.

Any attack on such a line posed immense problems. The joker in the deck was the very first hurdle—the Canal du Nord. As it was, there was only a mile-and-a-half stretch of it which was readily passable. Enemy fire concentrated on this small bottleneck could easily destroy the initial assault. Once this first objective had been taken, the corps would have to fan out into a ten-thousand-yard arc to the north and east and envelope the enemy's defence.

Currie decided on a very complicated attack which would require enormous discipline and organization. Four battalions, two from the 1st Division and two from the 4th Division, would spearhead the attack. Once they had seized the canal and the enemy's first trench line on the east bank, fifty thousand men, guns, tanks, and transport would have to be passed through the one-and-a-half-mile funnel. On the right the 4th Division would launch its attack with the two old 10th Brigade rivals, the 46th and the 44th.

Secrecy was absolutely essential. "Usually, a couple of days before an attack they'd be showing you pictures of all this," said Bob Stevenson. "They hadn't done that this time and when we got up there where we stopped, the advance party had laid tapes along there where we were supposed to line up. The sergeants had been briefed apparently because each sergeant was telling his platoon, 'When the barrage starts at five-twenty, you'll be going across the Canal du Nord. It's just right in front of you a short piece.'

That's about all the warning we had for that."

Thus, early on the morning of 27 September, the entire corps waited in silent suspense. Had the enemy guessed there was anything afoot? For the leading battalions it was tension at its peak. Sergeant Don McKerchar had something extra to worry about. "Lieutenant Goulden had been sent out to take some course or something, so I had to take the platoon over that morning myself. It was raining, it was cold and dirty, and it was my first experience at taking over thirty-odd men and I was worried, really worried about it. The canal was ahead of us, and we didn't know if there was water in it or not. Each section was given a rope. If there was water in there, somebody in the section had to get out and he had to pull the rest out, but I don't know how it was going to be done."

Bob Stevenson years later recalled those hours. "Just after we got lined up there, it started to rain. We had quite a little rain and I can remember trying to cover up the Lewis gun with my groundsheet. A fellow by the name of McTavish was my number two—him and I were trying to hide under the other groundsheet to keep out of the rain. It quit raining just shortly before zero hour. It was very dark and misty. We were always told when zero hour was but they don't need to tell you 'cause zero hour's when that barrage opens up. It was really a terrific barrage. I know it was the heaviest barrage I ever saw. It was a tremendous barrage!"

And so the 46th were off. A and B companies led in two waves, with C and D following. The battalion's objective was a sunken road which lay six hundred yards beyond the canal. This would mean smashing through the first line of trenches in the enemy's Canal du Nord line. Almost immediately enemy machine guns on the near side of the canal opened up, as did the enemy barrage.

"I hadn't gone ten feet before I got hit," reported Don McKerchar. "Seven pieces in my right arm and a bad bruise across the back of my head. I don't remember hitting the ground."

The artillery fire was unusually heavy and casualties occurred thick and fast. Charlie Russell, who had ridden the captured artillery horse at Amiens, was hit on the back by a large chunk of chalk. When Russell found out it was not a Blighty he had but merely a bruise, he got to his feet and went on, but in a very ill humour.

On the right, A Company enveloped a German strongpoint in front of Lock No. 4. Fifty prisoners were taken, although in doing so Lieutenant Warburton was killed by a stick bomb from one of the defenders. Already the company commander, Captain Martin, had been wounded. He was but one of many. In this ferocious episode Sergeant R. M. Lahue killed twenty of the enemy and captured the machine gun. Already streams of prisoners were coming back through the lines of advancing troops. Remembering the possibility of the canal being flooded, the men literally sprinted across in the mist.

"When we went up the other side we run into their barbed wire," Bob Stevenson recalled. "We had this really terrific barrage on it that tore it up pretty bad. We partly run into our own barrage. Once or twice before, I noticed them make mistakes like that—get going too fast and run into your own barrage. So we had to wait till it lifted which was of course only a few minutes."

"Sergeant-Major Rogers kept a lot of us young fellows from getting killed by our own barrage," Private Stan Colbeck of Llewelyn recalled. "He wouldn't let us advance until our barrage lifted. We had to carry scaling ladders as the canal was very deep where we crossed over. Myself and a pal named Brown, we carried the ladder so we were the first up and we had just gone a little way when a shell exploded right behind us. It hit us like a giant fist in the small of the back. I thought I was blown in two; I was all numb. I asked Brown if he was okay. He said he thought so. The screams behind us I will never forget. Brown and I were fine, but that shell wiped out our whole section."

After this it was comparatively easy going according to most of the survivors. The wire had been thoroughly demolished in enough places for the men to pour through. The leading waves met and dealt with some of the enemy, but the remainder of the attackers saw only prisoners. The noise of the barrage was so awesome that hardly another sound could be distinguished.

At least one platoon arrived at the sunken road under the command of a private. Private William Faithful had taken over when his officer and NCOs had become casualties. He had already personally attacked and killed the crews of two machine guns. Although wounded in this foray, he led his platoon on to the objective, but he died of his wounds shortly afterwards.

By 6:15 the 46th had seized the sunken road. It had taken only fifty-five minutes to cross what was one of the Germans' most renowned lines of defence, the Canal du Nord. But the cost had been high, as Mac McDonald noted. "The German machine-gunners were really first-class soldiers and did a very great deal of damage. We had quite a few casualties that morning."

Meanwhile the sunken road had to be consolidated, although the 50th Battalion had already leapfrogged and other Canadian troops were streaming past. Enemy dugouts yielded still more prisoners and the haul of arms was impressive. Four machine guns and five trench mortars had been captured. Then the rum issue arrived. "We needed it," was Private Colbeck's only comment.

Jock Rankin took stock of the situation, and only one solution to the manpower problem presented itself. He would have to consolidate. The companies were reorganized on a three-platoon basis, except B Company which had to be reduced to two platoons. This meant a reduction of one third in the battalion's firepower. Officers and NCOs came up from Transport to replace casualties.

On the west side of the canal, almost on the starting line, Sergeant McKerchar had regained consciousness. Although "badly holed" with seven pieces of shrapnel in his right arm, he was still worried about the platoon that he had led so briefly. "Somebody had dressed my head all up, but blood was still coming out of my coat sleeve. I was worried so much I went over there and they had got there all right. The captain saw me and told me to get out. I came back and met Sergeant Tomlinson at the dressing station and he says, 'Well Don, you finally got one, eh?' I asked him if he wanted to look at it. He says, 'Nope, you've been here long enough. You walk down there about five miles and you'll catch a train to the hospital.'"

During the afternoon an order arrived advising that the 46th was to attack again next morning at six. By three the depleted companies were on the road, where they shouldered their way through a swarm of transports and troops. The battalion was to support the 50th up to another sunken road, leapfrog and take over the advance, and then breach the enemy's Main Line of

Resistance, the Marcoing Line, where it crossed the Cambrai-Douai Road. The latter part of this move would be up a steady slope towards the enemy's main position. This time, C and D companies would lead.

Sharp at 6:00 A.M. the attack started under the cover of an artillery barrage. There was little opposition until the lines of khaki neared the twin villages of Raillencourt and Sailly on the right flank. The enemy there was putting up a terrific resistance and the battalions on that flank had been stopped. Thus the 50th Battalion leading the attack swung to the right in attempt to take Raillencourt from the flank. Meanwhile the 46th pushed ahead to the sunken road, where it had been ordered to leapfrog the 50th. All the while a murderous enfilade from Sailly and Raillencourt kept casualties mounting. The 46th's Lewis-gunners returned the fire, but it wasn't until the flanking battalions had taken the villages that the casualties temporarily ceased.

Although it was not known by the men, they were now leading the Canadian Corps. The situation was critical. On the right the 3rd Division's attack had bogged down against heavy resistance. A wide gap had appeared between the rest of the 10th Brigade and the 3rd Division. But the 46th men knew nothing of this as they went over the top from the sunken road. They were now expected to carry the attack through the famed Marcoing Line. Brigade and Divisional Headquarters were obviously optimistic, for little opposition was expected.

By this time it was nearly nine o'clock. "We moved forward under a very sketchy barrage," said Mac McDonald. "I suppose it always must be so in war—the first day of a big attack goes like clockwork; then, on the second, third, and fourth days the staffwork and organization seems to deteriorate. The longer a battle goes on, the worse it gets."

"We were going up this gradual slope," recalled Bob Stevenson. "There was a village just on top of this slope and quite a number of trees. It kind of looked like they had a machine gun behind every tree up there. They were really sweeping the ground there and we had quite a few casualties. I had just started firing the gun when I got hit. I got hit through the chin and down through the neck. That kind of put me out of action. For a moment I was kind of paralysed—couldn't speak and couldn't move—and it really bled, too, although it only bled for a short time. The blood spurted out all over the machine gun—covered it, you know. I could hear my number two saying, 'They got Stevie! They got Stevie! Pull him back out of the way.' These fellows in the shell hole grabbed me by the heels and yanked me back so my number two could move over behind the gun. When they yanked me back I kind of come to a little bit."

Stevenson had not only been hit in the chin, he also had a hole in his back, but his friends bandaged him up and he made his way to the dressing station, not caring to wait for the stretcher bearers—he had seen too many men bleed to death while waiting for those overworked Samaritans.

"That attack seemed to go in by fits and starts and never seemed to really get going," Lieutenant McDonald observed. "There was a tremendous lot of fire from German machine guns and rifles from the Cambrai-Douai Road and from some trenches just behind it and from a railway just behind the trenches."

By mid-morning the enemy had begun counterattacking the 44th and the right-hand company of the 46th. Although the Germans had suffered severe losses, they advanced wave after wave. All the A Company officers became casualties and Company Sergeant-Major F. D. Gibbons took over. After repulsing the attack, he led the company forward and captured five machine guns.

From this point on, the 46th found itself pinned down under terrific fire. The battle had become a bloody stalemate. Little artillery fire could be brought to bear on the numerous targets because the corps artillery was mostly on the move forward, but trench mortars came up and fired until their ammunition was expended.

There were desperate attempts to get the attack moving again. Charlie Russell, who had almost had a Blighty the day before, was sent with his partner to get assistance from a tank which was seen moving up. But in the hail of bullets splattering upon the tank, the crew inside never knew that two infantrymen were frantically pounding on their armour plates trying to attract their attention.

Charlie Russell died there in a hail of bullets and the tank rolled on unheeding.

Sergeant Tommy Rea from Edmonton got the momentum of the attack going once more. He organized new gun crews and set up posts under fire to counteract the enemy's fierce strafing. At one point he picked up a Lewis gun and charged, firing from the hip. The Germans fled before him, though not before a few were cut down. But even spectacular actions like this could not get the remnants of a battalion past the mighty Marcoing Line.

At this time Mac McDonald was rescuing a severely wounded officer, whom he dragged back under fire to some stretcher bearers. On his way back to the front, he single-handedly captured his first German. "He was a young kid; I should think fifteen or sixteen years of age, quite small, with a great big German steel helmet on his head and a long coat, and he looked frightened to death. He was crying and he was in a very bad state. I had a bit of a chat with him in my schoolboy German. Somebody must have told him that Canadians killed their prisoners because I couldn't get rid of him. I eventually got him back to the sunken road and handed him over, but he didn't want to leave me. He apparently thought as long as he was with me he wouldn't get killed by these barbarous Canadian infantrymen."

In general, the attack had come to a standstill. The *War Diary* summed up the situation. "The whole Battalion was held up by enemy machine gun fire, and there was no possibility of this opposition being outflanked on the Left as he was holding the Road in strength and was reinforcing from Sancourt. . . . On the Right enemy movement on the Douai-Cambrai Road was marked and his machine gun activity was intense. . . . Ammunition in all Companies ran out and parties were sent forward from time to time to keep up the supply and keep Lewis guns and rifles going."

So many casualties had been suffered that Major Jock Rankin was forced to amalgamate his companies. There was no longer an A or B or C or D Company; there was a Left Company under Lieutenant Tommy Hewitt and a Right Company under Captain Barter.

Mac McDonald was now given a thankless task. "During the afternoon Major Rankin sent me out to find the commander of the leading company on the left of the battalion, telling him he had to launch an attack up to the Cambrai-Douai Road and TAKE it. There was a bit of shelling, a lot of machine gun and rifle fire, and it meant going over a couple of hundred yards to where we thought the OC of the company was. Tommy Rea said he was going with me. I had to order him to stay put. It was like something out of *Beau Geste*. We shook hands and said goodbye. We had an arrangement long before this about where to write if anything should happen to either of us. I set out at an extremely fast gallop, resting in shell holes. I eventually found my man. 'You must be bloody mad,' he greeted me. 'What the hell are you doing here?' I told him. His reply to this order was absolutely marvellous. Never have I heard such a flow of really first-class profanity, but his last words were, 'If he wants the bloody road taken, tell him to come and take it himself!' If anybody showed their head, machine guns opened up. It was clearly and obviously absolutely impossible to take the road at that time."

McDonald returned to Headquarters, miraculously unscathed, and presented to Rankin a somewhat abridged reply from the company commander.

Jock Rankin was getting it from both sides. At 5:30 P.M. a message arrived from Brigadier Hayter that "he now had plenty of artillery at his disposal and that we had to capture the Douai-Cambrai Road that night."[27] Thus, at seven, under cover of a heavy barrage, the Left Company rushed the road and established posts there. The Right Company met fierce machine gun fire and was forced to filter small parties forward after dark. But it too succeeded in gaining its objective. And so the Douai-Cambrai Road was taken. The Hindenburg Line had been breached!

A few hours later General Erich von Ludendorff, the brain behind the Kaiser's army, demanded that the German government seek an immediate armistice. This, of course, was not known to the weary survivors of the 46th. Theirs was a strange mixture of pride and horror, pride at having once more done the impossible and horror when they looked about and saw how few were left to share that pride.

"In our particular company we had one officer, one sergeant, myself and I think eleven men," stated Jack Huckerby. "That was all that was left. I took two sections of machine-gunners into the line—that was fourteen men—and I brought out one man with me. I really believed it was the Suicide Battalion then."

Fortunately the 46th was blessed with a quiet night, as Mac described. "Just after dark Tommy Rea and I went to see what had happened, and as we approached the road we heard a peculiar noise coming from a house. We went to it very carefully. Company Headquarters had been established there and the sound we heard was the sound of a piano being played by one of our officers or men in the cellar. Apparently the piano had been moved down into the cellar by the occupants of the house. I well remember that the pianist was playing and singing tunes from *The Maid of the Mountain*. Where the Germans were, nobody knew and nobody seemed to care. The house must have been a German machine gun headquarters or post, for I picked up in one of the rooms a cardboard picture of a Golden Wedding, and on the back of that picture was written, 'A hearty welcome from the M.G. boys Regiment 451. We are pleased not to see you. We didn't want the war, but we hope to see you next year in London where I'm longing to take a Scotch whisky. Goodbye. Keep yourself well off. We are going home and be quiet.' It was signed, 'C. H. N. Cook at the Royal British Hotel at Dundee, Bonnie Scotland, from 1907 to 1911.' "

Although the fighting would go on until the corps was relieved on 10 October, the 46th Battalion would take no further part in it. From 22 August, when the Canadians had arrived in front of the Hindenburg Line, until 10 October when they were relieved, "Foch's pets" had suffered enormous casualties, their highest in the entire war. The total was 30,806, the equivalent of over thirty infantry battalions. There were only forty-eight battalions in the entire corps. For the 46th's part in the Canal du Nord operations of 27 and 28 September, 55 were killed, 306 wounded, and 9 reported missing. This meant that the battalion had suffered a total of 680 casualties since its arrival in front of Dury on 1 September. Thus the Hindenburg Line had cost the 46th more than Vimy Ridge and Passchendaele together.

In spite of these appalling figures, chests would have swollen with pride if the men had been able to read the corps *Intelligence Report*, which was only published years afterwards. "The enemy opposed this Division [4th] with the heaviest concentration of troops that has yet been encountered, in an effort to check our advance, and in fighting from 27th September to 1st October no less than elements of 9 Divisions were encountered and defeated, no less than 55 Battalions being directly engaged and defeated during the same period and approximately 2,000 prisoners taken."[28]

CHAPTER EIGHTEEN

Pursuit

> *We just followed after the enemy—when they went, we went. Everyone realized it was coming to an end and that it was foolish taking unnecessary chances.*
>
> Pte. Ted Oakley, 46th Battalion

"We were taken back to Arras in, of all things, motor lorries," Mac McDonald recorded. "This was indeed luxury to us. We were used to marching on our own two feet. It must have been a long way, for otherwise, I am sure we would never have been allowed to have a ride on lorries."

During this break the colonel, Dismal Dawson, returned to resume command of the 46th and Jock Rankin left. It would have been ideal, most of the men figured, somehow to have been able to keep both. Outwardly, the two were the antithesis of one another: Old Stone Face, impeccably turned out and silent; Jock, slightly scruffy, and easygoing. Yet beneath the misleading exteriors the two men were surprisingly alike. Both loved their men, both were respected, and both were known for their courage. Unfortunately a battalion cannot have two commanding officers, so Jock said goodbye to his comrades from Camp Sewell days and left for the 11th Brigade, where he took command of the 75th Mississauga Battalion from Toronto.

The 46th was to spend two weeks out of the line. Like most of the Canadian battalions it was woefully short of men. The hundred extra men "overposted" to each battalion during the summer had long since been used up. The flow of reinforcements had dwindled somewhat, and many of them were conscripts, though some of the new men were volunteers who had just come of age and others were men who had previously volunteered and had been rejected—usually on medical grounds. Nevertheless, all were lumped together by the veterans as conscripts and treated with contempt. It was a natural enough feeling on the part of those who had seen chums killed or maimed and who had themselves suffered. But it was not good for morale.

"I was sixteen. I was big and rough and ready, and they weren't too particular about ages," said one reinforcement. Yet on arrival at the front, he found himself treated with disdain. He described the conscripts he served with: "They were good men, but the poor devils, they didn't have a chance. They picked on them and kind of thought that they should have been in there earlier, regardless of why they weren't. It's too bad we took that attitude towards the conscripts."

Most veterans were willing to believe the worst, and occasional incidents seemed to bear them out. "This one chap was a zombie. He'd been called up. We were sitting in this dugout waiting for our tour of duty and I looked over. He had his rifle pointed down to his foot. . . . So I rushed over and I grabbed that rifle and says, 'What were you going to do?' He says, 'I was going to shoot my foot off so I wouldn't have to go over in the morning.' I says, 'You're coming with me, brother.' So I took him down to Captain Kennedy and he was sent down the line and I don't know what happened to him. But he did come back because I had him in my section."

Of course, volunteers had done the same thing in the past, but they had been regarded with a mixture of pity tainted with mild scorn, for they had endured what no man should experience until eventually they had cracked. For a conscript this fact was generally overlooked, and self-inflicted wounds were thought of as their badge.

The manpower barrel was running low and as a result many men were returned who, everyone agreed, should have been left in England. These were the men who had already been wounded twice. An example was Stevie, one of the signallers. He had been known as a jolly, easygoing type, but when he returned in the autumn of 1918 he was glum and morose. "It so happened that I had Stevie for my bunk-mate," wrote the former schoolteacher, Donald MacKay. "About a dozen times per day Stevie would say, 'If they are going to sign an armistice, I wish they'd hurry up. I'm a married man, have been wounded twice, and I think I have done my bit. It would be just my luck to get an R.I.P. in my last time in action."

However, *esprit de corps* never wavered despite the two camps of personnel. Old soldiers always stick together, and there was nothing like a spot of trouble for one or two, to make the rest pull as a team—as one incident showed.

Pat Gleason and two of his buddies had been overwhelmed by temptation. A half gallon of rum, destined for the regimental sergeant-major, proved to be too enticing for them to pass by, and they hid it by the waterhole where they would have to take the transport animals for water.

"This was a hot day, we were hungry and it didn't take much of that stuff until I had more than I should," recalled Gleason. "The other two were pretty well loaded also. The last I remember, Dunc was sitting on the ground hanging onto *two* horses. I said, 'Where's your other horse, Dunc?' He looked around and said, 'Oh, hell, one horse more or less don't matter in a war this size.' We managed to get back to camp okay, but I passed out on arrival. I just *might* have gotten away with it, had Captain Lett, the adjutant, not chosen that particular hour in which to inspect transport lines."

When Gleason and his chums recovered that evening, they were warned to appear before Colonel Dawson the next afternoon. "I was paraded into the colonel's tent first, leaving the two older chaps outside. The charge was read and I pleaded guilty. Then Colonel Dawson asked me what I had to say for myself. On the spur of the moment, I told him that three of us had gone to water our horses, and while there a couple of chaps from our home town of Yorkton came along and produced a bottle of some kind of liquor. Having scarcely ever tasted any before in my life, I told him I didn't know what the stuff was, but I had a couple of drinks of it, and that was the last I could remember. He turned to Lieutenant Gilbert, OC of Transport, and asked him how long he had known me. George really went to bat for me and informed Dawson that he had known me since I was a small boy, which was partly true in that he had seen me a couple of times when I was eight or nine years old when he had come to see my dad concerning a team of mules. He told Dawson he had never known me to take a drink in all the years he had known me.

"Dawson turned to me and said, 'Will you take my punishment or will you elect a court martial?' I said, 'I'll take your punishment, sir.' 'Very well, fourteen days Field Punishment No. 1.'*

"As I emerged from the tent and passed Dunc, he said, just loudly enough for me to hear, 'You young bugger! You BS'd him out of fourteen days! I was sure we'd get twenty-eight.' The others went in one at a time and received the same sentence. But, believe it or not, none of the three of us served one minute of it. Bill Milne, the transport sergeant, told us to keep our eyes peeled for the RSM coming around and if we sighted him to 'get to work at any damned thing.' As it turned out, the RSM came only once and it was that same evening. But we saw him first and really got busy cleaning harness, polishing buckles, bridles, and what have you."

Justice had been carried out, although everyone from Private Gleason to Colonel Dawson knew that theirs was a cock-and-bull story. But justice must not merely be done, it must be seen to be done. Thus everyone could witness that Colonel Dawson's sentence had been firm but fair; Lieutenant Gilbert had stood by his men; the RSM had ostensibly ensured that the punishment was being carried out; Sergeant Bill Milne had proved to be understanding; and the three privates would never try that trick again. Teamwork.

The 46th went back into the line on 14 October and the men soon found themselves on the west bank of the Canal de la Sensée, which ran through the village of Fressiers. Fighting had obviously been vicious and progress slow during the last two weeks, for their position was less than three miles from the Cambrai-Douai Road and the Marcoing Line which they had taken on 28 September. But on 17 October there was an air of excitement.

*Field Punishment No. 1 involved being tied during the daylight hours in a spread-eagled position on a wagon wheel.

"At 13:00 hours," recorded the *War Diary*, "a message was received that the 1st Division had succeeded in crossing the Canal de la Sensée, and evidences of the enemy withdrawal were asked for. All Companies were instructed to be on the lookout. 'B' Company reported at once that a German had been sniped by the C.S.M. one half hour previously. This was followed by a report from 'A' Company of a German officer being seen to visit certain posts, apparently giving instructions. Two motor trucks were seen passing down the Fressain-Aubigny-au-Bac Road. At 16:00 hours, the Battalion Observers reported three men leaving a post and running back with a Machine Gun. At the same time Brigade forwarded a report that the 11th Brigade had crossed at Cantin. Orders were received to attempt a crossing. An Engineer Officer who came to Battalion Headquarters in connection with a reconnaissance for possible localities for bridges was sent forward to Fressiers, and 'A' Company was ordered to supply a Work Party to work under his orders and construct with all speed a temporary bridge."

The bridge was finished that night, and C Company started the crossing. A dense fog began to roll in, creating an air of sheer suspense. Through the village of Fressiers the spectral figures moved. Silence reigned supreme as the wary riflemen slipped forward, taking cover, then advancing again, as they had been trained. They could see only a few feet ahead, and the fog seemed to play tricks on their straining eyes.

Meanwhile Battalion Headquarters had moved into Fressiers and an Advanced Report Centre was set up to keep in communication with the patrol, which was accompanied by the signalling officer, Bill Hepburn. The remaining companies had also crossed the canal by this time.

The enemy had vanished. C Company pressed on to the right, sending a battle patrol of fifteen men with a Lewis gun under Lieutenant Johnny Jones towards the village of Fechain. Through the fog they moved, along the cobbled road, trying to keep silent. Nevertheless, the large, steel-shod "ammunition boots" made an abominable racket in the eerie darkness. Then at 1:50 Headquarters received their report: Fechain was empty. The pursuit was on.

At this point new tactics came into play. "I remember crossing the canal, and we had with us, strangely enough, for the first time in the war, a thin screen of cavalry and a few cyclists who moved in front of the battalion," commented Lieutenant McDonald. This was not all, for besides these two eight-man patrols, the 46th had been given a battery of field artillery, a battery of machine guns, and two sections of trench mortars. All came directly under the command of Colonel Dawson.

Thus, at 9:30 on the morning of the eighteenth, the advance began. By 10:35 the town of Marcq was reported clear of the enemy, and the cyclists had sighted enemy in the vicinity of Monchecourt, two miles northwest of Marcq. By noon the 46th had reached the high ground to the north of Marcq, where they captured two machine guns. At about the same time the enemy began shelling the town. Machine gun fire from the vicinity of Emerchicourt stopped the advance. It was impossible to obtain enough artillery to cover an attack, so both the 46th and the 50th stayed put. On the battalion's left the 29th Battalion from the 2nd Division was also held up.

At ten o'clock that night the required barrage finally came down on the enemy line, and the 46th and 50th continued their advance. C and D companies led the way and captured their objectives and one machine gun at a cost of two casualties. At first the various companies had difficulty establishing contact with one another in the dark but the situation soon clarified. By dawn, patrols had begun probing ahead, only to discover that the enemy had once again vanished.

At eight-thirty the pursuit recommenced. There was little sign of an enemy and the day was a pleasant stroll to the veterans of the 46th. Through Mastaing they marched in column of route and on to Roeulx where, in the words of the *War Diary*, the battalion "was met by crowds of civilian population wildly enthusiastic over their liberation from four years of German tyranny."

The Germans had pulled out around noon that day and had obviously left in a hurry. "There were plenty of shot ponies and horses at the crossroads," noted Ted Oakley. "As soon as we got there out came the women with butcher knives and we were able to get some nice pony steaks and they sure tasted good after all the campaign rations we had been eating."

At Roeulx the men were billeted. "Everything was at our disposal," wrote George Kentner, now a sergeant. "The civilians were frightened of the bombs and shells, and slept in the cellars. We had a much-needed and enjoyable rest and were up again quite early in the morning, ready to be on our way. The town crier made his appearance, and summoning all the people of the village into the streets, made announcements regarding the conduct of civil affairs which might be observed since the withdrawal of Fritz."

By this time the 46th and 50th had been leapfrogged by the 44th and 47th. At eleven that morning the battalion moved out of Roeulx towards the important city of Denain less than two miles away, and by noon the men were being served dinner from the field kitchens in the Cité Bessmer, a suburb of Denain. Ahead, in the eastern outskirts of the city, the 44th and 47th were running into stiff opposition. As a result, the 46th had the remainder of the day to relax and find billets.

On the morning of the twenty-first, refreshed and ready for action, the 46th prepared to resume the advance through Denain. This proved to be an enjoyable experience for Kentner and his fellow veterans. "Forming up on the outskirts, we marched through the town. Our band led us through, playing the martial tunes we loved to march to. Imagine! The whole population of the town lined the streets and cheered us as we passed. Altogether, it was an inspiring event, that march through Denain, and it repaid us for a great deal of the hardships and suffering we had passed through."

Leaving Denain behind, the foremost ranks could see shells bursting in the town of Rouvignies on the road ahead. At one o'clock in the afternoon the battalion stopped there for dinner, and the search for billets began. "Mr. Spear and I went to one house and banged on the locked door," Kentner wrote. "After much knocking, the door was finally opened to us. Inside were three ladies, a couple of children, and a young girl of about sixteen. They had been hiding for a day and were not aware the Boche had vacated. They were unable to control their joy at seeing us. The young girl threw her arms around me and kissed me—which could have been embarrassing in other circumstances. One of the women took us upstairs where she showed us a tricolor she had kept hidden. We assured her that the Boche would not be coming back, so, gaining courage, she proudly unfolded it and suspended it from the window."

The search for billets was all in vain, for word had arrived that the 46th would be moving up that evening to relieve the 44th. It was a long, confusing march as the area was new to the men and there were no guides. Nevertheless, the 46th had taken over the line by 10:30 P.M.

The right flank lay in the village of Trith-St. Leger on the Canal de l'Escaut. Because the 51st Highland Division had not advanced this far on the other side of the canal (which ran east and west), the battalion's right flank was completely open to German attack. That was, providing Fritz could cross the canal. So the battalion scouts under Bobby Crowe investigated the length of the canal for possible crossings, but none was discovered.

It was a busy night on the left flank as well. Here, D Company sent out a patrol to the village of Le Vignoble, and by 3:35 Lieutenant Ronald Joseph Holmes had reported "all clear." Meanwhile the remainder of the company had been heavily shelled.

When dawn arrived the men on "stand to" could see before them the suburbs of Valenciennes, the fabled centre of France's centuries-old lace industry. The Canal de l'Escaut on their right curved round in a wide arc in front of them and headed north between the city and its western outskirts. Directly ahead of the left company was the Fauberge de Paris on the western bank of the canal. Colonel Dawson decided to seize this if possible, so he sent out a patrol from D Company under Captain W. W. Kennedy.

Into the outskirts of the Fauberge de Paris the dozen wary men advanced. There was not a sound from the deserted and looted houses. Presently a "whiz-bang" gun opened fire on the patrol. The men all knew by the sound that it was not far off and they expected to run into an enemy outpost at any moment. Suddenly machine gun fire spattered against the stone buildings and the pavé around them, and everyone dived for cover. Lieutenant Spear, Sergeant Kentner, and five men dashed across the street to form an advance post in one of the houses. From here they viewed Valenciennes. "Looking over the canal," wrote George Kentner, "we could see Boche transport wagons with their loads heading towards the rear. We could see and hear the trains shunting back and forth with their loads. Most of all, we could hear the noise of various explosions as the Boche executed his plan of systematic destruction."

The men of this isolated outpost soon discovered vegetables in the garden of the house and tea in the cupboard. By noon they had a feast simmering on the stove. Despite this, it was an unpleasant day, as Kentner recorded. "With his 'fishtails,' 'pineapples,' and small mortars, Fritz fairly brought our house down around us. No serious casualties occurred during the day, but it was a terrible strain on our nerves, and night found us pretty well worn out."

That afternoon the right-hand company had remained in Trith-St.Leger, but that was not to say that they had no excitement. It had been reported that a possible crossing had been found over the canal, and four officers went to investigate. Three of them were pinned down by an enemy post and it appeared certain that they would be captured. The remaining officer made it back to A Company where he took charge of a Lewis gun section and returned to the rescue. The Lewis-gunners moved through the flooded area in four feet of water but were able to find a position to fire upon the enemy post. This enabled the three other officers to slip back to safety.

While these adventures were taking place, Colonel Dawson received an order from Division to capture a bridgehead over the Canal de l'Escaut into Valenciennes. This would involve clearing out the machine guns at the crossroad, which were pinning down Captain Kennedy's patrol. Grenades and a light trench-mortar section were sent forward to the beleaguered party.

At 9:00 P.M. Lieutenant Spear, Sergeant Kentner, and their men stealthily slipped into the darkened street and crept towards the forbidding crossroad. The mortar barrage came down but missed the target completely. The advance continued, although the veterans knew that the enemy had now been alerted by the mortar fire. As the first of them stepped into the cross street in front of the German post, a hail of machine gun fire met them. Everyone dropped except Kentner and another who had run into a wire fence. Then came the "fishtails," and the patrol began to retire down the street. Lieutenant Spear and two men were badly wounded before they reached their outpost in the house they had left only minutes before. Spear died of wounds later that night.

It was at this point that the 46th's relief arrived. No one was sorry to leave, but the 85th undoubtedly cursed D Company for stirring up such a hornet's nest at Fauberge de Paris.

It was a long, weary tramp all the way back to Denain, and all were thoroughly disgusted to find the Germans still shelling the place. Nevertheless, everyone quickly found a billet and was instantly asleep. Despite the shells crashing about, Denain was sheer luxury.

Mac was unusually lucky. "Captain Hepburn, the battalion signalling officer, and myself were billeted in a little house which was absolutely spotlessly clean, and we slept in a double bed on snow-white sheets in the downstairs front room. I suppose they had brought the bed down because of the shelling. This was luxury for us."

The 46th stayed in Denain for several days and there was even time for a little socializing. It was there that Mac McDonald heard a story about a certain Lieutenant Blodgett. "Being a typical American, he was an outright republican. He didn't believe in the Royal Family. On one occasion when he was out of the line he got to an officers' club with a staff major, and this major saluted another staff major that was in this place. It was teatime so they sat down and had some tea. During the course of the conversation it turned out that this staff major was named Major Windsor. Blodgett told the story that after the staff major had departed, he said to his friend, 'What did you salute that chap for? He's only a major like yourself.' He said, 'Oh, he's the Prince of Wales.' Blodgett was suitably impressed and after that was always a royalist of the first water."

Edward, Prince of Wales, had been attached to the Canadian Corps for five weeks and the men were delighted. "They couldn't keep that bugger out of the lines!" Pat Burns enthused. "He liked the Canadians. In fact, he was so attached to us that he'd go right up to the front line. I was in the front line when he happened to come through. We stood at attention. He merely saluted; he didn't say anything, but he did stop and talk to a couple of the fellows. The Prince of Wales, imagine you, right in the front lines!"

On Sunday, 27 October, the prince formally entered the city of Denain. The 46th, along with the rest of the 10th Brigade, lined the streets and was later inspected by the heir to the throne. Sergeant Tommy Rea always referred to this as the battalion's proudest moment.

The next day the 46th was on "stand to" ready to move, but up at the front things were not running as smoothly as had been hoped. It was not until 29 October at 3:15 in the afternoon that the battalion left for Thiant. The following day the men waited. Although they did not know it, stirring events were afoot elsewhere. General Erich von Ludendorff, Germany's master strategist, had been relieved by the Kaiser; Turkey had surrendered and Austria was about to do so. The end was in sight.

For some men the end was closer than they could ever realize. The sadly depleted unit, now only 405 strong, was to play a major role in the capture of strongly defended Valenciennes.

CHAPTER NINETEEN

Valenciennes

It is comparatively seldom in the world's history that a man gets the chance to die splendidly. Most deaths are somewhat inglorious endings to not very glorious careers. A war like this one gives a man a chance to cancel at one stroke all the pettiness of his life.

Capt. Reginald Bateman, 46th Battalion

"As a key point in the Hermann Line, Valenciennes had been well-chosen. The Canal de l'Escaut barred approach from the west and north. Both banks had been wired, and on the far side trenches had been dug."[29] The Germans had added to these strong defences by flooding all the low land to the west and southwest. This meant that the only possible route of attack was from the south, opposite Mount Houy. Valenciennes was held by five German divisions, three of which were in the Mount Houy area.

The famous 51st Highland Division had attacked Mount Houy on 28 October but failed to hold the heights under heavy German counterattacks. The 10th Brigade would try it next. Thus, on 30 October, the 44th and 47th went into the line in front of the long ridge that barred the southern entrance to Valenciennes. The 46th and 50th were behind at Thiant and Maing respectively.

The plan for the attack was straightforward. The 47th and 44th were to lead off after a massive barrage and were to sweep over the ridge and Mount Houy. When they reached the road joining La Targette and La Briquette the 46th would leapfrog the

44th and press the attack into the southern edge of Valenciennes and the southeastern suburb of Marly. To their right, across the Rhondelle River, the 146th Imperial Brigade would advance across the open country. The attack would immediately be followed with an assault by the 12th Brigade across the Canal de l'Escaut from the 46th's old position in the Fauberge de Paris.

The 46th had a wide front, which encompassed Marly—a most formidable objective. This suburb included a steelworks that was known to be full of enemy troops. The task would have been difficult for a fresh, full-strength battalion. The 46th was neither fresh nor at full strength. Only 21 officers and 384 men were available for the operation. They were a mixed bag—conscripts, beardless youths, weary veterans, and a number of men returned from the hospitals of France and England.

The last day of October was spent in preparation, and on 1 November the 46th was in position. There the men endured a heavy bombardment of gas and high explosives, which caused some casualties. Then, at 5:15 A.M., a tremendous barrage crashed down upon the German position on Mount Houy. It was later calculated that the weight of shells fired by the Allies in the forty-eight-hour period covering the battle almost equalled that fired during the entire Boer War by *both* sides.

Because both the 44th and the 46th were rather "thin on the ground," the two COs had agreed on a means of making the best use of their slim resources. The 44th would concentrate on clearing Aulnoy on the right and Mount Houy on the left, and would provide only a thin line of attackers in the area between. Mopping-up would therefore be done by the 46th, who were determined to keep up to the barrage. Mopping-up would be most difficult along the roads that ran obliquely along the line of advance.

For this task, a special "mopping-up party" was formed from batmen, cooks, bandsmen, and "odds and sods." This party was put in charge of the battalion police corporal, George McIntosh. Tosh was a large Scots piper and the anchor on the champion tug-of-war team. His magnificent physique he modestly attributed to "plenty of oatmeal." Tosh was one of the most popular men in the battalion, despite being a military policeman, and was noted for his ability to keep the more feckless young soldiers out of harm's way, whether it be in the front lines or the *estaminets*.

The attack opened as planned and swept in against a demoralized enemy. Nevertheless, German machine-gunners, tough till the last, fought back viciously. The farther the advance went, the tougher grew the resistance. As expected, the opposition was bitterest along the two roads, both lined with the pulverized remains of houses.

On the right, A Company ran into trouble first, four hundred yards from Aulnoy. Heavy casualties occurred before Lieutenant Johnny Jones from Regina led his platoon from C Company around the flank to silence the enemy machine-gunners. By this time both A and B (on the left) had mingled with men of the 44th, and the advance doggedly continued on towards the proposed leapfrog position on the sunken road from La Briquette to La Targette. Officially, the 46th was still not in action, but up front it was a different story.

"The fighting that took place along the Famars-Valenciennes and Aulnoy-Marly roads was deadly work," wrote Colonel Dawson in his report. "Many of the enemy were killed by the parties of the 46th working with bayonet, bombs, and Lewis Guns. The area was packed with Germans. Every cellar contained numbers. Those that offered any show of resistance were killed and the rest sent back as prisoners.... At one point in the main road, a field gun was firing point blank at our men and also two trench mortars were in action with machine guns sweeping the streets. The Lewis Guns got in their work and No. 292383, Pte. W. J. Wood, pushed up close with his Lewis Gun, disposed of part of the crew and forced the remainder to surrender."

Company Sergeant-Major Nick Bretherton, an original member of the 46th, was as fiery as every. At one point, when the right flank was almost overwhelmed by a swarm of the enemy, Nick led a platoon forward to save the situation. Six of the Germans were rash enough to attack the little redhead. Two he bayoneted, and the remaining four surrendered to him.

Soon the leapfrog line was reached. From here on, the 46th would go it alone. It would have been classed as a hopeless affair if anyone had had time to analyse it: one battalion, now down to three hundred men, was to attack frontally a well-protected enemy that was known to number in the thousands. The decimated companies were reshuffled, with C and D in the centre now. In actual fact, platoons would be acting independently. It was a battle for sergeants and subalterns, not colonels and generals.

When the fifteen-minute barrage lifted, over the top they went. "Bob Irvin, Sergeant Irvin, he was a darn good fellow—came from Fort William," Private Skeates recalled. "He had some rum there and we emptied that bottle and we told our fellows, 'Come on!' and we went over. Machine gun bullets were like hailstones, coming four or five feet right in front of us. You couldn't believe it unless you had experienced it. Just like hailstones! But we beckoned our fellows on and we got them machine-gunners."

On the right the platoon followed the barrage forward, but in the brickfield south of Marly they ran into trouble: a group of nearly one hundred Germans had dug themselves in and had thus been untouched by the barrage. "Here followed a remarkable and most gallant attack by Major Gyles, C.S.M. Gibbons, Sergeant Cairns, and eleven other men," reported Colonel Dawson. "Fire was opened up from our Lewis guns and rifles in reply to the heavy Boche fire. Then C.S.M. Gibbons, Sergeant Cairns, and four other ranks with two Lewis Guns moved down to the right to outflank the enemy. This party made its way under covering fire to within 75 yards of the enemy and opened fire, causing such casualties that the remainder surrendered. Here, three field guns, one trench mortar, seven Machine Guns and over 50 prisoners were captured, and the ground was strewn with dead Germans."

The men continued on their way once again, Hughie Cairns always at the forefront. Presently the platoons (which were now little larger than sections) were in place on the right of the line. It seemed as if an eternity had passed, but on looking at their watches most were dismayed to discover that it was not yet nine o'clock.

The CO reported: "At 09:00 hours, I went forward to reconnoitre the situation in the front area. I found all Companies on their objectives. I visited 'D' Company and found their posts in position. While there, a runner came from 'B' Company stating that the Company was in position in the trench. All their Officers were casualties and only one Lewis Gun magazine remained for each Lewis Gun. I at once detailed Lieutenant Holmes, 'D' Company, to take command of 'B' Company with Lieutenant Morfitt to assist. At this moment, the armoured car reported back with a report that it had reached the Church in Valenciennes and that the city was full of Germans. In view of 'B' Company's need for Lewis Gun magazines, I made use of this car to bring up a supply from the dump. I found later that Lieutenant Gilbert had already sent forward tump-liners with supplies of all kinds and these were on the way."

By this time the signallers had arrived in the newly captured areas. Donald Mackay was accompanied by his grouchy buddy, Stevie, the twice-wounded veteran. "We went down into the basement. On the floor was a German soldier lying on his back. It was quite obvious that he was on his last gasp. As we walked past him he was making the motions for a drink. He was in bad shape. I saw him and I had water in my bottle so I went over and gave him a drink. But a lot of the boys thought it was a heck of a thing to do," MacKay related. "But I did it without thinking, you know—did it impulsively. I don't suppose he lived any time after that."

The youthful schoolteacher and his veteran buddy returned to the street to roll out wire for the field telephones. Almost immediately a shell hit nearby, throwing Stevenson into the ditch. "The shrapnel wound was high up in his thigh, and he was rapidly losing a lot of blood. We did the best we could for him. Our second attempt at applying a tourniquet was successful. Stretcher bearers came and took Stevie away, but he had lost a lot of blood. We heard later that he died at the dressing station. Thus, as he had predicted, it was for Stevie *requiescat in pace.*"

After the 46th had established its positions, Brigade ordered Dawson to send out patrols from his B Company's position. He considered matters in light of the information brought back by the crew of the armoured car that had reconnoitred in B Company's area, and due to the extreme weakness of this company and the vast superiority of the enemy—numerically, at least—the colonel decided against it. It was as well he did, for Sergeant Bob Irvin's twenty-four survivors were having trouble merely hanging on.

Dawson did, however, send out a patrol to explore the suburb of Marly. This patrol was led by a very young subaltern, John Phee Gordon MacLeod, who had risen from the ranks. Johnny MacLeod and his three men crossed the railway into enemy territory. Here they met Sergeant Hughie Cairns, who had gone out on his own initiative. Cairns was a remarkable character. Back home in Saskatoon, he had been a noted football player, and in the 46th he was known for his ability as a long distance runner, though he had also made his mark in the ring. He had enlisted in 1915 with the 65th Battalion in Saskatoon, and when that unit was transferred to the 46th *en masse* at Bramshott, he and his brother Albert were with them. Hughie had soon become one of the best-known characters in the battalion. "He wouldn't take responsibility for a bunch of men, but he could take apart a Lewis gun blindfolded. They used to have competitions throughout the division, and Hughie Cairns could beat everybody," said one comrade.[30] Hughie loved a good scuffle but he wasn't a bully, and he never, never stood in awe of anyone. He had already been recommended for one court martial but had come out of it with a D.C.M.

"I tell you the truth," wrote Harold Emery, "Sergeant Hughie Cairns was no band-box soldier. If you have a picture of Hughie Cairns looking like Gary Cooper in the picture about Sergeant York, why you have another think coming. He was a chunky chap about five foot eight, one hundred and seventy pounds, ruddy of cheek, and he wore a rather large-sized uniform—not too well fitting. He was good natured and a great buddy to his gun crew."

Hughie's brother Albert, known to the 46th as Abbie, was almost a mirror of Hughie. The Cairns brothers were inseparable. They had gone through thick and thin together, so when Abbie died of wounds he had received at the Drocourt-Queant Line, Hughie was heartbroken. "Hughie said he'd get fifty Germans for that," recalled one mate. "I don't think he ever planned to come back after Abbie got killed."

Certainly, this appeared to be the case on 1 November. Cairns had on two occasions leaped forward alone in the face of murderous fire, his Lewis gun held at the hip, spewing death. Besides the momentous fourteen-man attack under Major Gyles, mentioned previously, Cairns had single-handedly captured three machine guns and eighteen Germans, as well as killing seventeen. Now, on his voluntary one-man reconnaissance, he had discovered a courtyard packed with the enemy. This he told Lieutenant MacLeod and his patrol. MacLeod noted that Cairns had been wounded in the shoulder.

The young lieutenant, accompanied by Privates Fidler, Lavery, and Marshall, followed Cairns back to the courtyard, creeping to the wooden doorway which opened into the yard. Through this burst the five of them, Cairns again firing his Lewis gun from the hip. There was an instant of hesitation, and then the sixty-odd Germans in the yard threw down their weapons and raised their hands in surrender. They obviously believed themselves to be surrounded. The five Canadians knew that they would have to get them out of there quickly. A German officer, sensing the true situation, advanced as though to speak. All at once a pistol appeared in his hand and he shot Sergeant Cairns through the body.

Hughie sank to his knees but opened fire. He cut down the officer. The Germans dived for their discarded weapons. The five men of the 46th opened up on them and a vicious but unequal fight ensued. Still Cairns's Lewis gun could be heard above the din as it mowed down great swaths of grey-clad figures. A bullet shattered Cairns's wrist as he knelt in agony, but still he managed to keep the gun going. Then a burst of fire from across the yard smashed the butt of the Lewis gun, and Hughie Cairns collapsed in a pool of blood. MacLeod and one man frantically held the enemy at bay while the others dragged the bloody form of Cairns back through the gate.

At this moment reinforcements arrived. A stretcher party was formed, but one bearer was killed and Cairns was again wounded before the handful of surviving Germans finally surrendered. Hughie Cairns had got his fifty Germans—and more. He was carried out on a door from a nearby house. This stretcher party was followed by Hughie's grim-faced comrades and a handful of prisoners. The courtyard was a shambles, littered with a mass of dead enemy soldiers, while near the forlornly swinging gate was a darkening pool of blood.

Sir Arthur Currie was later to write: "I cannot refrain from telling you of the superhuman deed of Sergeant Hugh Cairns, late of the 46th Battalion, Saskatchewan Regiment. He was recommended for, and awarded the Victoria Cross for bravery before Valenciennes on November 1, 1918. . . . Throughout the operation he showed the highest degree of valour, and his leadership greatly contributed to the success of the attack. He died on November 2 from wounds."[31]

There were many other equally sad stories to be told. Amongst those killed was No. 472607, Tallis, Harold William, lance-corporal. The first of the six Tallis boys from Borden, Saskatchewan, to enlist, he was the fourth to die with the battalion. The fate of these six men, representing two generations of a family, reads like a history of the 46th:

> Edgar—died of wounds at M and N Trench
> Harold—wounded at the Somme, killed at Valenciennes
> Victor—killed below Vimy Ridge
> Arnold—wounded taking the Pimple, killed at the Drocourt-Queant Line
> William—returned to Canada in poor health
> Sidney—badly shellshocked.

Valenciennes, nevertheless, was a victory bought at a comparatively low price in Canadian blood, although hundreds of German dead were buried in the days to follow. "In that one morning our little depleted brigade captured about 1,800 prisoners and there were between 800 and 900 dead Germans in our area," wrote Lieutenant R. J. Holmes. "I never saw anything like it. We surely got ours back for almost a month of hard chasing and dirty fighting."[32] All this at a cost of 80 Canadians killed and 300 wounded. For the 46th though, the victory was costly. This half-strength battalion had suffered 33 percent of all Canadian casualties.

At ten o'clock that night the 46th Battalion was relieved by the 54th. It was a pitiful remnant that dribbled back. Of the 405 who had started out at 5:15 that morning, 34 had been killed, 2 were missing and presumed dead, and 90 were wounded. This was a total of 126 casualties—31 percent of the battalion's strength. Nevertheless, the 279 survivors felt proud. The 46th had captured seven field guns, six trench mortars, two anti-tank guns, and forty-five machine guns! The *War Diary* reported approximately 800 prisoners taken—twice the strength of the 46th. These prisoners represented five German infantry regiments and two of the famous machine gun sharpshooter units encountered and defeated by the Canadians. But most important, the battalion had broken Germany's last line of fortifications in France.

CHAPTER TWENTY

Peace

> *The reaction sets in. After I came home from the war I found myself waking up under the bed dodging shells which had never bothered me over there. When the whole thing was over, you'd have a nightmare about the war starting up again.*
> Pat Gleason, veteran of the 46th Battalion

It was mid-morning and Pat Gleason had just received orders to take a wagonload of ammunition to the ranges. The date was Monday, 11 November. "My wagon was already loaded, so it was simply a matter of throwing the harness and saddle on my long-eared friends and taking off. We were still within sound of heavy artillery, but just as I reached the ranges at 11:00 A.M. all firing ceased. What a strange and peaceful calm followed. Not a cheer went up from anyone. You know, I have a lingering suspicion that rough and tough as we all let on to be, that each, in his own way, was doing as I was doing—offering up a most sincere but silent prayer of thanksgiving that it was all over."

In this manner peace came to the front-line soldier. At eleven o'clock the long-waited Armistice took effect. For days there had been rumours that the Germans had requested one, and then, on the night of 10 November, word had been passed—at eleven the next morning the firing would stop. For the 46th it was exceptionally welcome news, for the battalion was scheduled to go back into action immediately.

Back in Valenciennes, where the 46th were billeted, the Armistice was greeted with a modest ceremony. Sergeant George Kenter wrote in his journal: "All parades were dismissed at 10 A.M., and we were told a short service would be held in the City Square to commemorate the greatest event we had known. In company with others I hurried down to the square. One could expect no elaborate celebrations in a shattered town like Valenciennes. At home they would all be holidaying and going mad with joy. But here things were different. There was no demonstration. A couple of bands [including the 46th's] were present and played a few appropriate numbers ending with 'Les Marseillaise,' 'O Canada,' and 'God Save the King.' A motley throng of civilians and soldiers filled the square. Our divisional commander, General Watson, with other staff officers and civic officials, stood on the steps of the Hotel de Ville. When the bands ceased playing the crowd dispersed. There was no shouting or cheering, but everyone wore a glad smile when they left the square. A few more serious of us reminded ourselves that we had just lived through one of the Greatest Moments of History."

Meanwhile, at Battalion Headquarters a familiar figure worked over the maps. Gordon Brown had returned and had been assigned to the Intelligence Section, preparing maps. He was busy plotting trajectories and marking positions for the battalion Lewis-gunners. "I was preparing this map for the next take-off for our boys when the word came through that the Armistice had been signed. That was the end of the map-making. There was no more of it. It was not many hours or minutes before we began wondering, 'When are we going to get home?' "

Home—that was the thought in everybody's mind. "The fighting is over, so let's get home." But there were many who would never go home. The statistics were grim: 5,374 men had served in the 46th. Of these 4,917 had been casualties—an incredible 91.5 percent. Only 457 men had served in the Suicide Battalion without being hit. These staggering figures included 1,433 young men who would stay forever in France or Flanders, or in graveyards in Blighty. Thus the survivors did not cheer on Armistice Day.

That night things were pretty quiet, although there were a few personal celebrations. "Mine was to sleep in a silk nightgown that night after a steak supper," Ted Oakley wrote, "the steak being cut from a pony the Germans had been using for transport and had been killed." Ted, like many others, topped off his meal with a bottle of champagne which had been liberated. A train of looted goods left behind by the Germans had been placed under guard of the 46th. When champagne was discovered, the men began to load rather than unload, and a merry time was had by all, at least until an officer arrived to restore order. He apprehended one private bearing a pail full of champagne. Fortunately for the unknown ranker, the pail had a hole in it and the evidence disappeared before the interview ended.

It was near the end of November when command of the battalion changed for the final time. Herbert Dawson moved up the ladder into a staff job. To everyone's delight, the new CO arrived in the person of Jock Rankin. If the army saw fit to take Old Stoneface from them after they had shared so much, then it could do no better than return Jock to the battalion.

Rumour had it that the 46th would soon be on the march to Germany to become part of the Army of Occupation, but as things turned out, the 4th Division fell victim to logistics. It, like most other allied units, was stationed west of the Rhine, and the 46th found itself in the small city of Wavre near Brussels in Belgium. There the men lived in billets which were a far cry from the accommodation of the same name that they had occupied back in 1916. The houses of the liberated Belgians were thrown open to the men, and feather beds, sheets, and home-cooked meals became the order of the day.

It was a period of sheer pleasure—except for the persistent yearning to go home and the minor irritants of a military routine that no longer seemed necessary. But one military event was welcomed. On 24 March 1919 the 46th was finally presented with the King's Colour. Each battalion traditionally carried two colours, the regimental and the king's. Both were large banners, the regimental in the battalion's colour, and the king's in the form of a Union Jack. Each colour bore the badges of the battalion and its Battle Honours. Like most Canadian Expeditionary Force units, the 46th had no Battle Honours from the past, and those of its own war had not yet been awarded. Despite this fact, the presentation of the King's Colour was the occasion for much pomp and ceremony. Brigadier J. M. Ross, the new commanding officer of the 10th Brigade, made the presentation. Because Ross was a Regina man, the event seemed a bit more personal to the men. This ceremony was followed by another the next day when the entire brigade was reviewed by Albert, King of the Belgians.

But the greatest day of all was 14 April. On that day one company of the 46th entrained for Le Havre en route to England. The next day the balance boarded the train at Wavre and followed their companions. At last the movement home had begun!

It was not a very rapid movement. On the seventeenth the men detrained at Le Havre. Three days later they were de-loused for the last time. But for seven more days they milled around the "bull pen" before orders came to move. Then, on 27 April, late in the afternoon, the 46th and 47th paraded to the docks. Their troopship was to leave at six that evening.

The next morning the haggard, seasick men of the 46th sighted the coast of Britain and by eight o'clock they had begun disembarking at Southampton. There they entrained for Bramshott. For the few remaining originals, the return journey brought back a flood of memories and visions of comrades they would never see again. At 12:15 P.M. they stepped for a moment back into the past as they alighted at Liphook Station. Nothing had changed. Longfellow's "spreading chestnut" still stood; the pubs were exactly as they had been four years earlier; and Canadians were still welcome.

The days at Bramshott were pleasant enough, but there was one overriding thought in everyone's mind—HOME. Finally, word came—the 46th would embark for Canada on Wednesday, 28 May. Several men opted to be discharged in Britain. Amongst them was Mac McDonald who was destined never to return to the prairies except in his dreams. Nearly all of those who had been convalescing in hospitals had already returned to Canada, as had the 1st, 2nd and 3rd divisions. Now, seven months after the Armistice, the remnants of the Suicide Battalion were heading home.

On schedule, the men boarded the *Empress of Britain*, and on

4 June the 46th stepped back on Canadian soil at Quebec City. From here the easterners still serving with the Saskatchewan unit dispersed homeward. Now, for most, came the final stage, the long train journey westward over the rolling farmland of southern Ontario, through the rugged Canadian Shield and onto the sun-drenched, silent prairie which seemed to stretch forever. God, it was good to be back!

Meanwhile, behind the scenes officialdom was wracked by its own war, for the 46th was to be demobilized in Regina. On 5 June the Moose Jaw *Evening Times* bore the accusing headline, "Regina Will Give 46th Battalion Fine Welcome." The citizens of Moose Jaw were incensed. Mayor Hamilton immediately wired the minister of militia. After all, Regina had already welcomed several Saskatchewan units. Why should it get the 46th too?

Next day the *Evening Times* trumpeted in inch-high letters: 46TH TO DEMOBILIZE HERE ON MONDAY. EFFORTS OF WAR VETERANS, CIVIC OFFICIALS AND OTHERS PRODUCE RESULTS—BATTALION WILL ARRIVE MONDAY AT 9 A.M. The city went mad. Monday was proclaimed a civic holiday. The men would be accommodated and fed at civic expense for two days if any wished to avail themselves of the offer. Two blocks of Main Street would be reserved by the CPR station for the men and their relatives to mingle for forty minutes after their arrival. Then the 46th would march up Main Street to the Armoury, their first home, where they would be demobilized.

An enormous dinner was planned for the men and any ex-members present. Seventy young ladies and members of the local cadet corps were ready to serve the meal. That afternoon the boys would be entertained at a professional ball game between the Saskatoon Quakers and Moose Jaw's Robin Hood Millers. The day would be wound up in the bunting-decked Armoury with a gigantic dance.

At 8:30 A.M. the CPR train bearing the 46th pulled into Moose Jaw. It was Monday, 9 June, the battalion's last day of existence. As the men emerged from the train they were met by a mighty roar. Ex-members became misty-eyed at the sight of the "jam label" shoulder titles, the well-known gleaming cap badges, and the rare well-loved face. The men and their parents, brothers, sisters, wives, children, and sweethearts shared the first few moments together after the long years of separation. But there were many others in the crowd who would never see their loved ones.

Then the Suicide Battalion formed up for its final parade, which was led by the returned 46th men, followed by Jock Rankin at the head of D Company. Next came the band led by G. B. McClellan. Behind the band marched A, B, and C Company, followed by the War Veterans Band, the Regina Garrison Band, and a host of other veterans. Former members of the battalion noted the absence of the 46th's popular pipe band. It was a shock to discover that only three pipers were left of the twelve who had piped them the weary miles across France. Sergeant Tosh McIntosh, Jimmy Logan, and Bill Patterson were all that remained.

The entire city had turned out and the cheering was tumultuous. Past the reviewing stand at the Bank of Montreal the column marched. The last salute was taken by the lieutenant-governor of Saskatchewan, Sir Richard Lake. At the Armoury, bleachers had been erected and these were full of schoolchildren. There the battalion formed up for the last time. Inside the Armoury several desks had been set up, each ready to receive a stream of men to be quickly demobilized. The men filed into their battalion's birthplace to emerge minutes later as civilians.

Some of them took immediate advantage of their new status, as Pat Gleason describes: "One of the sergeants was standing outside—one of the unpopular ones—and one of the boys came out. 'Well,' the sergeant says, 'did you get your discharge?' 'Yes, I did. Did you get yours?' The sergeant said, 'Yes.' 'Well, then you can go plum to hell. I'll have no more to do with you.' " And the world's newest civilian strolled off.

Thus, the 46th Canadian Infantry Battalion (South Saskatchewan) trickled out of existence. By the next morning the men had dispersed. Moose Jaw and the world were back to normal. Long-delayed peacetime activities were resumed and khaki vanished from the streets. The Suicide Battalion was already a memory.

The Bond That Binds

(By Sergeant Bill Chapman, 46th Battalion, Wavre, 27 December 1918)

There's a gladness in the memory of the good friends we have met,
But it's mingled with the sadness and the pain
For the boys now laid at Ypres, Vimy Ridge or Courcelette,
Who ne'er in life shall visit us again.

There is pleasure living o'er again some days we ne'er forget,
When friendships oft were sealed in bonds of blood;
Where we shared our fags and bacca, and never used to fret
When laid our beds together in the mud.

The friendships that were made in those uncertain potluck days
When we learned to draw our belts in for a meal
And laughed and joked together while death lurked round in the haze,
Are the friendships that we'll find as true as steel.

We shall go on our several ways to counter, woods, or farm
Perchance to meet no more upon the earth;
But the restless soul will wander, when the nights are still and calm,
Off through dreamland to where our friendships had their birth.

The counterman his ribbons will be offering for sale,
When o'er the scene will come a rapid change,
And his ribbons will hold cartridges, that pouring out like hail
Through the quick-fire gun he's getting into range.

He'll see the devil-dancing lights shoot up from No Man's Land
He'll feel the thrill come o'er once again,

As Bill and Tom and Jack and Dick are working hand-in-hand,
While the shrapnel's falling all round like rain.

He'll wake from out his reverie and think of all the boys
Who shared his joys and sorrows, laughs and woes;
And he'll give a thought to all of them who midst the battle noise
Were stood between their country and its foes.

And he'll feel the lack of something with a sigh and a regret,
And he'll know the feeling isn't something new;
For he'll want to grip the hands again of the boys he can't forget,
Who are bound to him with bonds of friendship true.

Yes, there's gladness in the memory of the good friends we have met
And there's pleasure living o'er again some days we'll ne'er forget;
There's a solace in the knowledge that these friends are ever true,
And you'll meet the world more bravely, when you know they think of you.

Appendix

There follows a list of some of the men who have appeared in this narrative. Of those not listed, many died young; others are hale and hearty today; some became Supreme Court justices while others spent much of their lives in jail. Lawyers, farmers, teachers, railroaders, businessmen, policemen, drifters, evangelists, cartoonists, generals, civil servants—every possible calling had its share of 46th men.

Bateman, Captain R.J.G. ("Reg"): Killed in action on 3 September 1918 at the Drocourt-Queant Line. His position as first professor of English at the University of Saskatchewan was memorialized by titling the senior professor of English the "Bateman Professor." A small book of his writings was published by friends and students in 1922, titled *Reginald Bateman, Teacher and Soldier*.

Blodgett, Lieutenant James M.: This one-time republican returned to live in Connecticut. His address reflected his new-found royalist sympathies: 119 Poplar Street, Lordship Manor, Stratford.

Bond, Private Colin ("Shorty"): Made a poor recovery from a bullet through the lung. Took up gardening in Moose Jaw. In the 1950s his lung was cured by a faith healer. Hale and hearty, and a "good Christian" until his death in 1976.

Bretherton, Company Sergeant-Major Nick, D.C.M., M.M. and Bar: Returned to Moose Jaw and joined the Saskatchewan Provincial Police and later the RCMP, taking part in several notable cases. Retired in Yorkton.

Broomhead, Private Jim: Became an optometrist but left that to join General Motors in Flint, Michigan, U.S.A. Worked himself up to general foreman. Through the years his arm, wounded at the Somme, remained almost useless. Retired in 1961 and died in 1977.

Brown, Private Gordon: After several attempts at farming, he eventually became prosperous. In 1978 he was living in Pelly, Saskatchewan, and although retired looked after the local RCMP detachment's jail "to keep busy." Has nine sons and daughters, all of whom served in the Canadian Armed Forces.

Burns, Private L. W. ("Pat"), (Lieutenant, RAF): Finished the war with the RAF in Egypt. Returned to Canada but took a job with a soft drink company in the State of Michigan, U.S.A. Came back to Canada at the outbreak of the Second World War and served in the RCAF as an instructor on Linx trainers. Active in the Royal Canadian Legion until his death in August 1976.

Butterworth, Private Jim: Injured in January 1918 and returned to Canada in January 1919. Took up farming and implement sales before becoming a grain buyer in the Peace River country for eighteen years. Became settlement officer for Department of Veterans Affairs after the Second World War. Retired to Calgary in 1961 and died in 1976.

Byng, Julian H. G., Baron Byng of Vimy: Commanded Third Army for duration of the war. Rewarded by the British government with a gratuity of £30,000. In 1921 appointed governor general of Canada. Became embroiled in a parliamentary question and was later recalled. Chief commissioner of Metropolitan Police (London) in 1928. Gazetted field marshal in 1932. Died in Essex in 1935.

Cairns, Sergeant Hugh, V.C., D.C.M.: Died of wounds 2 November 1918. Awarded the Victoria Cross posthumously, the last Canadian V.C. of the war. The city of Valenciennes named a street L'Avenue Hugh Cairns in memory of him. It was the only street in France named after an enlisted man of another country. The ceremony took place in 1936, and Cairns's parents, the premier of Saskatchewan, and the 46th's representative, George Gilbert, were all present. Cairns Field, Cairns Avenue, and Sergeant Hugh Cairns VC Armoury in Saskatoon are all named in memory of Hughie.

Colbeck, Private R. S. ("Stan"): Returned in January 1919 and took up farming near Dauphin, then firing on the CPR at North Bay, and then building scows and doing sawmill work in British Columbia. During the Great Depression he pedalled chocolate bars to factories and offices before joining the B.C. Provincial Police and later the Corps of Commissionaires. When the Second World War broke out, he enlisted and served with the 6th and 24th Field Regiments, Royal Canadian Artillery, before being discharged due to complications rising from a First World War illness. Next tried chicken farming before settling down as a bank messenger in Vancouver. Retired to the Okanagan Valley in 1967.

Colours: In 1919 the 46th Battalion's colours disappeared. Eighteen years later they were discovered in a vault in the Legislative Building in Regina. Colonel Snell's widow presented them on Coronation Day to the King's Own Rifles of Canada. Thereafter they hung in St. Andrew's United Church in Moose Jaw. On the night of 15 December 1963 they were destroyed by the fire which gutted the church. All that remained were the damaged staff heads which now repose in the officers' mess at the Moose Jaw Armoury.

Copp, Lieutenant John, M.C.: After being wounded in the head on 28 April 1917 before Lens, he returned to Canada to train troops. Was about to embark for France when Armistice was signed. Returned to Saskatoon to work for a trust company but eventually set up Copp Shoe Ltd. in New Westminster. Retired to California in 1969.

Currie, Sir Arthur, G.C.M.G., Legion of Honour: Honoured abroad but received no official welcome in Canada. Was attacked in Parliament by Sir Sam Hughes. Became principal and vice-chancellor of McGill University. In 1928 sued the *Port Hope Guide* for libel concerning his actions as corps commander. Died in 1933 in Montreal and received a state funeral. A memorial service was also held in Westminster.

Dann, Captain George: Invalided to Britain and posted to 19th Reserve Battalion in February 1917. Continued on training staff until September 1918. Returned to Moose Jaw and the Land Titles Office. Retired to Vancouver in the 1930s and died in a War Veterans' Hospital in 1950.

Dawson, Lieutenant-Colonel Herbert John ("Dismal"), C.M.G., D.S.O. and Bar, D.S.M. and Bar, Croix de Guerre (Belgian): Returned to Kingston, Ontario, and resumed position as director of studies at the Royal Military College. Commanded 7th Infantry Brigade (Reserve) in 1920 and retired in 1925. Died 18 September 1926.

Emery, Corporal Harold: Returned to hospital in Moose Jaw where he took a Vocational Studies course and graduated from the University of Saskatchewan. Worked twenty years in the Land Titles Office in Moose Jaw. Active with King's Own Rifles of Canada. Despite badly damaged leg, took up tennis and became provincial champion in 1935 and shared the doubles in 1934 and 1935. Retired in early 1950s as registrar of the Battleford Land Titles Office.

Featherstone, Private Jack: Returned to his farm, then in 1922 became a fireman with the CPR in Moose Jaw. Retired forty years later as engineer.

Forty-Sixth Canadian Infantry Battalion: The 46th Canadian Infantry Battalion paraded once again—on 19 April 1936 in Moose Jaw. The occasion was the presentation to the King's Own Rifles of Canada at the Moose Jaw Armoury of a trophy cabinet commemorating the 46th. The parade was commanded by R.S.M. Bill Jones and led by the KORC band under Frazer McClellan, the 46th's band sergeant.

Fountain, Lieutenant George: Commissioned in England prior to Armistice. Returned to Vancouver and obtained a degree in civil engineering. Became active in town planning, eventually becoming director of planning and head of Vancouver Planning Department in 1960. Since retirement in 1963 has served as a consultant.

Gillespie, Private Earl: Eventually joined the 46th in 1918 and returned home with them. Farmed with brother Fred at Central Butte and later at Tugaske. Died in 1957.

Gillespie, Private Fred: Transferred to 16th Battalion, Canadian Scottish. Returned to farm at Central Butte and Tugaske until 1941 when he moved to Moose Jaw and was employed by the post office. In 1967 was 16th Battalion's official representative at the rededication ceremony on Vimy Ridge. Now resides a few hundred yards from the Armoury where he enlisted in 1914.

Gillespie, Private Ruben: Missing in action with 28th Battalion at Hooge on 6 June 1916 when the enemy exploded a mine. Twenty-four other originals of the 46th were casualties that day, nearly all listed as missing.

Gillespie, Private Will: Killed in action with 28th Battalion at Hooge on 6 June 1916 when the enemy exploded a mine.

Gleason, Private Pat: Returned to Yorkton in 1919 and took up farming in 1920. Left the farm in 1924 and went back to school. Began teaching in Regina in 1925, but "six and a half years and four children later" his father talked him into coming back to the farm. Farmed and also ran the Tonkin post office until his retirement in 1973. "Completely retired" to Yorkton in 1975.

Haig, Douglas, Earl Haig and Baron Haig of Bemersyde, G.C.B., O.M.: Awarded £100,000 by the British government and received the Order of Merit and the ancestral home at Bemersyde. President of the British Legion. Died in 1928 and was buried at Dryburgh Abbey. Tributes also found at St. Giles Cathedral and Westminster Abbey.

Harris, Private Ernie: Recovered from seven wounds, with one arm shorter than the other. Awarded $7.00 per month by the Canadian government. Wounds forced him to give up his farm and work for the Saskatchewan liquor board. Retired to Swift Current. In 1975 was operated on to remove shrapnel, after which he declared, "To hell with it, I'm going to take the rest with me."

Hellings, Private Percy: Returned aboard the *Llandovery Castle*, which was stopped in mid-Atlantic and searched by German submarine. (On the return voyage the *Llandovery Castle* was sunk.) Settled in Moose Jaw eventually becoming a real estate man. In 1978 still retained his pawky wit and naturally jet-black hair.

Hea, Private Hartley: Returned home to Chatham, New Brunswick, by Christmas 1918. Took up a teaching position in Lang, Saskatchewan, in 1919. Held various teaching and principal's positions for thirty-five years and eight days. Retired to Victoria, B.C., in 1968.

Hope, Major John ("The Great White Hope"), D.S.O., M.C.: Returned to his law practice in Perth, Ontario. Became justice of the Supreme Court of Ontario in mid-1930s. Served as ADC to the governor general of Canada and became a brigadier-general in the militia.

Huckerby, Corporal Jack: Returned to Saskatchewan and farmed near Wowota until 1936. Became usher for the Legislature, then joined the King's Printer and Public Works Department. Served in the Second World War as RSM of the Regina Rifle Regiment on training staff. Head of Saskatchewan Government Messenger Service, retiring in 1964.

Jenner, Private Ernie ("Jinx"): Returned to Moose Jaw where he tried various jobs—used-car salesman, liquor vendor, mail service, etc.—and starred with the local baseball team. Served on training staff during the Second World War. Hale and hearty in 1978.

Johnson, Private George: With two other bandsmen, farmed near Camrose, Alberta. Joined Customs and Excise Department in 1930. Played with band of the 101st Edmonton Fusiliers and the Edmonton Symphony Orchestra. Retired to Victoria, B.C., in 1959.

Kears, Private Bobby: Served with 16th Canadian Scottish and was wounded on 9 April 1917 at Vimy Ridge and again April 1918. Returned to Moose Jaw and resumed work as a meat-cutter until retiring in the 1960s. Died in December 1976.

Kennedy, Captain William Walker ("W.W."), M.C. and Bar: Returned to law practice in Winnipeg. Elected as member of Parliament and made a widly publicized plea against the government's plan to reduce the pensions of war veterans.

Kentner, Sergeant George, M.M.: Took a job with the post office in Winnipeg but after a few months he left that to work in the Winnipeg office of Booth Fisheries. Went to Chicago with Booth Fisheries in 1923 and over the years worked himself up to vice-president and general manager. Retired to Fredonia, New York, in the 1960s.

McDonald, Lieutenant Eric D. ("Mac"): Demobilized in England and joined the West Riding Constabulary as a constable. He rose through the ranks to become divisional commander at Keighley where he retired in 1957. Honoured on the Queen's Birthday Honours List in 1952 with the Queen's Police and Fire Service medals. Died in late 1976.

MacKay, Private Donald: Returned to the teaching profession in various small towns in Saskatchewan. Retired in 1970 and lives in Wolsely.

McKerchar, Sergeant Don: Returned to Winnipeg where he worked for the Union Bank and the Grain Exchange. He eventually became an income tax expert and in 1975 still ran his own consulting service.

McLeod, Sergeant Neil: Returned to farming near Turtleford until the Dirty Thirties; then worked for Massey-Harris and the Relief Commission. In 1939 joined the Department of Indian Affairs as Indian agent at

Duck Lake and later at Fort Qu'Appelle. In 1957 was appointed regional head in Regina. Retired in 1961, but to keep occupied, works as a commissionaire at the University of Regina on the night shift.

Monger, Captain Harry, M.C.: The former RSM returned to Moose Jaw and served in the King's Own Rifles of Canada (formerly the 60th Rifles) as captain. In 1927 he retired after forty-three years' service in the forces. Died in 1955.

Musgrove, Private Bill: Tried various jobs—labour, farming, CNR caretaker, foundry worker, etc. Retired in Sackville, New Brunswick, in 1969. In 1976 moved to Burlington, Ontario, to be close to his sons and their families.

Oakley, Private Edward ("Ted"): Joined Alberta Government Telephones in 1923 and rose to head of Revenue Section in 1954. Retired four years later. Travels all over North America as judge of Roller Canaries.

Rankin, Lieutenant-Colonel James S. ("Jock"), D.S.O. and Bar, Volunteer Officers' Decoration: Returned to law practice in Weyburn; then appointed legal advisor to the Department of National Defence and assistant to the judge advocate general in 1929.

Rea, Sergeant Tommy, D.C.M.: Returned to Edmonton in June 1919. Hired as a farmhand but after three months came back to the city. Got a job with the City Telephone Department and remained with them till his retirement in 1953.

Skeates, Private Charles D. ("Charlie"), M.M.: Returned to barbering in Swift Current. During the Second World War served as a sergeant in RCAF in Canada and Britain, and made pocket money by barbering. Returned to his shop at the Healy Hotel until his retirement in the 1960s.

Smith, Lance-Corporal Alan A. ("Spike"), M.M.: Returned to Saskatoon and worked for the Soldier Settlement Board and later tried farming. Returned to government employment until he retired in Saskatoon. Still keeps busy with his son's firm as a "gopher" ("Go fer this, go fer that").

Snell, Lieutenant-Colonel Herbert: After losing an eye in the bombing accident, he left hospital to become commanding officer of the 9th

Reserve Brigade and landed in France in April 1917. Was temporarily attached to the 46th and 47th before taking over 4th Divisional Wing, Canadian Corps Reinforcement Camp and Divisional School. This meant that over 2,400 men were under his direct command. Returned in late 1919, but as his store in Moose Jaw had closed during the war, joined Gordon Drysdale Department Stores in Victoria. In 1922 joined the Robert Simpson Department Stores of Montreal, rising to become vice-president and general manager. Hospitalized in March 1932, due to complications from wounds, and died there on 12 November 1932, aged 52 years.

Spidell, Corporal Curry M. ("Spy"): Returned to farming near Mortlach but soon entered Acadia University in Nova Scotia. Planned to become a journalist but became a theological student in Rochester, New York. Served as a Baptist minister in various parts of the United States. When Canada entered the war in 1939, he volunteered but was "put on file." When the United States became a belligerent, Spidell rose to become senior chaplain in the Pacific Area. After the war became chaplain with the Bureau of Prisons. Retired in 1963 and settled in Nanaimo, B.C.

Stevenson, Private D. R. ("Bob") M.M.: Became a farmer near Wood Mountain. Met and married a girl from Grayshott, near Bramshott. Became a CPR engineer in Moose Jaw where he retired. Fit as a fiddle in 1978.

Syrett, Private Vic: Returned to school before joining Standard Oil, with whom he worked for forty years in various parts of the world. Retired to Australia in the 1960s and is now writing memoirs of his years with Standard Oil at their request.

Timberlake, Private Morley, M.M.: Returned to Canada and teacher-training in Vancouver. In January 1920 began a teaching career lasting over forty-one years. Retired as a principal in 1961.

Tingley, Private Bedford A. ("Bob"): Returned to British Columbia and became a fruit grower near Summerland. In 1937 became secretary-treasurer of School District No. 77 and retained this position until his retirement in 1964.

Tomlinson, Sergeant George ("Old George"), D.C.M., M.M.: Returned to Moose Jaw and became a railway mail clerk with the CPR. Remained active in the militia, eventually gaining a commission. At the outbreak of the Second World War he was among the first in the city to enlist and subsequently went overseas with the 10th Field Ambulance as captain quartermaster of the unit. Saw service in Italy but due to health reasons was later returned to Canada where he took up residence in Vancouver. Died in October 1974 while visiting his place of birth in Keighley, Yorkshire, England.

Vimy Crosses: Stood guard over the graves on Vimy Ridge until they were replaced by the Canadian Corps's memorial. In 1930 they were presented to St. John's Anglican Church in Moose Jaw, where they still stand.

Woodward, Lieutenant J. S. ("Woody"): Returned to Prince Albert for a time and then joined the staff of the *Western Free Press* in Vancouver. Later became the editor of the Saskatoon *Star Phoenix*, a position he held for eighteen years. Remained in good health and "enjoyed a dram" until his death in 1977, aged ninety-five.

Young, Sergeant Percy, M.M.: Served with the 16th Canadian Scottish. Returned to Moose Jaw where he rejoined the CPR as a switchman. An active member of the Legion. Retired from the CPR in 1962 as yard foreman.

Notes

1. *Moose Jaw Evening Times*, 28 May 1915.

2. E. S. Russenholt, *Six Thousand Canadian Men* (Winnipeg: 44th Battalion Association, 1932), p.9 (a history of the 44th Canadian Infantry Battalion).

3. See John Swettenham, *To Seize the Victory* (Toronto: Ryerson, 1965), p. 127.

4. *Letters from the Front* (Toronto: Canadian Bank of Commerce, 1920) Vol. 1, p.145.

5. *Keep in Touch: 46th Battalion Association Year Book* (Moose Jaw: 46th Battalion Association, 1934), p.27.

6. Colonel Dawson's report on the raid. From *War Diary, 46th Canadian Infantry Battalion* (Unpublished manuscript, 1916-18, housed in the Public Archives of Canada, Ottawa). Except where otherwise stated, extracts from the official reports of Colonel Dawson and other officers are all taken from this *War Diary*.

7. John Terraine, *Ordeal of Victory* (Philadelphia: J. B. Lippincott, 1963), p.229.

8. Russenholt, *Six Thousand Canadian Men*, pp.50, 52.

9. See Colonel G. W. L. Nicholson, *Canadian Expeditionary Force 1914-1919* (Ottawa: Queen's Printer, 1962), pp.191-92.

10. From the CBC series "Flanders Fields," written and produced by J. Frank Willis and edited by Frank Lalor (Toronto, 1964), No.8, p.28.

11. Winston S. Churchill, *The World Crisis* (London: Thornton Butterworth, 1927), Vol.3, pp.171-72.

12. F. A. McKenzie, *Canada's Day of Glory* (Toronto: William Briggs, 1918), p.26.

13. R. W. Gould and S. K. Smith, *The Glorious Story of the Fighting 26th* (St.John: St.John News Company, 1919), p.23.

14. In later years nobody ever admitted making this request. *See* Herbert Fairley Wood, *Vimy* (Toronto: Macmillan, 1967), p.139.

15. Gould and Smith, *The Glorious Story of the Fighting 26th*, p.23.

16. Will R. Bird, *The Communication Trench* (Amherst: Bird, 1933), pp.250-51.

17. Major-General E. K. G. Sixsmith, *British Generalship in the Twentieth Century* (London: Arms and Armour Press, 1970), p.106.

18. Leon Wolff, *In Flanders Fields* (New York: Ballantine, 1958), p.223.

19. Russenholt, *Six Thousand Canadian Men*, pp.116-17.

20. CBC, "Flanders Fields," No.11, p.7.

21. Wolff, *In Flanders Fields*, p.228.

22. Major J. E. Hahn, *The Intelligence Service Within the Canadian Corps 1914-1918* (Toronto: Macmillan, 1930), p.61.

23. *Ibid*, p.61.

24. *Daily Mail*, London, 15 February 1918.

25. Swettenham, *To Seize the Victory*, p.222.

26. Hahn, *The Intelligence Service Within the Canadian Corps 1914-1918*, p.229.

27. *War Diary (op.cit.)* 27-29 September 1918.

28. Hahn, *The Intelligence Service Within the Canadian Corps, 1914-1918* p.232.

29. Swettenham, *To Seize the Victory*, p.229.

30. CBC, "Flanders Fields," No.15, p.25.

31. Sir Arthur Currie. "Foreword" in Colonel George G. Naismith, *Canada's Sons in the World War*, (Toronto: Winston, 1919).

32. *Letters from the Front*, Vol.1, p.304.

Bibliography

Aitken, Sir Max, and Major Charles G.D. Roberts. *Canada in Flanders.* 3 vols. London: Hodder and Stoughton, 1916-18.
Banks, Arthur. *A Military Atlas of the First World War.* London: Purnell Book Services Ltd., 1975.
Barclay, Brigadier C.N. *Armistice 1918.* New York: A.S. Barnes & Co., 1968.
Berton, Pierre. *Vimy.* Toronto: McClelland and Stewart, 1986.
Bird, Will R. *The Communication Trench.* Amherst: Bird, 1933.
Canada in the Great World War, 5 vols. Toronto: United Publishers of Canada, 1920.
Canadian Broadcasting Corporation. "Flanders Fields." Toronto: written and produced by J. Frank Willis, 1964.
Churchill, Winston S. *The World Crisis.* Vol. 3. London: Thornton Butterworth Ltd., 1927.
Clark, Alan. *The Donkeys.* New York: Award Books, 1965.
Coombs, Rose E.B. *Before Endeavours Fade: A Guide to the Battlefields of the First World War.* London: Battle of Britian Prints International Ltd., 1976.
Dancocks, Daniel G. *Legacy of Valour.* Edmonton: Hurtig Publishers, 1987.
———. *Spearhead to Victory.* Edmonton: Hurtig Publishers, 1986.
Fitzsimons, Bernard, ed. *Tanks and Weapons of World War One.* New York: Beekman House, 1973.
Giles, John. *Flanders Then and Now.* London: Battle of Britain Prints International, 1987.
———. *The Somme Then and Now.* London: Battle of Britain Prints International, 1986.
Gould, R.W. and S.K. Smith. *The Glorious Story of the Fighting 26th.* St. John News Company, 1919.
Hahn, Major J.E. *The Intelligence Service within the Canadian Corps 1914-1918.* Toronto: Macmillan. 1930.

Harris. John. *The Somme: Death of a Generation.* London: Hodder and Stoughton. 1966.
Haycock, Ronald G. *Sam Hughes.* Canadian War Museum Historical Publication No. 21, Wilfrid Laurier University Press, 1986.
Keep in Touch: 46th Battalion Association Year Book: Moose Jaw: 46th Battalion Association, various years from 1922 to 1936.
Letters from the Front. 2 vols. Toronto: Canadian Bank of Commerce, 1920.
Lucas, Sir Charles. *The Empire at War.* London: Oxford University Press, 1921.
MacDonald, Lyn. *Somme.* London: Michael Joseph, 1983.
———. *They Called It Passchendaele.* London: Michael Joseph, 1978.
Malcolm. C.A. *The Piper in Peace and War.* London: John Murray, 1927.
McKenzie, F.A. *Canada's Day of Glory.* Toronto: William Briggs, 1918.
Morton, Desmond. *A Peculiar Kind of Politics.* Toronto: University of Toronto Press, 1982.
Naismith, Colonel George G. *Canada's Sons in the World War.* Toronto: Winston, 1919.
Nicholson. Colonel G.W.L. *Canadian Expeditionary Force 1914-1919.* Ottawa: Queen's Printer, 1962.
Roy, Reginald H., ed. *The Journal of Private Frazer.* Victoria: Sono Nis Press, 1985.
Russenholt, E.S. *Six Thousand Canadian Men.* Winnipeg: Forty-Fourth Battalion Association, 1932.
Sixsmith, Major-General E.K.G. *British Generalship in the Twentieth Century.* London: Arms and Armour Press, 1970.
Stewart, Charles H. *Overseas: The Lineages and Insignia of the Canadian Expeditionary Force 1914-1918.* Toronto: Little and Stewart, 1970.
Swettenham, John. *To Seize the Victory.* Toronto: Ryerson, 1965.
Terraine, John. *Ordeal of Victory.* Philadelphia: Lippincott, 1963.
Times History of the War. 22 vols. London: The Times, 1914-20.
Tuchman, Barbara. *The Guns of August.* New York: Dell, 1963.
University of Saskatchewan. *Reginald Bateman, Teacher and Soldier.* London: Henry Sotheran and Co., 1922.
War Diary, 46th Canadian Infantry Battalion, 1916-18. Unpublished: housed in Public Archives of Canada. Ottawa.
Wheeler, Victor W. *No Man's Land.* Calgary: Comprint Publishing Company for the Alberta Historical Resources Foundation, 1980.
Wolff, Leon. *In Flanders Fields,* New York: Ballantine, 1958.
Wood, Herbert Fairlie. *Vimy.* Toronto: Macmillan, 1967.

Index

Aconite Trench, 99-103
Albert, 44, 45
Albert-Bapaume Road, 44-46, 49
Allen, Sgt. George, 20
Amiens, battle of, 149-60
Ancre Heights, 47
Armes, Lt. H.P., 94, 100, 104

Bateman, Lt. Reginald, 128, 167-68, 211
Battalions:
  44th Bn., 19, 21, 25, 51-53, 82, 84, 94, 108, 153, 173, 178, 189, 195-96
  46th Bn. (South Saskatchewan), origins, 15; regimental march, 21; cap badge, 21; pipe band, 20, 44, 129, 208; casualties, 86, 120, 160, 168-69, 181, 202, 204; colours, 205; demobilized, 208
  47th Bn., 25, 56, 58, 76-78, 100, 108, 119-120, 159, 162, 189, 195, 206
  50th Bn., 25, 61-62, 77-78, 82, 84, 94, 100, 108, 120, 158-59, 188-89, 195
  65th Bn., 26
  196th Bn. (Western Universities), 72
Blodgett, Lt. James, 192, 211
Bond, Pte. Colin ("Shorty"), 142-44, 156, 211
Bramshott, 23
Bretherton, CSM, Nick, 86, 93, 197, 211

Brigades:
  10th Bgde., 25, 55, 75-77, 82, 94, 99, 104, 113, 149, 162, 177
  11th Bgde., 25, 55, 77, 80-82, 100, 187
  12th Bgde., 25, 77, 80-81, 100, 153, 159, 196
Broomhead, Pte. Jim, 32, 39-40, 45-46, 48-49, 55, 66, 211
Brown, Capt. Bob, 163
Brown, Cpl. Ewart, 165-66
Brown, Pte. Gordon, 107, 110-11, 115-17, 120, 127, 130, 137, 159, 164, 168-69, 204, 212
Bruay, 127
Burns, Pte. L. W. ("Pat"), 96, 103, 108, 113-14, 117, 119, 121, 130, 140, 192, 212
Butterworth, Pte. Dick, 26, 85
Butterworth, Pte. Jim, 26, 37, 56-57, 60, 85, 91, 212
Byng, Lt. Gen. the Hon. Sir Julian, 75, 212

Cairns, Cpl. Abbie, 26, 169, 200
Cairns, Sgt. Hugh, V.C., 26, 94-95, 198, 200-201, 212
Canal du Nord, battle of, 174-81
Cattell, Lt. Reginald, 40, 67
Colbeck, Pte. R.S. ("Stan"), 145, 175-76, 212
Colpitts, Cpl. Laurence, 79, 84-85
Copp, Lt. John, 31, 33, 47, 51-52, 54, 59, 85, 213
Currie, Lt. Gen. Sir Arthur, 97-98, 108, 173, 201, 213

Dann, Capt. George, 20, 38, 48, 56, 213
Dawson, Lt. Col. Herbert J., 29, 48, 57, 80, 84, 95, 117, 119-20, 123, 129, 158, 160, 183, 185-86, 197-99, 205, 213
Denain, 189
Desire Trench, battle of, 61-65
Dickin, Pte. Donald, 116, 120
Divisions:
  1st Div., 25, 100, 173, 187
  2nd Div., 100
  3rd Div., 25, 112, 177
  4th Div., 25, 43, 45, 96, 100, 112,

124, 149, 161, 173, 182
5th Div., 136
Drocourt-Queant Line, battle of, 161-68
Dury, 162-65

Elliott, Lt. A. J., 114
Emery, Cpl. Harold, 30, 32, 36, 47, 61, 76, 91, 113, 115, 120, 214

Faithful, Pte. William, 175
Featherstone, Pte. Jack, 128, 131, 138, 140, 151, 154, 214
Forty-Sixth Canadian Infantry Battalion (South Saskatchewan). *See* Battalions: 46th
Fountain, Lt. George, 94, 214

Gibbons, CSM F.D., 178, 198
Gilbert, Lt. George, 185-86, 199
Gillespie, Pte. Earl, 15, 214
Gillespie, Pte. Fred, 15, 214
Gillespie, Pte. Ruben, 15, 214
Gillespie, Pte. Will, 15, 214
Gleason, Pte. Pat, 74, 85, 139, 185-86, 203, 208, 215
Greves, Pte. Dick, 96-97, 160, 168
Gunning, Lt. R.H., 94, 100, 103
Gyles, Maj. Richard Walter, 61-62, 64, 80, 100, 156, 159, 198

Haie, Chateau de la, 69, 75
Haig, Field-Marshal Sir Douglas, 67, 99, 111, 125, 132, 158, 215
Harris, Pte. Ernie, 90, 102, 105, 108, 114-15, 120-21, 215
Harrison, Pte. William, 33
Hea, Pte. Hartley, 101-2, 215
Hellings, Pte. Percy, 90, 95, 101-2, 108-9, 111, 114, 215
Henstridge, L/Cpl. Walter, 118
Hepburn, Capt. William, 187, 192
Hilliam, Brig. Gen. E., 75
Hill 70, 100, 104
Hill 145, 80-82
Hindenburg Line, 161, 173, 180
Holmes, Lt. R.J., 190, 198, 202
Hope, Maj. J.H., 102, 119, 159, 167, 169, 215
Horan, Lt. James A., 51-52
Huckerby, Pte. Jack, 128, 180, 215

Hughes, Sir Sam, 14, 23, 43
Hughes, Brig. Gen. W.St.P., 26, 54, 75

Jenner, Pte. Ernie ("Jinx"), 142, 215
Johnson, Pte. George, 122, 216
Jones, Lt. John, 187, 197

Kears, Pte. Bobby, 22, 216
Kennedy, Capt. W.W., 94, 117, 121, 190, 216
Kentner, Sgt. George, 71-72, 78-79 83-86, 90, 123, 130, 142, 157, 161-62, 164-66, 168, 189-91, 204, 216
Kiggel, Lt. Gen. L., 125
Knight, Sgt. Arthur, V.C., 166

Lahue, Sgt. R.M., 175
Lens, 90, 100, 130
Leroy, Capt. O.E., 94, 115, 121
Llandovery Castle, 144
Ludendorff, Gen. Erich von, 180, 193

M and N Trench, 31, 35-36
McClellan, Bandmaster George, 17, 20
McDonald, Lt. E.D. ("Mac"), 21, 27, 32, 49-50, 56-57, 59-60, 146, 150-54, 158, 165-69, 176-81, 183, 188, 192, 206, 216
MacDonald, Pte. N., 37
McIntosh, Sgt. George, 196, 208
MacKay, Pte. Donald, 145, 185, 199, 216
McKerchar, Sgt. Don, 90, 92-93, 119-21, 123-24, 145, 167, 174, 176, 216
MacLeod, Lt. John P.G., 199-200
McLeod, Sgt. Neil, 74, 84, 86, 99, 122-23, 129, 153, 155, 157, 163, 169, 216
Marcoing Line, 177,
Marly, 196
Marqueffles Farm, 141-42
Marquion Line, 173
Milne, Pte. William J., V.C., 81
Monger, Capt. Harry, 20, 217
Mont Houy, 195-96
Musgrove, Pte. Bill, 30, 87, 93, 95, 217

Oakley, Pte. Ted, 53, 188, 205, 217
Oppy, 138-89

Passchendaele, 111, 124-25
Passchendaele, battle of, 114-21
Philbrick, Capt. Bertie, 38,
Pimple, the, 71, 82, 84-86, 130

Raillencourt, 177
Rankin, Lt. Col. James S. ("Jock"), 20-21, 31, 51, 53, 95, 162, 164, 166, 176, 179-80, 183, 205, 217
Rea, Sgt. Thomas, 179-80, 193, 217
Regina Trench, 47, 51-52
Regina Trench, battle of, 56-60
Reid, Capt. H.A. ("Tubby"), 94, 146-47, 157
Rising, Lt. Hugh, 146-47, 152, 165, 168
Ross, Brig. Gen. J.M., 206
Russell, Pte. Charles, 157, 174, 178-79

Sailly, 177
Scott, Lt. A.C. ("Tickler"), 30, 166
Scott, Sgt. Jack, 155
Sewell Camp, 19-22
Simpson, Lt. H.R., 131-32
Skeates, Pte. Charlie, 142-43, 169, 198, 217
Smith, L/Cpl. Alan ("Spike"), 83, 169, 217
Snell, Lt. Col. Herbert, 13-16, 21, 23, 25-27, 29-30, 89, 217
Somme, 44-54, 140, 155, 157-58
Somme, battle of, 56-65
Spear, Lt. R.G., 189-92
Spidell, Cpl. Curry ("Spy"), 73, 76, 142-44, 149-50, 155, 218
Steel, Lt. R.J., 53, 131-32, 147, 152
Stevenson, Pte. D.R. ("Bob"), 131, 133, 138, 146, 150-51, 156, 165, 171, 173-75, 177, 218
Sturley, Sgt. J.E., 165, 172
Syrett, Pte. Vic, 16, 29, 46-48, 67, 79, 104, 109, 111, 127, 152, 218

Tallis, Pte. Arnold, 26, 169, 202
Tallis, Pte. Edgar, 26, 37, 202
Tallis, Pte. Harold, 26, 202
Tallis, Pte. Sidney, 26, 202

Tallis, Pte. Victor, 26, 76, 202
Tallis, Pte. William, 26, 202
Taylor, Pte. Frank, 75, 85
Timberlake, Pte. Morley, 94, 163, 218
Tingley, Pte. Bob, 80, 218
Tomlinson, Sgt. George ("Old George"), 19-20, 24, 31, 65-66, 76, 176, 218
Triangle, the, 91-93

Valenciennes, 190, 195, 201
Vimy Ridge, 69-87, 104,
Vimy Ridge, battle of, 79-87

Walker, Sgt. A.R., 40
Woodcock, Lt. F.S., 51
Woodward, Lt. J.S. ("Woody"), 48, 50, 52, 219

Young, Sgt. Percy, 23, 219
Ypres, 107

Zouave Valley, 70